AF768786

110.00
13.50

The Difference Principle Beyond Rawls

The Difference Principle Beyond Rawls

Chris Wyatt

continuum

NEW YORK • LONDON

2008

The Continuum International Publishing Group Inc
80 Maiden Lane, New York, NY 10038

The Continuum International Publishing Group Ltd
The Tower Building, 11 York Road, London SE1 7NX

www.continuumbooks.com

Copyright © 2008 by Chris Wyatt

All rights reserved. No part of this book may be reproduced, stored in a retrieval system, or transmitted, in any form or by any means, electronic, mechanical, photocopying, recording, or otherwise, without the written permission of the publishers.

Printed in the United Kingdom by Biddles Ltd, King's Lynn, Norfolk

ISBN 978-08264-2942-1

Library of Congress Cataloging-in-Publication Data

Wyatt, Chris, 1963-
The difference principle beyond Rawls / Chris Wyatt.
p. cm.
Includes bibliographical references and index.
ISBN-13: 978-0-8264-2942-1 (hardcover : alk. paper)
ISBN-10: 0-8264-2942-4 (hardcover : alk. paper) 1. Liberalism. 2. Distributive justice. 3. Rawls, John, 1921-2002. 4. Cole, G. D. H. (George Douglas Howard), 1889-1959. I. Title.

JC574.W93 2008
320.51—dc22

2007046062

Table of Contents

ACKNOWLEDGEMENTS

I would like to thank Mark Erickson, James Hampshire, Neil Stammers and William Outhwaite for patiently reading early drafts of different chapters. Their comments were incredibly useful. I remain indebted to all four. Further thanks must be extended to Darrow Schecter for his review of the entire manuscript; his feedback was, as always, invaluable. Those familiar with Darrow's work will recognise his influence throughout this book. Thanks are also due to David Barker and all at Continuum for making the entire process of writing and publishing as least stressful as it possibly can be.

INTRODUCTION

Since the publication of John Rawls' *A Theory of Justice* (1971)—followed by *Political Liberalism* (1993) and *Justice as Fairness: A Restatement* (2001)—discussions on social justice and redistributive liberalism have taken centre stage in contemporary political theory. This book adds to an enormous body of literature. It does not question Rawlsian principles, but it does reject the liberal institutions he advocates. A debate is constructed in which his liberalism is contrasted with a non-statist socialism informed by the English theorist of guild socialism G.D.H. Cole.[1] These two authors visualise alternative macro socio-economic schemes. Although they are set within modern liberal and libertarian socialist frameworks respectively, they share a commitment to reducing vast inequalities in wealth. A key component of the two principles of justice Rawls articulates is the *difference principle*—that inequalities are only permitted if they benefit the least well-off. Rawls proposes that citizens deliberating without awareness of subjective characteristics—a collective lack of knowledge captured by the Rawlsian term the *veil of ignorance*—will be compelled to prioritise a society structured to accommodate this principle to other systems in which inequalities are allowed to concentrate with lesser degrees of regulation. This assertion will not be challenged. However, it is shown how the difference principle will be more easily realised in the left-libertarian scheme I shall be defending. The argument is that Rawlsian premises point to a more radical conclusion than Rawls acknowledges. As we shall see, Cole's libertarian socialist economy aims to allocate goods and resources through democratic means. Although this scheme has much to offer contemporary socialist discourse—and, of equal significance, political praxis—it must be recognised at the outset that certain revisions are required. Throughout this book these qualifications are introduced and analysed in detail. The resulting modernised, rejuvenated and revitalised version of Cole's scheme is referred to hereafter as New Economic Democracy (NED), the rationale of which will become clear as this introductory chapter unfolds.

1. Social Justice

It will be instructive to establish what I take to be the contentious issues in Rawls' theory. He is keen to promote liberal justice, what fairness means to individuals in liberal societies. The justice is distributive: it is concerned with the distribution of benefits and burdens. As all cases should be treated alike, it is ultimately about fairness. Such cases are morally urgent whenever the circumstances of justice apply, which is whenever self-interested people experience relative scarcity. Relatively scarce goods need co-operation in their acquisition. This requires considerations of justice, thus fairness matters. For Rawls, fairness is a morally neutral standard that determines how competition for relatively scarce resources can be conducted. He wants to show what fairness requires in people's social, economic and political arrangements. In normative terms, fairness is the central justifying principle. The highest praise to give any institution is to call it just. In the sense that justice is about what is due to people, it implies a formality in what they are entitled to. Inasmuch as the state is justified in using its coercive power to enforce people to perform their duties, state action is significant to duty. Justice identifies what people's coercively enforceable duties are. In Rawlsian liberalism this implies that the talented hold a duty to sacrifice a portion of their income to assist the less fortunate, a duty which can be enforced (Levine 2002: 179–84; Swift 2001: 9–15). Although I shall not dispute Rawls on any of this, alternative political arrangements are theorised in which to satisfy more thoroughly social justice understood in these terms. Rawls argues that parties in the *original position*—a hypothetical thought experiment in which individuals are all equally deprived of personal knowledge—will choose the difference principle, as it assures that the worst-off are the best worst-off when compared with the worst-off in other socio-economic set-ups. His defence of the maximin principle—*max*imise the position of those who have the *min*imum; the 'risk-averse strategy'—has great appeal. It seems likely that rational self-interested citizens would, under the appropriate conditions, choose the difference principle before all others. It is unclear though why parties would choose the kind of social liberalism Rawls insists they would. Indeed, a key premise of this book is that the difference principle can be applied more successfully to NED. In what follows, the argument is made that the worst-off in my scheme will be in a superior position than their counterparts in Rawlsian liberalism. So whilst Rawls' *concept* of justice—that basic rights and duties are assigned equally to all individuals—will not be contested, his more detailed *conception* of justice—the principles by which the concept is to be realised, justice as fairness—will be (1971: 5; Dreben: 330).[2]

For Rawls, a just constitution embodies a just procedure, within a contractarian setting, in which to procure a just outcome. The procedure is the political process of the constitution, and the outcome is just legislation; hence, if there are just circumstances and a just procedure, then the resulting distributions must also be just. A word of clarity though, as the emphasis is on processes, rather than outcomes: the aim of determining which particular basic structure is the most just is not Rawls' prime objective. Indeed, provided the guidelines to his procedural justice are strictly adhered to, any given outcome can be just:

> . . . it is not always clear which of several constitutions, or economic and social arrangements, would be chosen. . . . Institutions within the permitted range are equally just, meaning that they could be chosen; they are compatible with all the constraints of the theory. Thus on many questions of social and economic policy we must fall back upon a notion of quasi-pure procedural justice (1971: 201).

This, however, begs the question from the array of politico-economic arrangements that fall within the range of the 'just outcome family': which one can reasonably be considered more just? Rawls does not get drawn in to answering this question; he leaves it open, content to conclude that both his model of 'property owning democracy' (POD) and liberal socialism can secure the two principles and therefore be regarded as just societies. Nevertheless, he does stress that justice as fairness "tries to set out guidelines for how the decision can reasonably be approached" (2001: 139). He adds that in deciding between the two, information from history and political thought can be referred to; this is to supplement procedural justice (2001: 136–9). I will accordingly take up the issue directly and, using the sources Rawls allows, draw a more definitive conclusion. So whilst he does not directly address the issue of democratic institutional design, a tighter application of the Rawlsian method will reveal that the realisation of the two principles of justice require reforms in property rights more extensive than POD permits. POD is articulated through general principles, it is loosely defined; by way of contrast, the institutional arrangements in NED are specified with greater precision, they are more rigorously defined. My argument has both a negative and a positive dimension: it is negative in the sense that when the two principles of justice are applied to the basic structure of POD, they cannot fulfil their purpose; it is positive in the sense that when they are applied to the basic structure of NED, they can. Following the schema of quasi-pure procedural justice, it will be shown that between NED and POD, the former constitutes the just society. This is the only logical conclusion that can be drawn when the Rawlsian method is adopted and applied more closely.

2. Rawlsian Liberalism, Cole's Libertarian Socialism and New Economic Democracy

As we have just seen, Rawls acknowledges that in principle the difference maxim is compatible with both capitalism *and* socialism (1971: 271, 546).[3] Nevertheless, he regards the basic structures of capitalism as fundamentally sound. Regulations to accommodate his two principles of justice are required, but the three key institutions of private property, wage labour and a market economy are not regarded as fundamentally flawed.[4] POD retains these capitalist facets, which are overseen by a sizeable government constituted by four main branches: allocative, stabilisation, transfer and distributive. For Rawls these governmental divisions are fair as together they will ensure economic justice. It is clear that Rawls' liberalism is, in essence, a model of social democracy. Cole though is unimpressed by social democracy, arguing that parliamentarianism violates what he terms the 'functional principle'.[5] He is critical of statist approaches to democracy. "Mass democracy, I feel sure, is bound to be unsound unless it can be broken up into units of normally manageable size and complexity. We made, no doubt, many errors; but in that respect we were right and our critics wrong" (1958: viii). This statement, written shortly before his death and some forty odd years after he sketched his libertarian scheme, shows that throughout his life he retained his faith that socialism, so long as it is decentralised and functional, can be soundly built. It was between 1914 and 1920 that Cole developed his theory of how to break up democracy 'into units of normally manageable size and complexity'. His analysis led him to the advocacy of a libertarian socialism which incorporates a model of pluralist democracy. He remained adamant that this radical alternative can sustain its democratic attributes.

One of Cole's most important innovations consists in moving debates in political economy beyond the (socialist) plan versus (liberal) market straitjacket by showing how consumer interests can be aggregated in consumer councils at the individual, household, municipal and regional levels. He demonstrates that the liberal emphasis on political equalities needs to be institutionalised in the relations between producers and consumers, so that supply and demand can be co-ordinated without relying on supposedly invisible hands or the concentrated power of state planners. This is an ingenious argument. He takes the ideology of consumer power and choice that is normally used by apologists of capitalism and puts it to work for very different ends. Cole's model undermines capitalist social relations by de-coupling consumer choice from individual income, and by making consumer representation a right of citizenship rather than a prerogative of private wealth. Articulating consumer interests in a formally inclusive setting such as this establishes structural mechanisms in which political action can be channelled. This represents a vast improvement upon anything that is available at present. Consumers do have room to manoeuvre in market economies, but, one might be tempted to ask, what is more unwieldy than trying to organise and enforce a boycott of products that have already been produced and thrown out onto the market?

So, like Rawls, Cole recognises economic justice as a laudable objective and sketches institutions for its realisation. But in contrast to Rawls, he pictures a system of social governance which fundamentally remodels the public-private dualism. Cole shows that in order for democracy to be liberal in the pluralist sense, it will have to break with the property relations underpinning liberalism whilst retaining the liberal emphasis on freedom of speech, assembly, information and representation. He suggests that in order for liberalism to realise its stated aims, it will have to evolve beyond both a negative understanding of liberty and possessive individualism. Otherwise it will have to accommodate itself to demands for democracy in ways that will inevitably produce oligarchy, or worse, tyranny. Central to his scheme are self-governing bodies in which governmental functions are devolved and carried-out. The private sphere is transformed into a domain of co-operation and collective governance. Although the community would own productive property, the guilds would possess it collectively. This scheme establishes both a self-governing civil society and a state with pluralized component functions. In the manner in which it adheres to a re-politicisation and democratisation of the institutions in the civil sphere, it transforms the prevailing divide between state and civil society. Organisations like the guilds and consumer councils are constructed into the state's (commune system) set-up through mechanisms of representation and consultation. Administrative machinery is simultaneously distributed to these functionally demarcated spheres of democratic authority. Although Cole's system building has real strengths, it has to be acknowledged that in parts his suggestions for democratising the economy are disappointingly brief. In his later years he recognises as much. For example, the crucially important issue of democratically exerting control over investment policies, which is clearly vital to a politically organised economy, is not addressed in his writings. As he conceded shortly before his death, "[i]t surprises me now how little thought we gave in those days [1914–20] to the . . . control over investment, of which we were hardly conscious as a problem" (1958: vii). By way of correction, I will consider this matter in depth. It is also necessary to fill in some other gaps. Nine decades have passed since Cole first devised his scheme. During this time socialist discourse has evolved considerably. An engagement with this literature will serve to substantiate my argument.

The aim is to show why parties in the original position would opt for NED rather than POD. Here the contradictions in Rawls' model will be exposed. He insists that all sane people should enjoy equal participation in political affairs. "All citizens are to have an equal right to take part in, and to determine the outcome of, the constitutional process that establishes the laws with which they are to comply" (1971: 221). Yet he immediately acknowledges that "[t]he liberties protected by the principle of participation lose much of their value whenever those who have greater private means are permitted to use their advantages to control the course of debate" (1971: 222). Rawls is confident that his formidable governmental structures can effectively counteract the more extreme resultants of the free market, and so preserve the democratic constitutional process. His theoretical strictures on inequality are impressive, but his system still depends upon income from property ownership and regulated competition. These are precisely the institutional mechanisms which continue to be the key sources of inequality his system claims to contain. Consequently, it remains unclear how the intended outcome of the difference principle can be sustained in the market-based economy he subscribes to. In direct contrast, NED has the institutional arrangements whereby the desired reductions in wealth inequalities can more realistically be secured. Indeed, this book will show that it is this scheme, with its pluralist mediation of state and civil society, which is better equipped for accomplishing this laudable goal. Rawls' superb premises, we shall contend, point logically to NED, rather than POD.

Rawls' brief and fragmented comments on institutional design are not, as explained above, his primary concern (1971: viii). However, he does state that a theory of justice allows one to "derive a conception of a just basic structure . . . that can serve as a standard for appraising institutions" (1971: 263). This has been the subject of prolonged debate. The arguments that POD is, on the one hand, a disguised capitalism, or, on the other hand, a socialism with markets, are extensive. Rawls has been both critiqued and defended by socialists. Schweickart (1978; 1993), Nielsen (1991) and DiQuattro (1983) all show why Rawls should be (or is) a socialist. Although NED will implement one of Schweickart's key structural features—an ingenious scheme of democratic investment planning—this book will take the debate onto a new path. The organisational features of a non-capitalist consumer representation, the institutionalisation of producer-consumer dialogue through the modernised guilds and consumer councils—which forms a path beyond the constraints of the exhausted planning versus market impasse—a theory of political pluralism and a critique of state sovereignty distinguish it from command socialism, market socialism and other models of economic democracy. It can now be shown how NED gets its name. The economic and democratic aspects are self-evident. The newness refers to the direction Cole's libertarian socialism has been updated, i.e., to the innovations and syntheses that have gone into the theoretical construction of NED. The outcome is a scheme of economic democracy that is premised upon a fresh attempt to sketch the organisational aspects of, in Rawlsian speak, the 'good society'. It also constitutes what I believe to be an original response to Rawls, hence the term 'new'.

One final point of clarification: the reader will have noticed that the term 'socialism' has been dropped from the title of NED. This is deliberate. Although for the sake of convenience the terms 'socialist' and 'liberal' are used throughout, NED's attraction is not solely with the radical left. It will, I hope, be received sympathetically by democratic socialists, but it is also intended to have a wider appeal beyond the political ideologies of the traditional left and right. NED aims to restrict the role of the state (commune) to the absolute minimum, the task of redistribution falling to intermediate associations. Simultaneously, it seeks to protect overall liberty to the absolute maximum. These are both central to the liberal doctrine. The claim that NED can plausibly entreat the modern liberal is not then as bizarre as it first sounds. Libertarian liberals like Norzick will not be impressed by NED's extension of democracy into the private sphere. But for those of us who accept the need for redistributive planning, such a transformation is, as this book will argue, a prerequisite for the realisation of the difference principle.

3. Towards a Left-Libertarianism

It is imperative that a detailed and systematic left-libertarian response to Rawls is constructed. With the fall of the Berlin Wall in 1989, the implosion of the Soviet Union in 1991 and the evolution of the Chinese model of communism towards an odd version of state-managed capitalism, it would seem that there are now only authoritarian alternatives to liberal democracy. This impression has been ideologically reinforced of late by the efforts of the current American administration to distinguish between liberal democratic and non-democratic governments, and to threaten the latter with economic and military sanctions in the event of non-compliance with US strategic aims. Resisting the hegemonic projects of empire and countering the neo-liberal assault on social democracy is severely impeded by the fact that it looks like there is a single feasible mode of production with its own systemic logic, technological imperatives and corresponding mode of consumption. In sum, the state socialist model in Soviet Russia and Eastern Europe is gone, and social democracy increasingly appears to be a luxury that is only affordable when capitalism happens to be booming. As leading politicians of the European Union attempt to build socio-economic and political institutions that are generally compliant with the needs of global neo-liberalism in an effort to secure competitive advantages and new markets, it is opportune to outline a plausible economic and political alternative to liberalism that does not fall back on the spent forces of state socialism and social democracy. Several key questions emerge when discussing alternatives to neo-liberalism: is there a coherent and consistently non-statist understanding of political economy that eschews the authoritarianism of the Soviet model, on the one hand, though without relying on excessively naïve notions of human nature and spontaneous organisation found in anarchism, on the other? Is there an approach that transcends the trade sectarianism of syndicalism without embracing the compromised forms of self-management advocated by most market socialists? I wish to submit, for reasons that will become clear as this book unfolds, that there is. There is no better way of achieving this objective than through a debate with by far the most influential contemporary political theorist, John Rawls.

In liberal democratic capitalist societies a dichotomy has always existed between our personal economic affairs and our lives as members of the body politic. Liberalism, in both the 'Lockean universal rights' and the 'Millian developmental' traditions, may have solid arguments about the undesirability of excessive state intervention, but it has hitherto failed to resolve the problems that stem from economic inequalities and the unequal distribution of power embodied in capitalist property relations. State socialism attempts to solve these problems in an exorbitantly authoritarian way; unsurprisingly, the totalitarian state synonymous with this dictatorial form of socialism has now been both theoretically and empirically discredited. Rawls attempts to solve them within a social democratic framework, and in doing so is prepared to grant considerable redistributive functions to the state. The Rawlsian state is far more extensive than the 'night-watchman' state traditionally associated with liberalism. If the choice is between a weakly refined capitalism, state socialist command planning or POD, it is a no-contest; the last clearly has more intrinsic appeal. This book, though, adds another dimension to the equation. The theoretical attempt to unite the private sphere of production and the public sphere of citizenship within a non-statist scheme of communal ownership presents a viable alternative to both state socialism and state liberalism. Due to the well-documented problems commonly associated with centralised planning, there is no great controversy in stressing that the comprehensive state essential to command socialism should be repudiated. It is after all one of my key objectives to build upon the critiques of capitalism by developing a socialist alternative which maximises the material conditions of the worst-off, in a way that surpasses POD, yet in the process does not create a leviathan. The paradox is that a socialist of NED's kind could plausibly reject a liberalism of Rawls' kind for itself centralising too much economic power into the hands of the state; this is a case of socialism charging liberalism with a failure to circumscribe the role of the state! Herein lies the real irony.

The argument made throughout this book is important for a number of other reasons. *A Theory of Justice* treats utilitarianism as the main opponent, saying very little about Marxism(s). It thus avoids some potentially awkward issues. As such, commentators have rightly stressed a need for additional work along this path. "The need for a systematic Marxist response is especially great, since Rawls' work, when viewed as a defence of liberal, moral and political theory, has such ideological importance" (Daniels 1989: lii). The fundamental Marxist objection when considering justice is that it makes little sense to separate distribution from production. So whilst liberal justice endorses formal equality, it ignores material inequalities; as Rawls is keen to stress that inequality is the key problem a theory of justice must confront (1971: 7), this point becomes hugely significant. By developing a left-libertarian scheme which falls loosely within the Marxist-humanist tradition,[6] it will be possible to show how production, distribution and consumption can form central parts, distinct but not separated, in an associational socialist political economy. At the same time, it will enable one to picture what the bases to a decentralised alternative to global capitalist governance may look like in organisational terms. The multifaceted critique of corporate capitalism is largely what gives the increasingly expanding anti-globalisation movement impetus. However, at the normative level these polemics remain incomplete without a viable alternative. Even the undoubted brilliance of Marx's early writings leaves many organisational questions unanswered. This is precisely what is offered in the chapters that follow.

It is probable that NED will appeal to those, academics and activists alike, who have become disillusioned with statist attempts to realise socialist goals. The collapse of authoritarian state socialism and the debacle of democratic state socialism we are currently witnessing indicate that this is by no means only an issue of merely historical interest. As such, the pressing need to re-examine non-statist alternatives to liberal democratic capitalism could hardly be more urgent. For the two state socialist traditions of Leninism (revolutionaries) and social democracy (reformers), a centralisation of economic power was the key means to an end. These approaches have been dominant. Throughout the twentieth century, socialism was largely associated with social democratic reformism, Leninist vanguards, centralism, state planning, etc. NED, however, is fundamentally concerned with how to devise a system that empowers producers in their own spheres, whilst at the same time protecting the citizens as a whole. Following Cole, central to my thesis are questions concerning political pluralism, decentralised forms of participation and the critique of the doctrine of state sovereignty. As there has been a general disinclination from those working within the dominant state socialist perspectives to acknowledge that emancipatory politics are unlikely to flourish without a socialism based on ideas such as these, it is imperative that these themes are no longer marginalised in contemporary academic discourse. The arguments made in the coming pages are intended to offer a contribution towards the necessary corrective.

The book has five chapters. Rawls' theory of justice as fairness and his redistributive liberalism are outlined in detail in Chapter One. Chapter Two introduces Cole's libertarian socialism in all its facets. His quasi-anarchist critique of the state rejects the idea of sovereignty and formulates a theory of functional representation which deconstructs the modern liberal state. The main argument of his political scheme—to promote horizontal relationships and reduce and separate vertical ones—rests in the proposed dissolution of the kind of state that combines central institutions, commands ultimate authority and has the power to act with supreme force. Cole sketches a system of social governance embedded within a pluralist democracy. This chapter provides an elucidation of why he thought that the producer and civic guilds and the consumer and civic councils would constitute the right kind of economy, whilst communes at the local, regional and national level would provide the bases for a libertarian political alternative to the liberal democratic state. Chapters One and Two serve as primary introductions to the arguments of Rawls and Cole, and are intended to give the reader a thorough knowledge of both POD and libertarian socialism respectively. Chapter Three is where the critical discussions begin.

It is important to reiterate that I am *not* attempting to distinguish POD from Cole's scheme. Rather, the contrast is between the former and a contemporary left-libertarian model, NED, which, although informed by Cole's libertarian socialist writings, has been subject to revision. As the efficiency of NED is obviously crucial, these innovations are introduced and analysed extensively. Eight decades have passed since Cole first devised his scheme. During this time arguments within socialist circles have raged about the most appropriate way to manage the economy, the most tenacious of which is whether either a centrally planned or a market economy, or a combination of the two, can realise socialist goals. I shall discuss the similarities and differences between, on the one hand, Cole's scheme, and on the other, the ideal typical command economy and the doctrine of market socialism—paying particular attention to the latter. So, for analytical purposes, his scheme is located within a centrally planned–market economy debate. This analysis enables the identification of original syntheses. Two are particularly important:

A) the introduction of an intra-guild regulation of curtailed markets to distribute certain goods. Here the discussions centre on resolving the tensions between competition and co-operation in the economic realm.

B) the 'guildisation' of the idea of subjecting new investment strategies to communal and democratic adjudication, rather than relying upon the privileges of powerful wealthy individuals, as private property regimes do. The analyses on this issue focus upon demonstrating why the vital but potentially hazardous issue of asserting collective control over the direction of the economy is crucial to any contemporary alternative to capitalism.

As a corollary of this inquiry, it will become clear how a critical re-reading of Cole's libertarian socialist economy offers real solutions to the practical and theoretical flaws which impair both command and market socialism(s). The chapter concludes by confirming that rather than reliance upon expert planners or undifferentiated competitive markets, NED's political economy will consist of both participatory democratic planning and the innovative functionally demarcated markets.

Having established the rationale behind, and the bases of, NED, Chapter Four is where the debate with Rawls begins. In this chapter the political structures in both POD and NED are subject to critical scrutiny. I shall outline and apply Marx's critique that the modern state is a shield behind which capitalist power operates to POD. It will then be shown why the former is particularly damaging to the latter. Rawls is not at fault for being committed to a social hypothesis. But if some of the assumptions in it are false, his argument must be seriously questioned. So if any of the features Marxists have generally been keen to highlight are found—class antagonisms, exploiting nature of capital, etc.—it is hard to see how POD could sustain the principles of justice. The realisation of the difference principle is, as we shall see, hugely problematic when applied to class-divided societies like POD. Despite Rawls' proposals to distribute property as widely as possible, and his keenness to prevent large concentrations of wealth, it is shown why POD is unlikely to sustain either. As such, it cannot prevent the entrenchment of a ruling capitalist class. Attention then turns to a defence of the political pluralism of NED. Here the argument that NED harbours a real alternative to sovereign power is advanced. In my scheme the substance of sovereignty has been reconstituted so that it comes to rest largely with the interacting functional bodies in civil society. The commune's authority remains as a final court of appeal, but the manner in which it may assert itself is confined. Neither is there a small dominant class possessing the financial muscle capable of wielding a disproportionate influence upon the legislature. Far from undermining basic political liberties, I will suggest that NED enhances them. It is argued that this society is more realistically equipped to sustain Rawlsian principles of justice. The conclusion drawn is that the worst-off in NED compare favourably with their counterparts in POD.

Chapter Five discusses Rawls' mature theory of a political liberalism. The value of his idea of developing what he calls an 'overlapping consensus' is not denied. But it is claimed that, as it stands in POD, it is insufficient to fulfil the stabilising role Rawls ascribes to it. By way of contrast, the political structures in NED provide the means by which the required substantiation can be most effectively realised. It is shown that in terms of sustaining a sense of community, NED's thicker conception of the political represents a significant advance on POD. In addition, NED, as explained above, shares with the liberal doctrine a commitment to restrict the use of coercive political power; it also seeks to preserve liberty, understood as both a political and economic conception, to the greatest possible extent. With this in mind, this chapter consults a body of literature that discusses the most appropriate principle, 'neutrality' or 'perfectionism', to inform the policies of the state. The question of whether the state should non-coercively, yet self-consciously, promote particular conceptions of the good has become a key aspect of contemporary liberal theory. An engagement with this debate is the means through which NED's politicised civic services are articulated. The chapter would be incomplete without a defence of the labour relations I uphold. In NED, non-alienating co-operative labour has been elevated so that it is treated as a basic political right; it will be shown that this is not in violation of the neutrality stipulations of political liberalism.[7] The reasons for this are fairly complex, and are best accounted for in the latter sections of this chapter, after Rawls' position has been fully explicated. In the concluding chapter it is confirmed that the best worst-off will not be those in POD. As NED can assimilate the difference principle into its democratic structures with a plausibility that surpasses POD, the principles of justice are more applicable to NED. The conclusion drawn is that the good society can only be NED.

Notes

1 In light of the contemporary spirit in which this book is written, and to avoid giving any impression that the core ideas in Cole's social and political thought are in any sense antiquated, his guild socialism is referred to hereafter as 'libertarian socialism'. This will, I hope, also serve to dispel any misplaced preconceptions that production would be determined without due respect to consumer interests. I am grateful to Darrow Schecter for making the former suggestion (Schecter 2007: 20–1).

2 All references to both Rawls and Cole are in year and page numbers only.

3 This issue is covered more extensively towards the end of Chapter One.

4 Rawls' two principles of justice are explained fully in Chapter One.

5 This will be defined in Chapter Two.

6 See Chapter Five.

7 I take it that non-alienating co-operative labour must involve the training and application of both mental and physical skills. (For a full list of 'goods' obtainable from meaningful work, see Arneson 1987: 528–9.) Yet other than specifying the general organisational structures through which creative labour is most likely to prosper, I make no attempt to infer, empirically, what its precise content must be. I use the term as a normative concept, that workplaces and work relations are to be arranged so that labour becomes, for all citizens, as enjoyable, fulfilling and meaningful an experience as possible. I assume this to be in the interests of what Rawls calls 'the social bases of self respect'; which, as we shall see, is an indispensable 'primary good'. These terms are introduced in Chapter One.

CHAPTER ONE

Rawls' Theory of Justice

> No longer need it seem hopelessly hostile, a world in which the will to dominate and oppressive cruelties, abetted by prejudice and folly, must inevitably prevail. None of this may ease our loss, situated as we may be in a corrupt society. But we may reflect that the world is not in itself inhospitable to political justice and its good. Our social world might have been different and there is hope for those at another time and place (2001: 38).

This chapter provides an exposition of the key elements of justice as fairness. The theory Rawls presents in *Political Liberalism* and *Restatement* is somewhat removed from his original conception. But some continuity remains; in particular the principles themselves have not been extensively re-modelled (1993: 7). The alterations introduced "leave justice as fairness substantially intact, since its basic ideals and principles remain and only their finer formulation has been . . . revised and adjusted" (1993: xlviii–xlix); the principles of justice are now seen as political principles, rather than comprehensive moral principles as they were in *Theory*. What has changed is their justification. Rawls is concerned with establishing the just, basic institutions central to a 'well-ordered society'. This is achieved through an articulation of the shared notions that exist in common understanding. The "task is to *discover* and *formulate* the deeper bases of agreement which one hopes are embedded in common sense" (1980: 518). As he did in *Theory*, Rawls is still attempting to define principles of justice, but now he insists they must secure the reasonable grounds for reaching general agreement. Rawls' thought on a well-ordered society reflects the change of emphasis in his later work. A well-ordered society has a 'fair system of social cooperation', and is endorsed by a 'public conception of justice'. A public conception, which applies only to the 'basic structure of society', is collectively and actively accepted by all citizens seen as 'free and equal'. The basic structure refers to the main political, social and economic institutions and how they 'fit together into one system of social cooperation'. The principles of justice chosen in the original position are to provide the platform to a well-ordered society. This society though—and this point captures a key shift in his thinking—is also fair to the variety of conceptions of the good, as "democratic citizens holding different comprehensive doctrines may agree on political conceptions of justice" (2001: 5–10; 1993: 35; Levine 2002: 5; Dreben 2003: 335). Chapter Five introduces Rawls' revisions more extensively, where they are analysed. In this chapter, drawing from Rawls' main works taken together, the key *premises* of justice as fairness—the original position, the veil of ignorance, the two principles, the 'maximin principle', primary goods and the idea of free and equal citizens—are all introduced. This is followed by an account of his *conclusion* that the redistributive liberalism sketched is a just society. Particular attention is paid to how the Rawlsian liberal scheme aims to distribute goods and resources through both the market and the state, as these are the institutions analysed in the forthcoming chapters. The implications to my argument of Rawls' claim that his principles of justice are compatible with socialism, though incompatible with capitalism, are then reiterated. In regards to Rawls' method, the procedural device he applies to generate the appropriate institutional basis for his two principles, the 'four-stage sequence', is, as it is the means by which the advancement of my argument is premised, also covered extensively. We begin by defining his stipulations for the determination of just principles.

1. Rawls' Method

Reflective Equilibrium

Rawls states that to develop a theory of justice we must identify principles, the application of which will be in harmony with our intuitively valid judgements. Some of these we would never consider withdrawing. For example, the abolition of slavery and the elimination of starvation are matters we will all find intuitively sound, or as Rawls puts it, we 'view as fixed points'. A theory, though, is in equilibrium when it is sanctioned through judgements that are *considered*. Judgements need to be based upon more than our initial intuitions; they must be finalised through review. This is because when a citizen unifies their sense of justice, they will come to realise that considered judgements may have been realised through instincts or influences that are suspect or uncertain. They are also sure to find that their considered judgements conflict with one another, and that some are at odds with the given principles. When this occurs it is acceptable to concentrate further questioning and revision not only on the principles but on the judgements themselves. The equilibrium through which a theory is developed then is a *reflective* equilibrium. Firstly, this is in regard to a particular conception of political justice, one that requires the least revisions in a person's initial judgements, 'narrow reflective equilibrium'; and secondly, when alternative conceptions of justice are considered, 'wide reflective equilibrium'. In the sense that citizens 'affirm the same public conception of justice', it is general as well as wide. When applied to a well-ordered society, Rawls calls it a 'full reflective equilibrium'. It is through this reasoned reflection that a basic agreement upon a political conception of justice is secured (2001: 29–31; Kukathas and Pettit 1990: 7–8).[1]

Pure Procedural Justice

The different possible basic structures the original contractees choose from are identified and represented by principles. Rawls assumes that these principles must satisfy certain constraints, what he calls 'constraints of the concept of right'. Principles are to be general in form, universal in application, and they must be a public conception, i.e., openly and widely known to serve as a final court of appeal in cases of conflict. With the constraints of right in place, all possible candidates for determining the basic structure are, he insists, in the two-principle range. Given the publicity constraint, the basic structure is chosen through a process of 'pure procedural justice'. The reasoning is that if the circumstances and the procedure are both just, then so must be the resulting distributions, regardless of what they are. In pure procedural justice, there is not an independent criterion for judging particular distributions.[2] In Rawls' theory, distributive justice is settled through a pure procedure. Justice is not treated in terms of conformity to an ideal pattern of distribution. "The basic structure is arranged so that when everyone follows the publicly recognized rules of cooperation . . . the particular distributions of goods that result are acceptable as just . . . whatever these distributions turn out to be" (2001: 50). There is simply no ideal distribution which can serve as a benchmark to judge actual distributions. Rawls' conception of justice focuses on processes, not outcomes. The Rawlsian method of pure procedural justice asserts that any distribution must be seen as part of the wider scheme of co-operation from which it originates. It must be judged in accordance with the justice of the system, and not in any sense removed from it. "There is no criterion for a just distribution apart from background institutions and the entitlements that arise from actually working through the procedure" (2001: 51). The original position is designed so that the basic structure, which must meet the stipulations imposed by the constraints of right, is chosen under procedural conditions that everyone can regard as fair (1971: 88, 130–6; 1993: 72–3; 2001: 50–2; Kukathas and Pettit 1990: 65–8). With this awareness of reflective equilibrium and pure procedural justice, the means through which Rawls substantiates his theory can now be shown.

2. Rawls' Premises

Justice as Fairness

Rawls' objective is to reveal the principles of justice that contemporary dominant political and moral views should be based upon. His aim is to show that these principles are the outcome of a selection procedure that everyone can agree is fair, hence the term 'justice as fairness'. Rawls believes he is responding to the 'fundamental question of political philosophy' in relation to constitutional democracy:

> . . . what is the most acceptable political conception of justice for specifying the fair terms of cooperation between citizens regarded as free and equal and as both reasonable and rational, and . . . as normal and fully cooperating members of society over a complete life, from one generation to the next? (2001: 7–8).

As his political and moral ideology is a form of liberalism, the account of justice offered is a defence of the values of liberal democracy. Rawls' liberal problem is connected with finding fair terms for individuals and groups who hold competing, and often incommensurable, conceptions of what is 'the good'. Despite this, he believes it is possible for individuals to reach an agreement upon a common concept of justice. He is therefore concerned with demonstrating how generally agreed principles of justice could develop from the conditions of justice. His argument is that justice as fairness is appropriate for a well-ordered society in which everyone agrees with the same principles, and that social institutions can satisfy these principles (2001: 7–8, 16).

The Original Position and the Veil of Ignorance

The most distinctive feature of justice as fairness is its attempt to revive a notion of the social contract, in which a set of political and moral principles can be accepted generally. For Rawls, principles of justice are fair when they have been chosen in conditions where the parties involved have no idea how they will be affected by them. The idea is that justice as fairness will emerge from a collective ignorance. Rawls imagines a purely hypothetical and non-historical situation he calls the *original position,* in which the free and equal citizens are able to agree on the fair terms of social co-operation. In the original position, parties act as citizens' (not persons', but citizens')[3] representatives; as such, it can be thought of as a device of representation of different claims of justice (1993: 26). In this thought experiment, parties are subject to an informational constraint, the *veil of ignorance.* Knowledge about particular circumstances is denied. Parties do not know their class position, their race or gender, their physical or mental talents, or their personal conception of the good. The idea is to remove the bargaining advantages that are certain to arise in any society. There is equality as everyone is equally ignorant about their personal abilities and backgrounds, and so, to ensure fairness, all are symmetrically situated. Freedom stems from the shared ignorance about conceptions of the good, which are deliberately excluded so that everyone's right to frame their own conception is respected. In Rawls' words:

> The principles of justice are chosen behind a veil of ignorance. This ensures that no one is advantaged or disadvantaged in the choice of principles by the outcome of natural chance or the contingency of social circumstances. Since all are similarly situated and no one is able to design principles to favour his particular condition, the principles of justice are the result of a fair agreement or bargain (1971: 12).

Participants in the original position are not unintelligent, just constrained of personal knowledge and motivation. The only particular fact they are aware of is that the circumstances of justice apply; they know that most goods they are likely to need are neither in abundance nor in absolute scarcity, what Rawls calls the 'objective circumstances of moderate scarcity', and that they have 'the capacity to frame, revise and pursue a conception of the good'. General information though is obtainable—sociological, psychological and economic laws are all known. The idea is that parties know everything general, but nothing particular. Rawls' reasoning is that in the original position, the veil of ignorance insures that no one can influence the selection process to favour their own advantage. They are invited to advance principles of distribution by which they will be governed on their return to society. Rawls concludes that under these conditions, the fair principles he expresses would be chosen (1993: 23–7; 2001: 15–8, 84–5; Swift 2001: 21–23).

The Two Principles of Justice

Rawls insists that parties in the original position will only be concerned with their share of distributive assets. He argues that under the veil of ignorance they will attempt to obtain the greatest access to what he calls 'social primary goods' (see below). As this applies equally to everyone, the principles of justice chosen are agreed to in an initial situation that is fair. The social contract stemming from the original position therefore becomes the way in which the principles of justice are to form the basic structure of society. Rawls insists that two principles will emerge from the original position:

> (a) Each person has the same indefeasible claim to a fully adequate scheme of equal basic liberties, which scheme is compatible with the same scheme of liberties for all; and
> (b) Social and economic inequalities are to satisfy two conditions: first, they are to be attached to offices and positions open to all under conditions of fair equality of opportunity; and second, they are to be to the greatest benefit of the least advantaged members of society (the difference principle) (2001: 42–3).

The first principle specifies the equal liberties of citizenship, and the second contains what Rawls calls the difference principle, which addresses social and economic inequalities. Although the two principle are framed to operate 'in tandem and as a unit', the first principle is to have priority over the second, and the latter can only be applied after the parts of the previous principles have been fully satisfied (1993: 5–7; 2001: 42–3, 46).

The Maximin Principle

In order to enable themselves to decide from behind the veil of ignorance which principles will promote their good, the parties in the original position must approach society from the viewpoint of everyone since, logically, on returning to society, they could become any one of these people. So which principles is it rational to choose? Rawls suggests egalitarian or utilitarian principles would be rejected. The former is irrational, as some kind of inequalities in the difference principle may improve everyone's access to social primary goods (1993: 284). The latter is equally irrational, as no one has any way of knowing if they would be the one who is sacrificed for the greater good. Instead, Rawls believes it is rational to employ a *maximin* strategy whereby you *maximise* what you would get if you were one of the unlucky ones who on your return to society discovered you were in the *minimum*, or worse-off position (*max*imise + *min*imum = maximin). For instance, if the parties in the original position are aware of, say, six alternative socio-economic systems, all with varying degrees of affluence and inequalities, remembering that they do not know to which position or system they will be returning to, it is rational to presuppose that they would pick the system in which the worst-off were the least worst-off in comparison to the worst-off in the other five:

> To say that inequalities in income and wealth are to be arranged for the greatest benefit of the least advantaged simply means that we are to compare schemes of cooperation by seeing how well off the least advantaged are under each scheme, and then to select the scheme under which the least advantaged are better off than they are under any other scheme (2001: 59–60).

And the society with the best worst-off is the one containing the difference principle. Rawls therefore concludes that the parties in the original position would rationally choose the difference principle (1993: 282; 2001: 59–60, 97).

Primary Goods

Rawls asserts that as people in liberal societies are generally self-interested, they will seek to increase their distributive shares. The principles of justice are therefore needed to regulate the distribution of means, or primary goods. "These are various social conditions and all-purpose means that are generally necessary to enable citizens adequately to develop and fully exercise their two moral powers [see below], and to pursue their determinate conceptions of the good" (2001: 57). Primary goods are basic liberties and rights, freedom of movement and choice of occupation, powers and opportunities, wealth and income, and the social bases of self-respect. They are an appropriate index by which citizens' shares are objectively specified, and are treated as resources (1993: 181). Although they are instrumental for realising particular ends, they are not ends in themselves. These generalised means obtain what matters intrinsically, the various particular ends people hold. Rawls believes that individuals should be held accountable. He therefore insists that just principles ought to regulate how means—primary goods, not welfare—are distributed. Liberal justice respects the distributional consequences of individual choice. Distributing primary goods justly leaves individuals and associations responsible for their own holdings. Individuals are treated as ends, not means. So for Rawls it is the distribution of certain resources which matters for justice (1993: 188–9). As we have seen, parties know nothing of their personal conceptions of the good, but they are aware of the likely range of conceptions of the good, in which case they will realise it is in their interest to increase their amount of primary goods. Primary goods then are indispensable to the realisation of the various particular conceptions of the good. Yet some primary goods are clearly not within the range of the difference principle. This is why the first principle dictates the equal distribution of basic rights and liberties, which are separated from other primary goods. The first principle adheres to liberalism's central tenet of political equality. Regarding income, though, Rawls claims it is possible that unequal divisions may actually increase the distributive shares of the poorest sections of society. As it is the principle of maximin, and not equality, that is consistent with procedural justice, it is maximin that should prevail. Basic rights and liberties are separated from other primary goods because, unlike the latter, their distribution is not affected by inequalities. They come first and cannot be traded for income and wealth (1993: 75–6; 2001: 57–9; Levine 2002: 195, 202–4).

Rawls' principles of justice also demand that society be organised so that 'the social bases self-respect', a key primary social good, is equally distributed. The social bases refer to the public understanding of the two principles, which are known and endorsed by all free and equal citizens. A sense of self-worth "should be sought for the least favoured and this limits the forms of hierarchy and the degrees of inequality that justice permits" (1971: 107). He insists that abilities and talents must be paired with suitable roles or jobs. Cultivating requisite skills enables people to experience "the realization of self which comes from a skilful and devoted exercise of social duties" (1971: 84). The idea is that everyone should enjoy an equality of opportunity to enhance their natural capacities. "Each can be offered a variety of tasks so that the different elements of his nature find a suitable expression" (1971: 529). This reasoning, in accord with the 'Aristotelian Principle', infers that engaging in activities in which one is skilled is likely to produce more satisfaction and less frustration than those in which one is not (1993: 81–2; 2001: 60; DiQuattro 1983: 59–60).

Free and Equal Citizens

Justice as fairness pictures citizens engaging in social co-operation. In order to be capable of achieving this, Rawls ascribes them, in normative terms, two moral powers. One is the 'capacity for a sense of justice', the *reasonable*, and the other is a 'capacity for a conception of the good'—"the capacity to form, to revise, and rationally to pursue a conception of one's rational advantage or good", the *rational* (1993: 19). The reasonable, which is 'public in a way the rational is not',[4] presupposes and subordinates the rational (1993: 50–2). Citizens so regarded can take part in and honour a mutually beneficial social cooperation. That all citizens have the essential minimum required to fulfil the two moral powers is the sense in which they are regarded as equal. That they appreciate this in each other is the sense in which they are treated as free. "In specifying the central organising idea of society as a fair system of cooperation, we use the companion idea of free and equal persons as those who can play the role of fully cooperating members" (2001: 24). So, for Rawls, free and equal participants cooperating for reciprocal advantage is befitting to a political conception of justice (1993: 19–20; 2001: 18–22).[5]

The Four-Stage Sequence and the Priority of Basic Liberties

Having derived a conception of justice in 'abstraction from institutional forms' (1971: 195), Rawls moves on to establish the substantive content the two principles will endorse. Outlining a basic structure of society that he believes can accommodate the principles of justice, he details the just political and economic institutions. Corresponding to the former, the equal basic liberties of the first principle include political liberties like the right to stand for public office, to participate, to vote, etc.; freedom of consciousness and of thought; freedom of association and of movement; and so on. The list of basic liberties can be historically informed, taken from the most successful democratic regimes. Although the contractees in the original position are unaware of such particular pieces of information, they are known to us, and we may use them to spell out the principles of justice on offer. The list of basic rights and liberties can also be analytical. The task is to establish the liberties that are essential to the realisation of the two moral powers mentioned above. The basic liberties enable citizens to judge the justice of basic institutions and pursue a subjective notion of the good. Both principles are assigned to the basic structure, but the first principle applies directly to the constitution. The second principle is exercised only after the first principle has been satisfied, and the latter cannot in any circumstances be sacrificed for an increase in the former. As Rawls makes clear, "the equal political liberties cannot be denied to certain groups on the grounds that their having these liberties may enable them to block policies needed for economic growth and efficiency" (2001: 47). The first principle is concerned with constitutional essentials; the second principle is not. Both principles express political values, so why draw the distinction? Rawls' answer is that the basic structure has two co-ordinate roles, and each principle applies to one. The first role secures the equal basic liberties and forms a just constitutional regime. This involves the acquisition and exercise of political power, and equates with the first principle. The second role concerns the background institutions which provide social and economic justice, and these are in accordance with the second principle (1993: 229; 2001: 18–9, 44–8, 104–5).

To highlight the link between just principles and a just constitution, Rawls pictures a 'four-stage sequence' in which the principles of justice are adopted and applied. This strategy is integral to justice as fairness. It is a schema of intermediate stages which occur in a definite series, and "sketches what kinds of norms and information are to guide our political judgments of justice" (1993: 397). Firstly, the principles of justice are chosen behind the veil of ignorance in the original position. Secondly, at the constitutional convention, with the two principles now determined, the original contractees are given knowledge of the general economic and political factors of their society. From here they choose the political constitution in which the rights and liberties of the first principles will be assured, a constitution that "satisfies the principles of justice and is best calculated to lead to just and efficient legislation" (1971: 197). With this partial knowledge of their basic structure it then becomes possible, at the third stage, to frame laws determining economic and social policies as the constitution, informed by the two principles, requires and permits. At the fourth stage, with the particular situation now fully known—the veil of ignorance becoming progressively weakened as it passes through the sequential descent of the four-stage process—rules are applied by administrators and laws interpreted by the judiciary. The first principle is applied at the constitutional convention, whereas the second principle is only introduced at the legislative stage (1971: 200; 1993: 397–8; 2001: 48; Kukathas and Pettit 1990: 47–9). This is Rawls' proposal for how the political and economic arrangements of a just society can be determined. To help illustrate how the Rawlsian method will be used to show why NED is the just society, it will be useful to take a closer look at this four-stage sequence.

At the second stage of the four-stage succession, delegates choose a constitution. Within the constraints of the two principles, they frame a system detailing government power and the rights of citizenship. Although they still know nothing particular, the veil of ignorance has been partially lifted. Together with a general knowledge of social theory, they are now aware of certain facts of their society—its natural resources, its economic infrastructure, its political climate, etc. With their theoretical knowledge and a familiarity with societal facts, delegates "are to choose the most effective just constitution, the constitution that satisfies the principles of justice and is best calculated to lead to just and effective legislation" (1971: 197). For Rawls, a just constitution incorporates a just procedure aimed to secure a just outcome. The procedure is the political process of the constitution, and the outcome is just legislation. The two principles represent an independent criterion for the procedure and the outcome. That is, in the framing of a just constitution, the two principles act as an independent standard for the expressed outcome, a standard needed to make the problem of constitutional design easier.[6] This is the Rawlsian method of procedural justice. The initial task is to design a just procedure; this must incorporate the certainty that the constitution embodies the equal liberties of the first principle. The political system, which Rawls assumes to be a constitutional democracy of some description, would be an unjust procedure if it failed in this regard. The idea then is to choose from the just procedural arrangements those that stand the best chance of realising a just legal order. This requires that the delegates are aware of the general beliefs, interests and political tactics prevalent in their society. But as they are still ignorant in regards to particular citizens, themselves included, the original position is unaffected (1971: 196–8).

At the legislative stage of the four-stage order, proposed bills are judged by legislators who, as usual, are denied all information on particularities. They enact laws only as the constitution permits and the two principles require. In relation to the constitutional convention, it is far harder to tell if the second principle is being applied successfully; there is more room for reasonable disagreement in the evaluation of complicated social and economic variables. It is easier to reach agreement on the practice of the political arrangements of the constitution. Rawls therefore imagines a division of labour between stages in which different questions of justice are posed. These correspond roughly to the two elements of the basic structure. The first principle acts as a primary standard for the constitutional stage. The convention must protect the fundamental liberties of each citizen, and ensure that the political process is a just procedure. The second principle resonates with the legislative stage. It dictates that, within the constraints of the first principle, economic and social policies maximise the conditions of the worst off. At this stage complete economic and social facts are known. "The second part of the basic structure contains the distinctions and hierarchies of political, economic, and social forms which are necessary for efficient and mutually beneficial social cooperation" (1971: 199). Rawls confirms that the ordering of the two principles is exhibited in the sequences of the constitutional and legislative stages. The last stage is where rules to particular cases are applied by administrators and judges. At this stage no limits on knowledge remain, and all citizens are fully aware of their circumstances and characteristics (1971: 198–9; 1993: 229, 397).

Justice as fairness attempts to establish the ideal social co-operation by stressing model conceptions of both a well-ordered society and a moral person, as discussed above. The original position organises the connection between moral citizens and a well-ordered society by capturing how ideal principles of justice would be chosen. Although the principles apply universally, there is a context, the society modelled in the original position. Rawls refers to this context as reasonable. It is a society in which all the original contractees choose the fair terms of co-operation, implying that benefits and burdens must be shared in an 'appropriate fashion'. There is, though, more to social co-operation than establishing the fair terms of co-operation, 'the reasonable'; there is also a concern to advance one's own good, Rawls calls this 'the rational'. The reasonable, involving as it does reciprocity and mutuality, presupposes and subordinates the rational as it places limits on the range of ends that citizens may strive towards. At every point in the four-stage sequence, the reasonable subordinates the rational. In all four stages, agents are increasingly restricted as the tasks become more specific. In each case, as the veil of ignorance weakens, the constraints of the reasonable become stronger. This is because in a well-ordered society, the principle of equal basic liberties is applied before any subjective pursuit of the good. In the original position, reasonableness restrains rational reflection (1980: 520–30; 1993: 339–40; 2001: 6–7, 18–9, 80–4; Kukathas and Pettit 1990: 126–32).

To summarise, the political constitution will enforce the first principle, the state being conceived as an association of equal citizens. The government can only restrict liberty to maintain public order. When security is seriously threatened, so is liberty. This implies that it is only just to constrain a liberty in the interests of liberties more widely conceived. In addition, equal liberty implies that all citizens are given the chance to participate in the political arena; legislative power is to be held accountable by the usual separations of powers, systems of checks and balances and a declaration of rights. A just political constitution grants government the authority to pass and enforce laws, yet also limits its powers as liberty demands. These constitution essentials are, Rawls maintains, the traditional devices of constitutional democracy. An economic system is just if it sustains the second principle, and the just political system upholds this economy through legislation. Equality of opportunity is realised through subsidized schooling, regulating the activities of enterprises, averting monopolies and the provision of a minimum income. For Rawls, the maintenance of a just economy requires four branches of government (see below). It is clear that economic justice is embodied in the ideal-typical institutions of a welfare state. This is how the two principles are to govern the basic structure. Finally, the distinction between the two principles is drawn because a) they are applied at different stages and accord with the two co-ordinate roles of the basic structure, b) establishing the constitutional essentials is more urgent, c) it is easier to see if they are realised and d) it is less difficult to reach agreement about what they should be (1971: 271–7; 1993: 230; 2001: 28, 49; Kukathas and Pettit 1990: 49–51).

3. Rawls' Conclusion

Capitalism Renounced

Although Rawls is defending modern liberalism, POD (1971: 274), he infers that a theory of justice is not incompatible with socialism. This section explains why he believes both systems could be just. It should first be noted why he rejects capitalism. He begins by pointing out that both 'laissez-faire capitalism' and 'welfare-state capitalism' violate the two principles, and therefore cannot be considered just. Although the latter has some regard for equality of opportunity, they each fail to secure the fair value of the equal political liberties. Huge inequalities in the ownership of productive assets ensure a command over the economy, and consequently political processes, concentrates within a small class. Furthermore, economic and social inequalities are not regulated by the notion of reciprocity. Given this, Rawls makes it very clear that although welfare-state capitalism and POD both sanction private property in productive assets, they are not the same. He infers that "the background institutions of property-owning democracy work to disperse the ownership of wealth and capital, and thus to prevent a small part of society from controlling the economy, and indirectly, political life as well" (2001: 139). Rather than redistribute income to the least well-off 'at the end of each period', POD ensures the widespread ownership of the means of production 'at the beginning of each period'. Rawls' intent is to enable all citizens to manage their own activities within a setting of a 'suitable degree of social and economic equality':

> In property-owning democracy . . . the aim is to realise in the basic institutions the idea of society as a fair system of cooperation between citizens regarded as free and equal. To do this, those institutions must, from the outset, put in the hands of citizens generally, and not only of a few, sufficient productive means for them to be fully cooperating members of society on a footing of equality (2001: 140).

The anti-monopolisation of productive resources is, for Rawls, essential if the basic structure is to actualise pure background procedural justice (2001: 137–40).

Redistributive Liberalism

Despite Rawls' repudiation of capitalism, the complex of social, economic and political institutions he proposes to realise the two principles are not extensively dissimilar to those of capitalist society, even though they are in need of moderation:

> As these institutions presently exist they are riddled with grave injustices. But there presumably are ways of running them compatible with their basic design and intention so that the difference principle is satisfied consistent with the demands of liberty and fair equality of opportunity (1971: 87).

This scheme involves widespread ownership of the means of production. Although land and capital are not equally held, they are broadly distributed (1971: 73). The idea is that divisions will not be so great that a small group will be in a position to control productive resources (1971: 280). As we have seen, social classes are identified by reference to the share of primary social goods, and can be compared on objective grounds (1971: 91–2). These classes are termed 'relevant social positions', each one representing different levels of well-being. There are any number of these, all of which are distinguished by occupation, wealth and income differentials. Hence the clearness of Rawls' class theory: it simply involves breaking everyone down into different degrees of well-being. It is within this constitutional democracy, where the government oversees a market economy, that Rawls believes his two principles will be realised. The government is to supplement markets by allocating labour and resources. Here private enterprises operating in labour and capital markets are kept competitive through taxation and income transfers. Although inequalities of life-prospects will still exist between those in different social positions, Rawls believes they can be just if they do not violate the second principle. Take the example of two youths of equal talent, one the son of a barrister, the other a son of an unskilled manual labourer. Unequal life-prospects are justified if decreasing the inequality makes the latter worse-off. The assumption that inequalities provide incentives which ensure an efficient economy, the end result being a greater distribution of material benefits to everyone, presupposes limits to redistribution. Rawls' welfare-state transfer payments needed to 'mitigate the inattention of a market economy' must not threaten the growth and efficiency of the productive process. Limits occur when the taxation policies needed to fund transfer payments interfere with economic efficiency, not least by reducing incentives, to the point that lower-class expectations do not increase, but decline (1971: 98; DiQuattro 1983: 54–7; Macpherson 1973: 90–1).

Rawls regards this well-ordered society as a social co-operative union which embodies a mutual benefit principle, an 'idea of reciprocity between citizens'. Unlike market principles of distribution, in which social fortune, pure luck, natural capacity, etc. are all powerful determining factors, the distribution sanctioned by the difference principle is conditional. Rewards that cannot be shown to be related to performing a social function are simply not allowed. Those in the most advantaged stratum enhance the common good by improving the conditions of the least advantaged. Greater returns, though, are not permitted purely on the basis of the best-off benefiting the worst-off. Rewards are not only through this disproportionate contribution criterion, they represent compensation for the cost of fulfilling social obligation. Those who contribute more to the common good deserve a larger share themselves. This is to compensate for the greater costs encountered in the fulfilment of their socially necessary labour. Incentives are deemed to be just because they align with this compensatory facet of the difference principle:

> . . . the difference principle includes an idea of reciprocity: the better endowed . . . are encouraged to acquire still further benefits . . . on the condition that they train their native endowments and use them in ways

> that contribute to the good of the less endowed. . . . Reciprocity is a moral idea situated between impartiality, which is altruistic, on the one side and mutual advantage on the other (2001: 76–7).

Rawls' position is that a perfectly competitive market embedded within just institutions satisfies this compensatory requirement. In the Rawlsian scheme distribution is not determined ultimately by the market. The state, via its policies of taxation and redistributive payments, its provision of public goods and catering to need, takes preference over the market. It is the state which limits inequalities; the market is relied upon only where it corresponds to just principles. The compensatory nature of the difference principle highlights why it would not be fair to establish an equal incomes policy. Certain individuals should receive more because their contribution towards realising consumer demand involves sacrifice. The argument here is that in the original position, citizens would agree that unequal distribution is fair when disparate burdens and workloads are taken into account. Rawls also makes a clear distinction between private and public goods, arguing that the production of the latter is a question that must be decided irrespective of the system of ownership of productive resources. Public goods are not aimed towards individuals in line with their personal tastes; they are made generally available independently of particular preference. Almost any good can be public if the state provides it. This is the orthodox communist vision. In direct contrast, Rawlsian justice needs the market because of its allocative function. The difference principle compensates rewards in proportion to the intensity, labourers, boredom and danger of various jobs. By enlarging the public goods sector, the system of proportional reward is simultaneously undermined. Extensive provision of public goods is at odds with the distributional aspect of the difference principle (1971: 270). So although Rawls' well-ordered society does produce public goods, their quantity is restricted (1971: 72–5, 101–2; 1993: 16–7; 2001: 49, 76–7; DiQuattro 1983: 57–65, 70–1).

Nevertheless, Rawlsian liberalism still requires a formidable state. It is composed of four government branches; each has its own set of functions. The four branches are constituted by various agencies, which are responsible for realising certain social and economic conditions. The *allocative* branch keeps the economy competitive. It relies on taxation and subsidies to correct the deviations caused by monopolies and externalities. The *stabilisation* branch addresses the macro-equilibrium of the economy. This branch seeks to establish goals like full employment. The role of these two branches is to sustain a stable and efficient market economy (1971: 275–6). The *transfer* and *distributive* branches are directly responsible for implementing justice. The former ensures that everyone is maintained above the social minimum. Its role is to provide public goods to fulfil the immediate needs of those poorly served by market distribution. "Since the market is not suited to answer the claims of need", Rawls acknowledges, "these should be met by a separate arrangement" (1971: 277). The distributive branch is concerned with the wealthier section of society. By using various taxes on inheritance and expenditure, its task is to avert those large concentrations of wealth potentially inimical to the stipulations of the first principle and the first part of the second principle—political liberty and equality of opportunity, respectively. This branch also requires revenue so that it can make available the transfer payments required to fulfil the difference principle. So, "the aim of the branches of government is to establish a democratic regime in which land and capital are widely . . . held. Society is not so divided that one fairly small sector controls the preponderance of productive resources" (1971: 280). The Rawlsian state provides public goods where collective provision is preferable to the market. Beyond this, Rawls believes it is fair to allow the price system to settle all other consumer expenditure (1971: 275–8).

Justice as Fairness and Socialism

> We must ask whether a liberal socialist regime does significantly better in realising the two principles. Should it do so, then the case for liberal socialism is made from the standpoint of justice as fairness (2001: 178).

Rawls does not refer to Cole's libertarian socialism at all.[7] The nearest he comes is a short discussion on what he calls 'liberal socialism'. Nevertheless, his brief comments are clearly applicable to my argument. Rawls rejects state socialist command planning as it cannot sustain the principles of justice, and he is right to do so. He is, though, sympathetic towards more liberal variants of socialism. Although the means of production are socially owned in liberal socialism, he adds that "economic power is dispersed among firms, as when, for example, a firm's direction and management is elected by, if not directly in the hands of, its own workforce" (2001: 138). In Rawlsian liberal socialism, firms are situated within a system of competitive markets. In terms of ideal descriptions—when something is working well, both POD and liberal socialism include arrangements whereby the principles of justice can be satisfied:

> Both property-owning democracy and a liberal socialist regime set up a constitutional framework for democratic politics, guarantee the basic liberties with the fair value of the political liberties and fair equality of opportunity, and regulate economic and social inequalities by a principle of mutuality, if not by the difference principle (2001: 138).

In making a practical decision between the two systems, information drawn from historical circumstances and the traditions of political thought can be considered, which, presumably, is to supplement pure procedural justice (2001: 136–8).

The just society does not, he insists, have to be premised upon the private ownership of the means of production (1971: 65–6). Socialism with communal ownership, however, would still need to be set within a market economy. He defends markets for their efficiency and their ability to uphold liberties and equality of opportunity. Socialism is distinguished from a private-property economy on the grounds that "the size of the public sector under socialism . . . is much larger" (1971: 266). A further distinction is how the two systems would implement markets. Socialism will use markets to distribute consumption goods, but markets will not decide the direction of production, this being the prerogative of planning. A private-property economy will use the market for both. Rawls does not commit himself in advance on whether a private-property system or socialism, or the many intermediate forms, is preferable to the requirements of justice. It is clear though that due to the orientation towards market motivations, and in regards to the redistributive role Rawls ascribes to the state, his socialism is clearly in the social democratic tradition. As we have just seen, central to his just society is a set of statist regulators devised to maintain liberties and equality of opportunity, restrict monopolies, provide a minimum income, correct market externalities, realise full employment, provide equal chances of education, prevent financial equalities from being large enough to undermine the equal value of the political liberties of the first principle and ensure a widespread ownership of the instruments of production. For Rawls, given that individuals are generally self-interested and have limited altruism (1971: 280–1), these formal arrangements will meet the stipulations of the two principles as well as can be expected. In Rawlsian liberal socialism the instruments of production will be publicly owned, firms will be directed by workers' councils and constitutional democratic decision making will 'determine the general features of the economy' (1971: 280). Market forces, though, will still dictate the conduct of firms. So although Rawls does suggest that the two principles of justice can be realised in a socialist society, it is one that shares certain key institutions of a capitalist market system. This issue will be dealt with in Chapter Four, where Rawls' just society is analysed (1971: 274–5; Macpherson 1973a: 344).

These are the essential features of, and rational behind, Rawls' theory of justice. In the preceding chapters his premises will be defended and used to justify the institutions of NED. In the process, his conclusion, POD, will be rejected. In order to achieve this, it will be helpful to first set out the institutional contours of Cole's libertarian socialism.

Notes

1 Space limits restrict me from going any deeper into the idea of reflective equilibrium. For interesting discussions, see the articles by Norman Daniels, Joseph Raz and D.W. Haslett in Corlett (1991).

2 This is not to be confused with the principles of justice themselves, which for Rawls are substantive, and therefore more than procedural (1993: 192).

3 This captures a shift in Rawls' thinking from *Theory* to *PL*.

4 The public–non-public distinction is fully explained in Chapter Five, where it is analysed.

5 In *PL*, the 'moral citizen' has replaced the 'moral person' of *Theory* (Dreben 2003: 325).

6 Rawls confirms elsewhere that as the two principles in justice as fairness are not procedurally neutral, they are clearly substantive (2001: 153).

7 He does, though, use the expression 'wage slavery', a term that was condensed into 'wagery' by the guild socialist S.G. Hobson (1971: 281).

CHAPTER TWO

Cole's Libertarian Socialism

> I was against centralism whether it manifested itself in the dictatorship of a class . . . or in an overweening advocacy of the claims of the State as representing the whole body of citizens. I believed that democracy had to be small, or broken up into small groups, in order to be real, and that it had to be functional for this to be possible—that is, related to a definite and particular activity and not to an indiscriminate medley of purposes combined in a single body deemed to be superior to and different in its motives from all others. To this conception of democracy I have adhered all my life (1958: vi/ii).

This chapter provides an exegesis of Cole's libertarian socialism. It provides an account of his objection to socialist collectivism, the doctrine of state sovereignty and undifferentiated representation. As we shall see, he asserts that genuine freedom is dependent upon self-governance, and that to have a substantive content, democracy must apply to the economic domain as well as the political. In the scheme Cole devises, there is no ridged divide between state and civil society. Democratic participation is extended to the economic and civil realms, yet restricted to the various functionally demarcated bodies individuals belong to. Self-governance is to apply both within and between these functional agencies. The challenging goal is to reconcile socialist planning with individual freedom. As well as workplace democracies, the idea that consumer interests must be represented as a right of citizenship, rather than determined through prerogatives of private wealth as they are in market economies, is expressed in organisational terms. In his initial scheme the state was to perform the role of representing consumers, but in his mature guild theory other agencies of consumer representation had replaced it. Realising consumption was not a single undifferentiated activity, he felt obliged to construct a new structure to accommodate such diversity. Here he contrives a system of councils to represent consumer interests. In *Guild Socialism Restated* (GSR), Cole confirms that a radical decentralisation must apply equally to the spheres of production and consumption. His socio-political structures underwent painstaking elaboration to find the appropriate structures to suit the new theory. In this innovative organisational setting, the modern liberal state is comprehensively rejected, the rationale of which is explained below. His critiques are augmented through the development of two interrelated arguments, functional representation and political pluralism, both of which are also clarified below. The politico-economic structures sketched in GSR are then introduced. There are, accordingly, four sections to this chapter: 1) 'The Democratic Domain', 2) 'The Functional Principle', 3) 'Political Pluralism' and 4) 'Cole's Rejection of the Consumer Representing State and His Amplification of the Functional and Pluralist Principles'.

1. The Democratic Domain

> We have never really believed in democracy; for, if we had, we should have tried to apply it, not to politics alone, but to every aspect of human life. We should not have been democrats in politics and autocrats in industry: we should have stood for self-government all round (1972: 160).

Cole suggests that within the capitalist system, workers are motivated to work through fear (of starvation) or appeals to their greed (greater financial reward). Such motives are, he maintains, both inadequate and undesirable. He therefore suggests a new motive: 'free communal service'. It is communal in the sense that goods will have a use value—a use that is determined through democratically arrived at demand, and not through personal profit. It is free in the sense that freedom is inseparable from the principle of industrial self-government. These two principles of service (to the community) and freedom (in the workplace) are incomplete without each other. The fundamental principle of libertarian socialism's productive ethic is that the good of the community must take precedence over the private interests of the individual. Rather than production being based around private individuals striving for personal returns, it should be premised on the manner in which the whole community can meet its own basic needs. Cole's reason for adopting this principle is best clarified by taking note of his polemic against the bureaucratic and centralist forces of socialist collectivism. He believes the fundamental evil in society is slavery, not poverty, the former being the disease, the latter only the symptom. "The many are not enslaved because they are poor, they are poor because they are enslaved" (1972: 41), and that "[o]ur preoccupation with poverty is the cause of our long wanderings in the valley of the shadow of reformism" (1972: 42). Believing poverty to be the root evil in society, collectivist socialists seek a solution through redistributive measures, believing a reformed parliament can protect workers' interests. In their eyes, as modern methods of production are on such a large scale and are so complicated, the individual craftsman's freedom cannot be revitalised. The gist of their argument then is that it hardly matters how industry is organised. Rather, the aim is to secure the greatest efficiency in production in order to manage the widest product distribution possible. For Cole, as long as the social problem is thought of as fundamentally a question of distribution, the more immediate inequalities in the productive realm will remain largely intact. This position completely misconceives the nature of freedom:

> Freedom is not simply the absence of restraint; it assumes a higher form when it becomes self-government. A man [sic] is not free in himself while he allows himself to remain at the mercy of every idle whim: he is free when he governs his own life according to a dominant purpose or system of purposes (1972: 157).

To be industrially emancipated, the workers must therefore be able to choose their own leaders[1] (1972: 36–8, 40–5, 156–9; 1921: 2–3; 1921a: 2–3).

Democracy, on the other hand, places trust in human nature. It asserts that we are fit to govern ourselves. Cole's puzzlement is why the collectivists, who are supposed to adhere to the democratic principle, appear so sceptical and doubtful towards human nature:

> They admit the right of the worker, as a citizen, to a vote in the choice of his political rulers; but they refuse to the same man the right to elect his industrial rulers. The contradiction is flagrant: the explanation of it is discreditable (1972: 160).

Moreover, on its own political democracy is futile unless it is premised upon industrial democracy. Not surprisingly, he regards representative democracy as inadequate as long as it is limited to the confined domain of politics, thus leaving all other aspects of social life untouched. He is then critical of the traditional economic and political socialist theories of the state: the doctrines of collectivism and parliamentary representation respectively. His scathing appraisals stem from the same position, the radical democrat. For Cole, full democracy can only be achieved within a system of workers' control. Such a system cannot be attained if the means of production are either privately or state owned. Democracy is not just about deciding what products get produced, but about the actual process of production itself. It is a statement about people's social relationships, a general theory of society, not simply an insufficient theory of government. Citizens must be part of the decision-making process or lose part of themselves. In contrast to social democracy, Cole prioritises local producers' democracy over national consumers' democracy. This urgent appeal for workers' control leads straight to the question of state sovereignty (1972: 160–2).

2. The Functional Principle

To allow the guilds their stature, Cole attempts to put the state in its 'proper place'. He suggests that as it is not the only institution within the community, it should not have an absolute right to command the individual's loyalty. He not only rejects the view that the state sustains citizens in the community, he also rejects any notion that people can be totally represented by any single organisation. Rather than treating the state as the universal sovereign of the community, he views it as just one association among many, none of whom have a legitimate claim to supremacy. Within this diversity of association, the state is certainly granted an important role, but it cannot claim a 'solitary grandeur'. "There is no universal sovereign in the community, because the individuals who compose that community cannot be fully represented by any form of association" (1972: 12). It is this concept of representation that is the foundation for Cole's democratic model. He asserts that over time the democratic idea has been lost in an inaccurate theory of representation, a theory that held that one person could 'represent' another absolutely. To Cole, the claim that an individual as a whole can be adequately represented is a dangerous sham. The alternative idea is that only particular functions and purposes that citizens have in common are capable of proper representation. Therefore the conditions that would produce either effective representation or misrepresentation are, with the former, that representation is 'specific and functional', and with the latter, that it is 'general and inclusive'. Misrepresentation occurs when the initial reasons for granting representation lose their precision and distinctiveness. Parliament is the worst offender, for its apparent omnibus representation denies the principle of function that is essential for real democracy. It is precisely because the state sees itself as being all-inclusive and because parliament is premised on the absurdity of universal representation that it fails (1972: 7–12, 14; 1920: 13–5; Wright 1979: 58–60).

So, in Cole's thesis, the concept of function is the real principle of democracy. As citizens all have many different purposes and wants, they form various different groups and associations. They can express their various interests in each appropriate association, every one representing a different aspect of their divergent purposes. As no single interest can express the individual as a whole, it must be structurally possible to allow expression for a multiple of interests. There is no single general concept of citizenship. This results in the establishment of a number of associations to satisfy people's needs. In this entanglement of associations, every one will exist for a certain specific purpose, a purpose that will demarcate the function of the association. The character of the whole must find expression in the interrelations that occur in the various institutional settings. Sovereignty exists only in the interaction between these bodies. Even then, such communal sovereignty is incomplete because none of the groups that make up society can perfectly represent the general will of the community itself. Any notion of state sovereignty is therefore inconsistent with the principle on which libertarian socialism is founded (1972: 13–5; 1920a: 47–54).

3. Political Pluralism

As the political theory of collectivism incorporates the doctrine of state sovereignty, Cole is emphatic that libertarian socialist political theory must offer a viable alternative. He begins this task by engaging with Rousseau's theory of associative and general wills. Very briefly, Rousseau recognised that social life is the expression of organised will. His conception of the general will, and its affiliation with the body politic, is the key to understanding his social theory. For Rousseau, although an associational will may for its members be general, it is nevertheless individual in relation to the state. Due to his concern that associations may conspire against the general public, he insisted that they should always be subordinate to the body politic, which consequently becomes sovereign. Like Rousseau, Cole sees the associative act as having a double relation. In terms of the association that carries it out it is general, but in relation to the wider society it is particular. The key difference is that for Rousseau loyalties to particular associations must be inferior to those connected to the body politic, whereas for Cole any obligation to the state cannot account for all of the other social obligations. On this reasoning, as the state holds no claim to superior obligations, it loses its omnipotence. "The State, I contend, even if it includes everybody, is still only an association among others, because it cannot include the whole of everybody" (1914a: 154). Cole's objective then is not to replace the state with a rival incumbent, but to particularise it. In contrast to Rousseau, he argues that the general will cannot express itself completely in any singular piece of social machinery. He suggests that all organised machinery, governmental or non-governmental, can only partially express the general will. So the state, as the national geographical grouping, can adequately represent the features of common life that can be represented geographically. However, things are different in the areas where actions affect people unequally. Here the state cannot represent the common will. Industry, for example, affects everyone in different ways. Every separate industry has its own unique interests, and industry as a whole has its own general outlook that cannot be represented by the geographical group.[2] This functional difference calls for a special association to control the industrial sphere. Cole reiterates that the general will embodies a range of lesser and conflicting particular wills. These wills are, as indicated above, differentiated by function, and are indispensable for the full expression of the general will. "With Society, the complex of organised associations, rests the final more or less determinate Sovereignty. We cannot carry Sovereignty lower without handing it over to a body of which the function is partial instead of general" (1914a: 157). The suggestion is that only in society as a whole can a complete fullness of powers be contained. Indeed—and for Cole this was

Rousseau's error—we cannot place in the political body that which only the whole of society can incorporate (1914a: 140–4, 151–9; 1920a: 132).

To recap so far, Cole views collectivism as the granting of complete sovereignty to the state, the territorial association (and syndicalism the same, only with the producers, the professional associations). He does not accept that either grouping is by itself enough. Some common requirements are accomplished better by one and others by the other. This pluralist approach is central to Cole's theory of libertarian socialism. The key features are that associations should be the recipients of obligations, that the functional principle is society's main differentiating criterion, that the state is merely one functional association amongst many, that associations have the right to self-government and that inter-associational relations should enjoy a sympathetic co-ordination to meet community requirements. There was of course, as explained below, also the guilds' position within this scheme (1920b: 36–9; Wright 1979: 39).

4. Cole's Rejection of the Consumer-Representing State and His Amplification of the Functional and Pluralist Principles

As his political thought matured, Cole came to realise that consumption is not a single undifferentiated activity. Insofar, he no longer saw an adequate vehicle capable of representing consumer interests in the government system. Instead he called for radical functional decentralisation in this sphere, which, along with production, must be given full expression. It is the organisation of libertarian socialism revealed in *GSR* that represents his most complicated attempt at system building. The basic structure of society outlined here has three branches of economic and social activity that are to form the bases of a federal and decentralised structure. They are: 1) the producers' organisations, the economic guilds, 2) two distinct organisations to represent the consumers and 3) the civic services, which will represent citizens' non-economic interests. This model is functional throughout, broken down into territorial units which are institutionally linked at different levels, bringing consumption and production into harmony. The co-ordinating agency, a system of communes, consists of representatives from the guilds, the consumer and the civic bodies. We will look at each in turn, starting with the industrial guilds.

In order to explain a guild's structure and communal bases, it will be instructive to explain how Cole believes they will come into being. This involves clarifying the fundamental differences between a guild and a trade union. He begins by drawing a distinction between essential and non-essential forms of association—those which are, and those which are not, intrinsic to society. We have seen that the *content* of the association's interest helps reveal its specific function (political, vocational or appetitive). He now adds that it is its *method of operation* which identifies essential and non-essential forms. This principle exposes the difference between administrative and propagandist concerns:[3]

> By an *administrative* association I mean an association which is primarily concerned, not with the advocacy of any particular opinion, but with the doing of some particular job, the arranging and conducting of some particular part of the work which has to be done in Society (1920a: 73).

For Cole, it is the administrative associations that are primary, and essential, whereas propagandist associations are only secondary, and non-essential. Propagandist associations are not essential because they do not themselves execute vital social functions. Administrative associations though do, as they deal with interests that are vital to everyone. Although the organisations of producers are essential, it does not follow that all trade unions are. To clarify this claim, Cole makes a further distinction, this time between 'several' and 'associative' wants. Although both give rise to associations, their social value differs substantially. Associations with a several bond represent their members in only one capacity; they are not concerned with the satisfaction of their additional needs. Associative wants, on the other hand, need a tight and lasting co-operation from associates. This creates a communal spirit, and their respective associations constitute a more essential section of the structure of society. Cole generalises that when people co-operate to fulfil a want on an associative basis, the want in question is usually in the general interest. These associations are therefore the most central to society and command a higher status (1920a: 34–7, 65–7, 72–9).

On this criterion, even though trade unions *whose wants are several* may be principally administrative in function, Cole nevertheless refers to them as *non-essential*. The guilds too will be concerned with administration, although as they will be characterised by *associative wants*, they will be *essential*. Cole is now in a position to describe how the guilds will emerge. He observes that the several and associative distinction is not fixed in concrete terms. Most associations contain both, although to different degrees. "But, in proportion as an association finds and fulfils its function in Society, the 'associative' basis tends to become predominant, and the motive of 'severalty' sinks into the background" (1920a: 79). For example, when trade unions operate to improve the conditions of wage-earners, they correspond to several motives. But when they push for a control in the running of their industries, hence becoming industrial unions, their motives become associative. Cole thereby calls for a radical reconstruction in the structure of trade union machinery. He cites the struggle between craft and industrial unionism, and appeals for an amalgamation on an extensive scale. Rather than adhering to the craft union perspective, which asserts that skilled and unskilled workers should have separate organisations, he develops the idea that both skilled and unskilled workers should be jointly organised in one union. This position is known as industrial unionism. Both these positions stress a different kind of trade union organisation. Craft unionism collectivises all the workers who are engaged in the same kind of work—clerks, carpenters, tailors etc. Industrial unionism goes further, it places all the workers who are co-ordinating their activities to produce the same kind of products into one organisation—miners, railway employees, shipyard workers, etc. (1972: 54–6, 58–60; 1920a: 73, 76–9).

Cole endorses industrial unionism not just because craft unionism lacks the strength to confront the mass formation of capitalism, but also because the latter is ill equipped to make a claim for industrial control. "Only an Industrial Union, embracing the whole personnel of an industry, can assume control over that industry" (1972: 62). If trade unionism is simply protective, and if its job is only to improve workers' conditions within the wage-system (corresponding more to several motives than associative), then either craft or industrial organisation can meet these requirements. But if its task is more than just protecting its members' material interests, and if it includes the establishment of self-government in industry (with associative wants now taking precedence)—and for Cole this is exactly the role it should be taking—then it has to be industrial unionism:

> Only by the impetus of their own intelligence and economic power can the workers pass from the era of collective bargaining to the era of collective control, to Guild Socialism from the wage system . . . a body consisting of clerks or mechanics or labourers drawn from a number of different industries can never demand or assume the conduct of industry. It can secure recognition, but not control (1972: 64).

So to assume control, the trade union structure must be industrial. These are Cole's reasons for supporting industrial unionism (1972: 60–5). To confirm, *when an industrial union is formed and puts into practice the idea of collective control, once it takes over the administration and democratic regulation of its particular industry, thereby institutionalising its associative basis, it becomes a guild.* Hence:

> A National Guild would be an association of all the workers by hand and brain concerned in the carrying on of a particular industry or service, and its function would be actually to carry on that industry or service on behalf of the whole community (1920b: 46–7).

For example, the railway guild will include managers, porters, technicians, engine cleaners, signal-men, etc. It is assigned by the community the job of administering an efficient railway. So long as it fulfils this task, its internal arrangements (like choosing its officers) and its methods of administration will remain its own business. The general basis of guild organisation is that it is industrial and represents a distinct service (1920b: 43–7).

With this position established, Cole elaborates upon the structure of a guild. He adds that for democracy to be real, every member of the guild must exercise it directly. The freedom of the small unit is therefore vital. Guild members are scattered all over the country, and the local workplaces—factory, mine, dock, station, classroom, etc.—are the principle component of industrial democracy.

With the local workshops mostly conducting their own affairs, the larger guild organisations will co-ordinate production to match supply with demand, supply raw materials, sell products that were not directly sold from the factories themselves, establish general regulations of organisation and productive methods and represent the guild in its external communal relations—such as other guilds and consumer bodies. The district committees who form the basis of the larger guild structures will represent the various factories and different classes of workers. Likewise, the national committee will follow suit so that every district and sectional point of view is represented. The industrial guilds will be co-ordinated through the Industrial Guilds Congress (IGC). This will be the ultimate representative confederation on the productive side. It will act as the guild legislature, and, on solely guild matters, adjudicate in its capacity as a final court of appeal. It will also interpret the basic principles of guild practice, as well as determining the pay to the different grades of workers in and between the guilds. Like the guilds, the IGC would have guild councils at the local and regional levels (1972: 60–5; 1920b: 43–54, 59–62, 69–73).

Turning now to the equally important issue of safeguarding consumer interests, Cole sees consumption as possessing a principle of differentiation analogous to, yet different from, production.[4] It has two main divisions: a) a household that includes individual choice, which he calls 'personal and domestic consumption', and b) where consumption and use is undifferentiated and supplied in mass, which he calls 'collective consumption'. Separate organisations are needed here, and Cole names them the 'co-operative council', to represent the former consumption, and the 'collective utilities council' to represent the latter. Their function is firstly to safeguard consumer concerns like the quantity and quality of production, the prices charged and the variety of need, and secondly, to protect them from the producers. To be genuinely democratic, it is essential that, like the guilds, these organisations are decentralised and local. Cole is just as adamant that self-government must also apply to the civic services. He sees the need for an education guild, a health guild and a guild for every non-economic civic service, such as drama, music, medicine and sanitation. Along with the consumer councils, every locality needs a council to represent citizens' general interests in education and health. He duly calls these bodies the 'cultural councils' and the 'health councils' respectively. Their role is to articulate the civic viewpoint and co-operate with the relevant guilds to ensure that supply meets demand. In choosing their consumer and civic council representatives, Cole suggests that the citizens vote by way of wards within the town. Each citizen is duly granted four votes, one for each council. Every member of the four councils would be a ward representative, and would represent a particular function (1920b: 79–92, 101–10, 123–6).

These then—the producer, consumer and civil services—are the three main branches of economic and social activity. It is within this scheme that Cole offers an alternative to the sovereign state. He insists that in a truly democratic society, the state serves the people by mediating between organised producer and consumer interests—and, when it does this in practice, it is no longer the state in any conventional sense. In this case the state does not accommodate a sovereign undivided general will which corresponds to representation in general. Democracy is realised only when our interests, both in terms of producers and consumers, are organised on a functional basis. Cole accordingly rejects the doctrine of state sovereignty, as it is not functionally democratic. For the same reasons, he also rejects the existing structure of the state. He does not see the state as an association from which information regarding the overall organisation of society can be derived. So in his guild writings, the state is not given the role of integrating society, for groups cannot be free so long as one group regulates the others. There are three key reasons why the modern state has no place within his social and political thought. Firstly, it violates the functional principle; secondly, it is an inappropriate body to represent consumer interests (this is an unsuitable way of returning a political content to civil society); and thirdly, it is unfit to co-ordinate the interests of the various functional bodies. He is however obliged to show how all the above groups will co-operate as part of a single system and express the communal spirit. He must then construct a new co-ordinating governmental system. This is articulated in the shape of a system of local, regional and national communes. These are constituted by democratically elected representatives of all the essential functional bodies. Cole infers that a local commune would be a co-ordinating, and not administrative, body. The guilds would manage their services, and their co-operation with the relevant councils would largely determine their policy. Nevertheless, the commune would still have these essential tasks: a) to allocate local resources—*financial* functions—b) to act as a court of appeal in disputes between the different types of functional bodies, c) to determine the boundaries between the functional bodies, d) to decide issues that have no functional bases and e) to control coercive machinery like the police force (1914: 140–5, 151–4; 1972: 13–8, 160–2; 1920b: 127–9).

As in Cole's view society has many associations fulfilling various functions that cannot be regulated by a single body, he seeks to pluralize the state. The self-governing bodies will, through mechanisms of representation and consultation, be the means by which democratic social governance is realised. Administrative apparatus is, concurrently, diffused into the democratic functionally demarcated spheres of authority. Government functions are therefore devolved to and carried out by such bodies. The commune will unite these groups locally, co-ordinating the producer, consumer and civic elements, which together constitute the totality. As it is to have few direct administrative functions, Cole predicts a lack of opportunity for a centre in which a large bureaucratic and coercive apparatus could develop. The national co-ordinating body, the national commune (which would consist of representatives from the industrial and civic national guilds, from the economic and civic national councils and from the regional communes) would, he contends, be quite unlike the existing state. The civil service for instance will not simply become the commune's direct servant; it will be disseminated between the various functional associations. All the functional groups, along with the communes, will therefore have their own small civil service. Consequently, the national commune "would be a much less imposing body as the central organ of Society than the Great Leviathan of to-day, with its huge machinery of coercion and bureaucratic government" (1920b: 135–41).

The private sphere is now premised upon co-operation and collective governance. In the manner in which this scheme establishes both a self-governing civil society and a pluralized state, it transforms the prevailing divide between state and civil society. Hirst summarises Cole's position deftly:

> If the 'state' is thus dissolved into a multi-centred plural public power, so 'civil society' is transformed from a private domain governed by competing individual wills in the market into a federative structure of social cooperation between quasi-public bodies, the guilds (Hirst 1994: 103).

This dual process is crucial. It is the publicisation of civil society and the pluralisation of the state's component functions that constitutes the unification of the private and public spheres. Cole has devised a structure of economic governance which transcends the doctrine of state sovereignty. The division is transformed by circumscribing the central powers of the state and by increasing the powers of middle-range institutions of democratic social and economic governance. Although the community would *own* productive properties, the guilds would *control* them collectively. So whilst a civil society consisting of self-governing associations needs a genuine yet secondary public power to regulate their interactions, its role is mainly to co-ordinate and to protect individual and associational rights. Cole's communes do not determine all the activities in their territories, and herein lies his repudiation of the sovereign state (1972: 36–8; 1920a: 124–7; Hirst 1994: 103–4, 167–8).

This chapter has laid out the basic economic and political structures that constitute the essentials of Cole's scheme. The second half of Chapter Four will, after the discussion with Rawls has begun, critically reflect upon the libertarian socialist commune. The immediate task though is to introduce and analyze the revisions that are needed to breathe fresh life into Cole's proposed economy. It is to this task, the construction of NED's political economy, that we now turn.

Notes

1 In order to do this in a more than symbolic way, workers will need suitable apprenticeships where they learn for whom and about what they are voting.

2 To clarify, Cole argues that state ownership does not have to imply state control. He points out that during 1919, the railwaymen were in favour of state ownership, but they sought the

control, management and administration of their service. This means the state will assume ownership of the railways on behalf of the using public, whilst as producers, or in this case providers of a service, the railwaymen get the function of management. It is only when state ownership is combined with state control that sovereignty is established and the workers are left with no direct control (1919: 1–2).

3 For example, states are largely administrative, whereas political parties are mainly propagandist (1920a: 73).

4 This distinction is not one of individuals, for the differentiation is—as with producers—between interests.

CHAPTER THREE

The Political Economy of New Economic Democracy

Throughout his life, Marx remained adamant that the fundamental dynamic in civil society is economic. Following in his footsteps, writers in this tradition have referred to civil society as a web of economic, social and ethical arrangements considered separately from the state. Although civil society in Western European countries incorporates more than economic relations—voluntary associations, (new) social movements, etc.—it is still largely characterised by market considerations and private ownership of productive resources. Even if for some theorists economic factors are not fundamental, there can be no doubt that for most people they exist, and that they are strong. In order to validate the claim that the worst-off in NED would be in a superior position to the worst-off in POD, there is, I think, an obligation to analyse its economic proposals in some detail. Indeed, to be taken seriously, any model of socialism needs to show how its economy will allocate goods and resources. NED is no exception. I shall begin by establishing the terms by which Cole proposes to fulfil this vital task. In the ninety or so years since Cole formulated his libertarian socialist scheme, social relations have changed dramatically. Theories of socialism have consequently progressed accordingly. Although Cole's scheme has much to offer contemporary social and political thought, certain revisions are required. An insight into why these are necessary will be gained by critically engaging with the literature in which contentious socialist issues are debated. Arguments within socialist circles have raged about the most appropriate way to manage the economy, the most tenacious of which is whether either a centrally planned or a market economy, or a combination of the two, can realise socialist goals. As a corollary of this evaluation, I will distinguish Cole's scheme from both centralised command planning and market socialism. The argument is made that it contains certain features which, although in need of amendment, can nevertheless find expression within the plan-market controversy and make a valuable contribution to contemporary socialist theory. Only after this discussion will it become clear how NED offers real solutions to the shortcomings of these other two socialist approaches. That is, it is shown how an element of participatory democratic planning can be used for allocative purposes, rather than reliance upon expert planners or recourse solely to competitive markets. I then move on to discuss a further issue that relates to the democratisation of civil society: 'democratic investment planning'. The issue addressed here is how NED can approach the vital but potentially hazardous issue of how to finance its industries and services democratically. There are three parts to this chapter: 1) 'Democratic and Participatory Planning', 2) 'Democratic Investment Planning' and 3) 'Analysing Democratic Investment Planning'. As we proceed I shall indicate throughout where modifications to Cole's scheme are needed and how they are incorporated into NED.

1. Democratic and Participatory Planning

The first two sections in this passage focus on Cole's unique non-statist proposals for democratically regulating the economy and for the determination of prices. This is important because it distinguishes his scheme from, firstly, the market economy, where supply and demand regulate prices, and secondly, from command planning, where a centralised state assumes this responsibility. This will lay the foundations for the themes to be analysed in greater detail throughout the chapter. Before these sections conclude, as the possibility of an over-centralisation is not fully extinguished, a few preliminary remarks are offered which serve to reinforce the decentralised aspects of his scheme. Centralisation will still exist, though to a limited extent. In the case of the collective utilities council, centralisation is largely unavoidable; indeed, it is even desirable. Such tendencies can, however, be offset by the predominately decentralised co-operative council, which accounts for the larger markets. The third section discusses command and market socialisms, the rationale for which is provided at the time. I begin by explaining how Cole intends to organise production and exchange.

Cole's Libertarian Alternative

The guild constitution, Cole initially asserts, must co-ordinate production at a national level efficiently. Simultaneously it must also preserve diversity, which can only be achieved by granting the locality and the craft freedom of expression and adequate representation within the guild as a whole. He acknowledges that if his system of organisation cannot secure independence for the smaller units within the guild, national guilds will fail. The guilds must maintain the distinctness of each works and each locality. He maintains that as such independence can be secured by distributing *functions* rather than *powers*, the national organisation of industry and the local organisation of production are reconcilable. For Cole it is the co-ordination of supply and demand that has to be organised nationally, and "not *production*, but *trading* that must be under a national control" (1972: 202). The thing to organise nationally is exchange:

> The quantities of various commodities that are to be produced and the prices that are to be charged for them—these are the questions that must be asked and answered in respect of the whole industrial life of the nation. The organisation of supply and demand and the control of prices in consultation with the consumer will therefore be the main business of the National Guild authority, and of the District Committees which will work in conjunction with it over a smaller area (1972: 202).

Cole is keen to point out that in order to avoid the evils of large-scale modern industrialised production, the single works must be made up of a self-governing group of workers. Their need is mainly to govern production, rather than exchange. The latter is to be done by the district committees and the national executive, in co-operation with the corresponding level of the state authorities, depending on whether the market is local or national. But as production takes place in the various works within each district, they must be free to organise their own productive techniques. The 'standardisation and centralisation of exchange', he asserts, will remove the need for the 'standardisation and centralisation of production'. The idea is that goods and resources can be exchanged efficiently, whilst simultaneously enabling workers to enjoy a sense of freedom within their self-governing works (1972: 181–4, 201–4).

These are Cole's initial proposals for the organisation of production and exchange. However, by the time he writes GSR, his system has changed. The guilds are no longer to be in dialogue with a consuming representing state, but with two separate bodies: the co-operative council for those domestic products which require an individual preference, and the collective utilities council where consumers are not required to express their personal tastes. Yet as far as the guilds are concerned, there are distinct similarities. The local workplaces of the guilds, he repeats, are to carry out production, whereas the duties of the larger guild organisations, which are not so much controlling as co-ordinating bodies, include the adjustment of supply to meet demand and the determination of total output, through dialogue with consumers (1920b: 48, 59–62; 1920c: 4).

The Determination of Prices

As we have just seen, along with the regulation of quantity and quality of production and the arrangement of distribution, the fixing of prices is to be determined by the guilds in conjunction with, initially, the state, and in his mature scheme, the corresponding consumers' council. For illustration purposes, he considers the example of a single commodity: milk. The distributive guild is to deliver milk, which it will buy from the agricultural guild. The consumers have the co-operative society to deal with the milk question. The distributive guild will combine the amount it gives to the agricultural guild with its own distribution costs and will then propose a price to the co-operative society. If they agree, this becomes the selling price.[1] If not, the matter goes before the appropriate-level commune. Before this though, other considerations may arise:

> If the Co-operative Society is satisfied that the distributive cost allowed for by the Distributive Guild is reasonable, but thinks that the price paid to the Agricultural Guild is too high, it can either alone, or jointly with the Distributive Guild, take the matter up with the Agricultural Guild directly, and . . . failing agreement, carry the matter to the Commune (1920b: 142).

The distributive guild may, on its own, take the matter to the agricultural guild, but this, being a matter between two guilds, would go to the industrial guild congress rather than the commune. In one of these ways, through constant dialogue, Cole is sure a just price will emerge (1920b: 88, 141–2; 1920e: 1). This constitutes the basis of Cole's economic proposals. Although it is a planned economy, the emphasis is on dialogue and negotiated co-ordination. This approach to economic and social system building has real strengths; it does though, as specified above, require revisions. The reasons why, and the form they may take, will become clear as the critical evaluations of the planned market economies and democratic investment planning proceed. In the remainder of this section I shall address the issue of centralisation.

Firstly, an excess of centralisation remains a possibility. The fixing of prices, the regulation of quantity and quality of production and the arrangement of distribution is to be determined by the guilds in conjunction with, initially, the state, and the corresponding consumers' council in his mature scheme. It has been observed that "[s]ince these are functions of the national guilds, then, it seems that consumer-consultation is dispensable for the local units of production, at least in so far as they serve national markets" (MaCain 2001: 5). The local workplaces of the guilds are to carry out production, whereas the larger guild organisations are to ensure supply meets with demand. Again MaCain raises a serious concern:

> This qualification seems to me to be very strong, as it seems to imply that the plan is disaggregated by the national guilds, establishing output quotas by factory and workshop, thus leaving very little really for the self-governing workshops in their autonomy to decide (MaCain 2001: 5).

Although Cole insists that the functions of the larger guild organisations should only be minimal for each industry, and that the factories may exchange some products between themselves, it is true that the larger organisations are to "lay down general regulations, local or national, governing the methods of organisation and production within the Guild" (1920b: 60). As such, it is possible that workers within the factories are likely to find the opportunity for self-assertion fairly restricted. A major problem is that if the majority of guild socialist markets are national, the system will simply, and quickly, centralise. If so, some of the commonly cited objections to centralised planning may be levelled at this particular feature of Cole's scheme.[2] So, although Cole is comprehensively opposed to centralisation, the problem requires further reflection (1920b: 60–1).

So, it must be distinguished which kinds of decisions are appropriate for national level consideration. Devine (1988) addresses this issue. Echoing Cole, he too puts forward a theory of democratic planning based on negotiated co-ordination. His general position is that the alternative to democratic planning is coercion by either state administration or market forces. Although he recognises that some decisions should be taken centrally 'where necessary', decentralisation is to be preferred 'wherever possible'. Devine suggests that national level decisions can be taken in relation to general macro-economic matters: social policy in health and education; social policy in the infrastructure of the transport, communications and energy sectors; and social policy in pollution control and other environmental protection and conservation projects. Within this framework, far more detailed decision making can be left to decentralised self-governing organisations. His proposal is that decisions will be made locally unless there are valid reasons to make them at a wider level—such as when decisions affect wider groups (Devine 1988: 15, 22, 54, 193, 212). Cole's assertion that consumption needs to be dichotomised into two broad acts enables us to expand on this distinction. That is to say, the outlook required for these two distinct forms of consumption—domestic and collective—is different. Although he fails to elaborate in any great detail on this particular issue, his insistence that the localities should be equipped to preserve their autonomy is clear enough. For example, he repeats that "by far the greatest part of the work of the community would be carried on and administered locally or regionally" (1920b: 136). Before 1919 he proposed that exchange be conducted by the district committees and the national executive, depending on whether the market was local or national (1972: 203). The particular markets that were to fall into either category though remained unclear. But with the distinction of domestic and collective consumption drawn, it seems that in the former case exchange and distribution can be conducted efficiently by the local guild and council organisations. In the case of the co-operative council, there will be a need for large decentralised local organisations. This, as we shall see, constitutes an important amendment.

In this latter example, as the markets are local, demand ratios would be calculated by the substantial local co-operative councils. It follows that national output quotas only need to be established where national markets are involved, or as Devine says, where decisions affect wider groups. Such markets will fall mainly to the collective utilities council. In these cases, along with what Devine refers to as general macro-economic matters, regional and/or national co-ordination seems indispensable. It should also be noted that as localities and regions "would not be self-sufficient, not all the demand originating in an area would be spent on goods and services produced there, while some local production would be sold outside the area" (Devine 1988: 214).[3] But for the majority of domestic products that are produced in every region (or at least most), there is no need to calculate national, and in some cases even regional, output quotas. Perhaps this is what Cole has in mind when he claims that the larger guild organisations "would, where it was necessary, co-ordinate the production of various factories, so as to make supply coincide with demand" (1920b: 59–60). Note the line 'where it was necessary'. Many products were to be 'disposed of directly from the factory', or, as the National Guild League puts it:

> The workshop is not isolated from the rest of the control of industry. The organisation of the workshop is very closely connected with the organisation of the works as a whole. *With the business of buying and selling* as well as the actual business of production (NGL 1917: 69).[4]

For the majority of products for the domestic market that are regulated by the co-operative council, national quotas do not need to be established. In which case, as the workshops within the guilds are in dialogue with their counterparts in the local co-operative councils, their decision-making autonomy would be preserved. They would not therefore be severely threatened by the national elements. Finally, as domestic consumption constitutes the larger section of the market, it is these decisions that are in the ascendance.

The Plan-Market Controversy

This section begins by rejecting the socialist ideal of centralised command planning in its entirety. Attention then turns to an alternative socialist doctrine which holds that socialism can, and indeed should, allocate goods and resources through a market forces economy. A particular strength of markets is acknowledged, the price mechanism, and a notable inadequacy, the general disregard for the needs of the poor. Only after this discussion will it become clear how NED has the potential to preserve the benefits of the market, whilst simultaneously transcending its deficiencies. Traditionally socialists have upheld a planned system because they believe it can provide an opportunity for the conscious framing of economic activity to meet predetermined needs. Their argument is that through planning, society's productive resources could be organised effectively. In the old Soviet Union and Eastern European bloc countries, this took the form of centralised administrative command planning. Such an approach to planning the economy has now been so comprehensively discredited that we may pass over its structure and deficiencies briefly. In command planning, the organisation and co-ordination of production takes place through an administrative hierarchy: decisions are passed down from the centre through intermediate bodies, and then on to the production units. The consignment of goods and services to, and between, productive units is determined vertically from above, rather than horizontally through direct contact between the units themselves. It is here that most of the systems' difficulties appear. Although in their rejection of capitalism the command planned countries dispensed with the private ownership of the means of production, they merely succeeded in replacing one form of management, capitalist, with another, bureaucratic. Indispensable to its hierarchy are relationships that are necessarily based upon superiority and subordination. In this approach to planning, neither workers nor consumers can participate effectively in economic decision making (Devine 1988: 55; Albert and Hanhel 1991: 4). The general objection is that command planning is not, and cannot be, democratic.

As a consequence of the biased flow of information and lack of adequate feedback channels, centralised planning proved to be grossly inefficient: it provided few incentives for risk-taking and therefore lacked technological innovation, and it saw the repression of individual freedom and independence, widespread shortages and a general disregard for consumer satisfaction. In light of such well-documented problems, the epistemological arguments against command planning are now well known and widely accepted as accurate. Briefly, with the constant introduction of technological innovations, economic life changes continually. Materials are put to new uses, requiring new capital goods in the production of end products. This in turn has a bearing upon sources of supply. The new knowledge about supply and demand cannot be communicated fast enough to a central authoritarian body (Devine 1988: 12, 55; Butler 1983: 71). I do not wish to dispute these claims. However, agreement with the critics of central planning, notably Hayek, on these points does *not* involve a compulsion to reject all forms of planning. On the contrary, as the planning in Cole's scheme is decentralised, democratic and premised upon producer-consumer dialogue and negotiation, it cannot be confused with the kind of centralised authoritarian planning outlined and criticised here.

Having rejected command planning, it now needs to be shown how the argument that a socialist society may incorporate a market forces economy can be constructed within the boundaries of socialist discourse. During the last three decades, debates have intensified within socialist circles about the possibility of overcoming the inherent problems of command planning by retaining the use of a market mechanism in the economy. The suggestion has been made that the socialist / capitalist distinction is not so much about markets, but is concerning the ownership of the means of production. Under the appropriate organisational setup, it is claimed that an economy driven by market forces is not only compatible with socialism, but should actually be its defining characteristic. This doctrine is generally referred to as market socialism. Although there is more than one version of market socialism, they share certain common characteristics. They are market societies as commodities are brought and sold, and they are socialist in that the capitalist class in no longer dominant—workers, or their elected managers, make the decisions. The market socialist David Schweickart (1998) summarises the essential features of market socialism. He notes that the three main defining institutions of capitalism are: a) the market economy, b) private ownership of the means of production and c) wage labour. In contrast, a market socialist economy places great limitations on, or seeks to eradicate completely, private ownership of the means of production. One of its central claims is that the means of production can be socially owned by worker-controlled enterprises that would operate within an economic system of market competition. When wage labour is replaced by workplace democracy, with the workers receiving a share of net proceeds, it is 'worker-self-managed' market socialism. Although there are theoretical variations within the doctrine, market socialists agree that as central planning is fundamentally flawed, and as markets can be dichotomised from capitalism—that is, the market is likely to change when set in a complex of property relationships distinct from those of capitalism—market socialism is the best option available (Schweickart 1998: 10–1; Ollman 1998: 99).

Given the failings of command planning and the inherent dangers affiliated to it, the endeavour by market socialists to disassociate themselves from this authoritarian socialism is not surprising. To their credit, the attempts of market socialists to theorise how a system of workers' control may operate in a decentralised setting represent a vast improvement upon centralised command planning. In the next section of this chapter, 'Democratic Investment Planning', there will be recourse to critically evaluate market socialism's maintenance of a competitive ethic. For the more immediate purpose, I will consider the price mechanism and the inattention to the needs of the least well-off.

Markets have traditionally been defended for their efficiency. They have, as their supporters from both the political left and right claim, informational and motivational benefits. In the network of prices, markets have a sophisticated communication system. Prices can summarise large amounts of information, usually from people who do not know each other, very simply. When there is a large demand for a good, its price will rise, denoting its under-supply. This in turn indicates to producers that higher profits can be secured by increasing the production of the good in question. In this sense there is an incentive for producers to respond by increasing the production of the desired good. At the other end of the scale, when over-production occurs, prices tend to fall. This signals to the producers to cut back the production of these products and turn their attention elsewhere. The price system then communicates to individuals in the marketplace basically what others want. Markets, it is argued, distribute purchasing power to consumers. Through their choice, they can relay to producers what to produce. So one of the strengths of markets is their ability to supply information on consumer demand quickly and efficiently, whilst simultaneously providing incentives for producers to respond to. These, it seems, are solid enough reasons for continuing with a market of some description. However, there remains a particular weakness of a market forces economy. Although markets do serve the above functions, there are non-market and other social factors which are particularly pertinent, especially the issue of production for need. The provision of needs in non-market terms is a vital element of socialist discourse, and is a substantial element of the left objection to markets. The argument is that as there are certain basic goods all individuals need, they should be provided for collectively—and not through markets, which satisfy wants. In a market system, demand is articulated through purchasing behaviour, which is determined unequally by the ability to pay. The problem is that the individual difference in the ability to pay undermines demand as an indicator of need. Market forces may meet consumer *demand*, but it certainly does not follow that they respond to social *need*.[5] Producers cannot respond to those needs which are not expressed through purchasing activity due to lack of personal finance. In these cases, markets cannot be responsive to consumer need (Martell 1992: 157–9; Butler 1983: 46–8; Hoover 1989: 210).

Capturing these concerns, Paul Hirst (1990) recognises that the market, as an information system, accounts for choice whilst minimising constraint and intervention. For these reasons the market is often contrasted, favourably, to bureaucratic collectivism. But as this comparison is made in regard to a perfect market, it has certain improbable assumptions: that in the free market there is no large-scale unemployment, and, moreover, that no one is denied essential goods and services due to their inability to pay for them. His contempt is evident: "[o]ne should not", he insists, "be mesmerised by such drivel" (1990: 94). He concludes that markets may be the most effective way to distribute some goods and services, but alternative systems are more appropriate for the distribution of others.[6] It is on this crucial issue, the catering to need, that NED offers a real alternative to the doctrines of command planning and market socialism. In NED, the use of market criteria in productive decision making will continue to have a role, especially when demand is in relation to personal wants, desires and tastes. But in the case of catering to needs, democratic and participatory planning will be the norm. This will be the diametrical opposite to centralised command planning. Basic needs can be articulated democratically from below through negotiation between the co-operating bodies devised by Cole. On a related issue, Martell points out that

> . . . market research needs to be carried out in order to identify needs which are distorted or unrepresented in patterns of consumer market demand. Such mechanisms can be sensitive to the diversity of needs as they are defined by people themselves, resorting to neither the statist imposition of preferences nor the distorted perceptions of market forces (Martell 1992: 159).

The consumer and civic councils are ideally suited to undertake such market research. As decentralised functional organisations, they would only need to articulate local information to the corresponding workplaces. They are well placed to respond to the particular knowledge of local circumstances, and would not have to comprehend and accommodate the ramifications of national plans. Cole's institutionalisation of producer-consumer dialogue, therefore, remains central to NED.

Summary

In this passage I have established that although a minimum degree of centralisation will persist, the more substantial decentralisation of politico-economic decision making can be sustained. This was an important task as it renders the plausible critiques of command planning inapplicable. It was explained why NED will adopt Cole's proposals for determining the items that are produced in order to satisfy basic needs. Although, for the reasons indicated above, markets will continue to play a role in NED, as decision making in relation to needs is *not* dominated by market considerations, they will not be its defining characteristic. The question remains, however: how will the goods produced to satisfy basic needs be funded?

2. Democratic Investment Planning

In this section we shall see how Cole proposes to deal with the matter of capital, i.e., how guild socialism will finance its industries and services. It will then be shown why certain revisions are required. In order to show how they will be introduced, Cole's considerations on capital will be compared to Schweickart's scheme of democratic investment planning. The similarities between Cole and Schweickart will be confirmed, as will one very important difference: the tensions between co-operation and competition. Through a critical discussion, I will suggest how NED will accommodate a suitable compromise between the two positions.

Cole's Capital Provision

Cole states that it is vital to maintain the correct ratio between production for immediate consumer use and production for use in additional production. He adds that the allocation of the communal productive resources would be the business of the local, regional or national commune, 'as the case may be'. The communes will decide upon the allotment of production to consumable, and then to capital, in each industry and service. In order to fulfil this task, every guild would be asked to prepare a budget. These budgets would include what they need to produce for immediate use, and what they need for 'extensions and improvements'. During these preparations the guilds would consult each other. The appropriate councils would then have the opportunity to criticise and suggest amendments. Finally, all the budgets would go before the commune's finance committee. "The various budgets will there be brought into harmony with the estimated national production, and after any necessary further negotiations have taken place, the complete budget will come up before the Commune as a whole for ratification" (1920b: 145). So, the provision of capital would be conducted and managed by the commune (1920b: 143–5). It can now be appreciated how NED aims to subsidise the products that will be sold below their cost price. To reiterate, the goods and services whose prices are determined through democratic planning would be those whose supply is essential for the satisfaction of physiological needs, such as hunger. Unlike the commodities which are produced to fulfil personal wants and desires, it would not be left to market forces to settle the issue. Rather, as Cole proposes, the regional and national representatives of the relevant guilds, the distributive guild, the collective utilities and co-operative councils would deliberate and determine the just price. It is important to stress that "[i]t might be considered desirable . . . to sell a particular commodity at . . . less than the natural price based on its cost of production" (1920b: 142–3). This would indeed be the case with those foods that have been democratically established as essential to the maintenance of physical health. MaCain clarifies and expands the issue:

> The determination of prices may lead to operating cross-subsidies . . . This involves a system of direct lump-sum transfers among the guilds, to cover the costs of production of some goods for sale below their 'natural' prices. These transfers are decided like other economic magnitudes under guild socialism—by direct negotiations among the guilds with arbitration by the next, more inclusive body in the case of impasse (MaCain 2001: B4).

In relation to payment and taxation, Cole suggests that the local, regional or national IGC would—along with its other main tasks of establishing the essential principles of guild organisation, legislating where central co-ordination is required, representing the guilds in their external relations and adjudicating on inter-guild disputes—determine the level of payment between the various grades of workers and between the guilds themselves. In addition, the guild's congress would survey 'the whole field of economic conditions'. The communes would then have the chance to effectively criticise. After the commune has made its allowances to capital, and decided what a guild pays to its members, any surplus would pass to it for re-appropriation. It follows that the guild system does not tax individuals. The commune taxes at source and draws the agreed amounts from the labour-power of the guilds. Cole concludes his short discussion on the financial powers of the commune by noting the following:

> Let me again emphasise the fact that, in practice, the greater part of all this detailed financial work would not be done by the Commune at all, but directly and in consultation by the various functional bodies. Only moot points needing settlement and general questions of principle would normally come before the Commune (1920b: 147).

These are Cole's financial proposals. The main idea is to enhance inter-guild co-operation. If a guild is particularly successful and secures higher profits than it initially thought, they would simply be passed to the commune. In this way, Cole hopes the guilds will not come to regard each other as rivals. The aim is rather to abolish competition and promote the maximum degree of co-operation. His belief that free communal service is in itself enough to provide adequate motivation to work is evident (1920b: 70–3, 146–7).

Schweickart's Capital Provision

Although I am in sympathy with Cole's overall ideas and the co-operative direction he is aiming for, I also recognise that his faith that people could be motivated in the absence of financial incentives of any kind is perhaps too optimistic. It may not be that the provision of a financial incentive is the only method of motivation; in an established socialist society it may not even need to take preference. But it is significant, especially initially. As such, it seems plausible that the guilds be permitted to return a percentage of their profits to their workers. This would constitute another significant moderation. An insight into what forms such alterations might take can be attained by comparing Cole's economic proposals to the system of democratic investment planning devised by David Schweickart (1998). He is a market socialist whose model of 'economic democracy' prioritises worker self-management. Although co-operatives will compete, such competition is to occur against the backdrop of a democratic investment plan. This constitutes a second dimension, which is to complement workplace democracy. The necessity of such an addition has found support within socialist circles. For example, Howard states:

> . . . a society of worker-owned cooperatives, exchanging their products in a market, could still be an alienated society. The workers might still be egoistic, mainly concerned with profit and consumption, alienated from other cooperatives and from the general interest, relating to each other indirectly through a direct relationship to things, commodities exchanging for prices in the market (Howard 2000: 77).

Vast inequality of income, through differential capital intensity, would also persist. In addition, problems like environmental destruction, pollution, unemployment, etc., would continue to be 'external' to economic decision making and profit maximisation. So although Howard is a proponent of workplace democracy, he concludes that the additional measure of democratic investment planning is required to complement it (Howard 2000: 77, 106).

What then does this entail? The totality of productive assets is collectively and publicly owned, with each firm paying a tax for their use. *New* investment is financed externally, through a national investment fund that is bankrolled by the capital asset tax. Unlike capitalism, which depends on private saving funds for investment, Schweickart's scheme relies on taxation:

> Economically this tax functions as an interest rate on capital—and thus obviates the necessity of paying interest to private savers. . . . The proceeds of the capital-assets tax constitute society's investment fund, all of which are ploughed back into the economy (Schweickart 1998: 17).

The entire capital assets are regarded as collective property, although they are utilised by the various work forces that control them. There is not a money market that unites private savers and private investors. The capital assets tax generated funds for new investment are dispersed through democratic channels. It is important to emphasise that planning "is not for the whole economy; the planning is only for the new investment to be undertaken, that is, investment not financed from depreciation set-asides" (Schweickart 1993: 73). Firms are free to spend their depreciation set-asides on any capital improvement they see fit. This spending is considered ongoing investment, and is distinguishable from the bank-financed new investment. Established firms will only be affected by the planning if they decide to expand operations which cannot be supported by their depreciation funds. Explaining how funds are to be dispensed, Schweickart states that social control over the supply of decentralised investment funds will be realised by interconnected plans and banks. Decisions about which projects to favour will be taken democratically at three general levels by elected legislatures. Here, investment hearings will occur where expert and popular opinions can be expressed. To begin with, the national legislature will determine how much is to be set aside for national projects (pollution control, transport maintenance, etc.). It can also mandate the encouragement of certain types of projects (those that are environmentally friendly, for example) by making suitable funding available. The rest is distributed to the regions on a per-capita basis: if a certain region has 8 percent of the national population, then it receives 8 percent of the investment fund[7] (Schweickart 1993: 68, 71–4; 1998: 16).

Regional legislatures will do likewise. Now only the decisions about where to channel public capital and which particular projects to encourage are made on a regional basis. The regional authorities will receive the former sums and the remainder will go to localised communities. For their part, these communities will also decide how much is to go into local public investment, as well as how much is needed to finance their own encouragement grants. Finally, communities will allocate funds to the banks in their localities. Every bank will get a portion of the investment fund received by the community; the exact amount will depend on how many firms are affiliated to it and by its record at making sensible grants in the past. Every enterprise within this area chooses one of these banks to affiliate itself to.[8] The selected bank will not only render the usual services of holding the firm's sales income and providing it with working capital, it will also, significantly, retain its depreciation reserve. Banks are free to make grants (grants, not loans) as they please, charging a basic use tax in the majority of cases, although this rate may be reduced for encouragement projects. As per their criteria, they will use a 'projected profitability and employment creation'. It is to these banks that enterprises will appeal for new investment capital (Schweickart 1993: 75–6).

This is the basis of Schweickart's proposals. The market would still set prices, but there is no incentive to invest in the firm in the hope of extracting profits. In contrast to capitalism, the course of investment is not under the command of the market. The manner in which funds are returned to communities is democratically planned. This investment mechanism is, he contends, preferable to unrestrained market forces. Workers, acting as citizens, can help determine the formation of the investment fund, and in this sense participate in directing the economy. There is not the dichotomy between owners and non-owners of wealth stemming from property ownership. These measures are intended to limit inequality. Whilst a given firm could secure a higher profit than others, it is divided among the firm's workers. As profits cannot be converted into capital wealth, firms cannot make money just by having it. In regard to political equality, individuals will not have so much or so little that they are dominating or dominated. Not only are the workers' co-operatives run democratically, but this is complimented by socially controlled investment (Schweickart 1998: 16–8; 1998a: 127; 1998b: 171; Howard 2000: 14, 107, 156).

Synthesising Cole and Schweickart

The comparisons with Cole's project are salient. Both schemes recognise that investment finance should derive from source (either the labour power of the guilds or the co-operatives' capital assets tax), and crucially, both schemes recognise that the use of society's communal productive resources should be under democratic control. Cole is keen to reaffirm that the balance between saving and spending will, along with the reasoned allocation:

> . . . be done by the method of real self-government, each service and interest having a full opportunity of putting its point of view, and taking part in the communal decision. Moreover, this will take place locally and regionally, in respect of local and regional services, as well as nationally (1920b: 146).

In a similar vein, when referring to investment rates, Schweickart states that "[t]his rate is set democratically—not by market forces. That is to say, the decisions as to the overall rate of reinvestment are under conscious control and subject to democratic debate" (Schweickart 1998b: 170). Nor is this all. The two schemes object equally to the idea of reinvesting returns in the hope of securing higher profits. Both Cole and Schweickart are equally opposed to the notion of converting profits into capital wealth. On this issue though there is a crucial difference. In Cole's scheme extra profits simply return to the local commune, which will facilitate further democratic deliberations about future allocation and reinvestment, while in Schweickart's scheme they are shared out among the co-operative's workforce. This distinguishes the latter model from the former. As with the guilds in Cole's scheme, Schweickart's workers control their firms, they do not own them, but unlike Cole's guilds, the worker-governed enterprises will be in open competition.

It is on this specific question, whether a competitive ethic should be expressed in a democratic socialist society, that a compromise between the positions of Cole and Schweickart will be suggested.[9] It is first worthwhile to take note of why this issue continues to divide socialists. In their critiques of market socialism, Ticktin (1998) and Ollman (1998) raise similar concerns. Ticktin questions the argument that competition ensures consumer satisfaction. As competition forces the competitors to prioritise the goal of making money, manufacturers will only market those goods that are likely to secure a profit. In a similar vein, Ollman notes that in markets, people compete to get as much for the products they are selling as they can, and, simultaneously, to buy their goods as cheaply as possible. In the process, they become indifferent to the plight of their competitors. Consideration for others inhibits the ability to compete. Echoing these sentiments, Martell (1992) points out that market socialists claim that competition is a trait of capitalism, and that producers working within co-operatives will develop more of a communitarian spirit. It is more likely, he counters, that whilst such co-operatives could harbour an internal ethic of community, they would remain just as disposed to 'sectional self-interests and competitive considerations' as their capitalist counterparts (Ticktin 1998: 61; Ollman 1998: 83–4; Martell 1992: 160).[10] Whereas for Schweickart:

> If enterprises do not compete, they have little need to innovate. They do not have to worry that if they do not keep abreast of the new technologies, their rivals will capture their markets, so the negative threat of failure is not there (Schweickart 1998: 14).

The question is: should society sacrifice co-ordination for competition, sacrifice competition for co-ordination, or attempt to find the correct balance between the two? There is no easy answer to this arduous question, and those that are put forward are unlikely to satisfy everyone. Nevertheless, it is my contention that NED has the potential to shear a path between the two extremes. Such a path is, I think, the most desirable option, for there are merits to both the above arguments. On the one hand, a limited and tightly controlled degree of competition probably is a suitable method to inspire motivation and generate innovation. On the other hand, it is also highly likely that if competition is intense, competitors will indeed become apathetic too and detached from the circumstances and difficulties of others. The suggested compromise draws from the work of contemporary associational socialist theorists who address these questions. Briefly, Hirst asserts that associational socialism will still have a restricted role for competition between work units providing goods and services. But by introducing powerful anti-monopoly provisions and placing a limit upon the accumulation of personal fortunes, it seeks lesser inequalities in economic and political matters and the avoidance of concentrations of authoritarian power. Associational socialism "would accept market exchange but seek to encourage cooperation, mutuality, reciprocity and charity. In the right framework cooperation can compete effectively with materialistic individualism" (Hirst 1990: 101). Amplifying the sentiments which are likely to be generated in co-operatives into a wider solidarity needs, as Martell puts it, 'comparable communal structures' to link them in the wider setting (Hirst 1990: 100–1; Martell 1992: 159–60). It is upon these premises that a path between co-ordination and competition can be steered. NED, even with a restricted role for competition, can still sustain the comparable communal structures which are a prerequisite to the encouragement of co-operation, reciprocity and mutual respect.

Firstly, competition *between* the guilds themselves will for the most part be virtually non-existent. The coal and steel guilds are both in service to the community; they are not in open competition to produce coal and steel. Providing raw materials are allocated appropriately, which would be determined—through the guild's congress—by the guilds collectively, *inter-guild* competition will hardly exist. Guilds would be designated assignments by the elected investment fund legislatures, who will be incorporated into the IGC at the three general levels. The opportunity for the two consumer councils to monitor investment decisions applies unreservedly. As with all other economic considerations in NED, only in cases of impasse will the communes be asked to adjudicate. How then might a measured degree of competition be implemented? The answer lies in *intra-guild* competition. In NED the majority of guilds have localities in each town. It might for pragmatic reasons be appropriate for certain heavy industries to, following the steel plants, concentrate in particular regions. The norm though would be for the greater number of guilds to have workplaces in most towns. They would, in accordance with Schweickart's suggestions, be affiliated to community banks, which would be organised along guild lines. Community banks would therefore be guild banks, and the firms connected to them would be of a similar industrial type. Each individual national guild would be responsible for overseeing competition in its own domain. Not only will the guilds be allowed to retain a percentage of their profits, but the distribution to the various localities will include a performance criteria. Although everyone would, as Cole says, receive a standard income, the local branches that perform the best would be rewarded with higher financial bonuses. In some cases this could take the form of different localities *between* towns, i.e., the town 'A' branch of a particular guild may have produced finer products and generated higher revenue than its town 'B' counterpart, and should therefore be rewarded accordingly. This would probably be the case with the production of specialist work, like stone-masonry, for example. In other cases, especially with the production of more standardised goods, there may be any number of workshops *within* the same town. In either case it seems reasonable to allow the more productive workshops to retain a pre-established percentage of their net proceeds.[11]

As the localities within a guild will often be competing for the same market, this would inevitably introduce a competitive ethic into the internal relations of the guild. The question then emerges as to whether such experiences would duplicate capitalist sentiments. The failure to keep ahead of their intra-guild competitors could, in a sense analogous to capitalist firms, be detrimental to business. There is good reason to doubt this. It will be the role of the works or district committees to ensure that competition is not only equitable, but that it does not exceed the pre-arranged specification. Guidelines would be imposed by ensuring that information flows to every locality equally, and that no single workplace comes to be in an advantageous position whereby it can exploit its market position to further its own self-interests. As representatives from every locality constitute the works committee at the town level, information channels will be secured. The works committees are in a good position to prevent sectional interests from advancing to the extent that the plight of other guild members is disregarded. In other words, they can provide suitable comparable command structures capable of generating solidarity sentiments. If competition between the various workplaces within a guild still proves to be too intense, there are other structural arrangements which lend themselves to the guild organisation. A case in point is Roemer's 'bank-centred market socialism'. The finer details of this scheme need not concern us here; I merely wish to draw attention to one particular facet central to it. Firms will cluster together and form financial groups. Each of these financial groups will have at its centre a government main bank which will act as principal monitors. These shares are to be apportioned to the bank, to the firms' workers and to the other firms who constitute the financial group. Every company has a board of directors made up of representatives from these three constituencies, and all three will likewise receive a share of total profits. To begin with, workers of a firm will have their wages supplemented by their allowance. In addition, for the other member firms, their share will augment their other incomes. The same dynamic applies to the main bank: the higher the profits, the greater its allotment. All three categories have interests in monitoring each other sufficiently. As the main banks are state banks, their incomes are public. The general public will receive returns in line with a predetermined political formula. So workers will have four sources of income: wages, a percentage of both the profits of their own firms *and* the other firms in their cluster (the former being the greater) and a social dividend (Roemer 1994: 49–50, 76; Schweickart 1993: 324–5).

Roemer's egalitarian scheme, partly because it has a role for a stock market, is not Cole's libertarian socialism. But his idea that workers should receive proportional multi-incomes is certainly applicable to NED. The key difference is that the firms that cluster together to form financial groups will be functionally demarcated in order to be apposite to the guild organisation, and the main bank will be a guild bank. As firms stand to gain from the success of other firms in their guild, an intense competitive ethic is unlikely to emerge; even if it did, given the reasonably equal distribution of incomes, it would not be to the lasting detriment of any one workshop.[12] There is more to Roemer's scheme than the aspect just outlined. For instance, he introduces measures successful firms can take if a firm in their cluster performs poorly continuously.[13] Our principle interest though is the way in which his above idea, once introduced into the structure of a guild, can help restore the desired degree of co-operation.

This is significant, as the following observation from Ollman will testify. In social democratic mixed economy, there are private and public ownership sectors operating under market rules and a national plan respectively. This is also not Cole's libertarian socialism. However, NED does include a public sector (in relation to needs), and a co-operative private sector (in relation to personal wants and desires). The question Ollman poses is how to prevent the market, driven by its logic and dynamism, from spreading and covering what is supposed to be safeguarded. In mixed economies this includes areas initially designated to the public domain. His argument is that as the market holds a privileged place, the private sector soon takes priority. The problem is whether people can be expected to maintain the kind of mutual concern necessary to co-operate, whilst simultaneously preserving the desire for private advantage and mutual indifference which are the 'qualities' of good competitors. The claim is that although it is possible for a person to display contrasting sentiments, the mix is nonetheless a volatile one. Market thoughts, like any others, cannot simply be suspended at will. Beliefs, values and emotions are difficult to compartmentalise, and when there is a clash, one set usually wins. So all the time market sentiments are fortified daily through market dealings, the key features of socialism are unlikely to proceed vary far (Ollman 1998: 103–4). Although he is right in the case of a social democratic mixed economy, there are notable differences with NED. In relation to the issue of private sector encroachment, the works and district committees of the guilds can ensure that the production of need and want goods is undertaken by the localities evenly. In this sense public and private goods are provided equally by the same groups of producers. On occasions when this is not possible, as the teams of workers producing mostly public goods could be denied the opportunity to secure performance-related bonuses, corporate welfare measures (tax benefits, generous subsidies, low interest loans, etc.) may be introduced to compensate these disadvantages. The determination of such affairs would, like other economic considerations in NED, be subject to democratic adjudication. As workshops would be prevented from reinvesting their profits and thereby from expanding, as competition is limited to and overseen by each guild, and as the provision of need goods is to take preference over those produced through market consideration, the market loses its privileged place. It is these facets that help impede the tendency for the market to broaden and encompass the public sphere.

Summary

NED will retain its stance that the distributions of investment funds continue to be democratically determined, and that the workplaces are not permitted to reinvest their profits. It will, however, incorporate two of Schweickart's key ideas—that a percentage of a guild's profits are kept within the guild for internal distribution as it sees fit, and that the guild's localities would continue to pay a capital assets tax to fund future investment. It differs from Schweickart's scheme in the sense that competition would be monitored more closely; the guild committees would invigilate competition within their own demarcated industrial sphere. These measures should go some way to ensuring that the benefits of both co-operation and competition are successfully utilised. The pursuit of such a balance is preferable to an economy which is either entirely planned or purely market driven. Democratic investment planning is, I propose, one of the most tenacious strengths of NED.

3. Analysing Democratic Investment Planning

Having established that NED's proposals for financing industries and services through self-governing organisations (guilds and consumer / civic councils) participating in communal decision making are to be assimilated to the kind of democratic investment planning advocated by Schweickart, this section will critically evaluate this proposition. I begin by confirming that the abolishment of the capitalist class and the placement of constraints upon the self-expanding value of capital represent a significant step towards the end of capitalism and the realisation of NED. Attention then turns to the problem of providing incentives for efficient investment in public ownership schemes like ours. As we shall see, this issue is intensely debated within contemporary socialist circles. For structural convenience, I will introduce it and explain the format to the following critical evaluation as we proceed.

Eradicating the Capitalist Class

Schweickart is keen to stress that publicly generated capital does not, unlike capitalist privately generated capital, move geographically to where it can secure the highest returns. The investment fund is legally mandated to return to the communities where it initially originated. These communities are not compelled to compete for capital. With this alternative method for raising capital, capitalists are no longer indispensable. In democratic investment planning:

> . . . there is no 'privileged class' . . . i.e., a stable class of people with more power than the combined power of the elected officials . . . there are no capitalists, nor is there any other set of non-elected officials who possess

> anything like the power of the capitalist class under capitalism (Schweickart 1998a: 127).

Once capitalist ownership has been replaced with workers' co-operatives, as there will no longer be a capitalist class extracting a surplus value, capitalism would be abolished. With the capitalist class now obsolete, markets can be reshaped in workers' interests. Such a development, with the appropriate vertical demarcation, represents a significant step towards the realisation of NED. Regarding the vitiation of the capitalist class, there is no question that Cole would have embraced such a change. He too dislikes class domination and the 'perverted' power of the capitalist class (Schweickart 1998: 19–20; 1920b: 121–2). Not every socialist, though, is convinced that the elimination of the capitalist class necessarily signals the end of capitalism. Ollman, for example, argues that market socialists like Schweickart severely underestimate the extent to which capitalist practices, feelings and problems would persist within market relations. He claims it is capital, rather than just the capitalist class, that is the real essence of capitalism. Capital is not merely wealth, it has a 'self-expanding value', it is wealth invested in the hope of securing greater wealth. This, Ollman suggests, guarantees that wealth will be self-centred; it becomes obsessed with its own growth. His point is that the power of capital is the ability to expand regardless of who is in control—capitalists, state *or* workers' collectives. The logic behind competing co-operatives compels workers to follow the capitalists and adopt the same relation to capital. As soon as goods are made to sell at a profit—profits which are then reinvested—a rhythm is established which will continue to cause the ills that capitalism has hitherto been unable to solve: unemployment, economic crisis, ecological destruction, vulgar greed, a widening gulf between wealth and poverty, etc. So for Ollman, workers' problems are caused not just by the power of the capitalist class, but by the domination of capital and market operations (Ollman 1998: 106–9; 1998b: 179–82).

In a direct riposte, Schweickart maintains that within his system of democratic investment planning, capital as self-expanding value would not exist. Capitalists may be compelled to reinvest much of their profits to increase the value of capital, but enterprises are not subject to the same degree of unremitting pressure to expand. Co-operatives are legally restrained from reinvesting their profits. They are distributed among the workforce. New investment, it will be recalled, is funded by the 'capital assets tax-generated investment pool'. Although there are capital assets—i.e., the material means of production each co-operative controls—there is not the kind of capital which has an inherent expansionary tendency (Schweickart 1998b: 169–70). Echoing Schweickart, Lawler (1998) argues that a system of workers' co-operatives, organised nationally by a workers' government (the communal system in NED), will not compete and exploit each other in order to amass vast amounts of capital. Under capitalism, capital may shift to where greater returns can be secured, but worker-managed enterprises will not be inclined to move and labour for less wages in the hope of accumulating increasing amounts of capital. For Lawler the market itself is not at fault. The problem is "the domination of the market by powerful financial and industrial powers beholden to no one and motivated by their own insatiable requirements" (Lawler 1998: 142–3). It is true that NED has a limited role for both intra-guild competition and a market to satisfy consumer demand. As a corollary, many goods will be produced in order to be sold at a profit. Ollman's concern that capitalist sentiments would persist within market relations is not, therefore, extraneous. But as workplaces are legally restricted from reinvesting their profits, capital as wealth to create more wealth, the inherent expansionary tendency, will not exist. This is the crucial difference. Without the device of democratic investment planning, market socialism is likely to remain 'economic liberalism without capitalists' (Hirst 1990a: 174). But with this mechanism installed, a significant step is taken in the theoretical direction towards NED. To reiterate, the satisfaction of physiological needs would be met through non-market mechanisms, and the guild committees can where necessary closely regulate competition. The competitive rhythm established would be far less intensive than the cut-throat nature of capitalist competition. The abolishment of the capitalist class does, I maintain, constitute an advance towards NED.

Incentives and Efficiency

The second issue is the objection that schemes of public ownership (including by implication NED) do not provide the incentives for profitable investment that private ownership does. This is now generally referred to as the 'soft budget constraint'. Within the literature on market socialism in which public ownership is discussed, this issue appears to be one of the most disputatious. The remainder of this section is devoted to its exploration. A critical evaluation is provided, by means of which I conclude that NED's scheme of public ownership is, from a libertarian-socialist perspective, preferable to private ownership. First used by Kornai, this term refers to the tendency of political authorities to grant regular loans to firms that are economically wasteful, and, following the efficiency criteria, should have been left to close. In other words, the budget is softened to rescue insolvent enterprises. The mechanisms for budget softening include soft subsidies, which can be made discussible; soft credit, with easy re-negotiation of debt; soft taxation and soft administered prices. This financing is implemented as it is hard to end poorly performing projects because previous investment will be lost. The fear is that as managers expect to be bailed out in the face of losses, they come to work within these built-in soft expectations. There is, the argument goes, little incentive for management to eschew expensive investment ventures with high risks of failure. The problem is how managers of public firms can be motivated to secure financial efficiency.

> Private ownership is an essential requirement for a hard budget constraint. A private owner can be left to his fate; it is his problem, not

> the state's. Softening of the budget constraint is the result of deep state involvement, since the state bears ultimate responsibility for the fate of the firm (Kornai 1993: 53).

In regards to NED the word state is replaced with political community. Kornai's concern though is not inconsequential. Louis Putterman goes as far as to say that all schemes of public ownership of capital will be impeded by the soft budget constraint (1993: 162). To reiterate, in Schweickart's scheme of national investment funding, funds are dispersed to regions, from regions to local communities, and then to local banks. Howard summarises: "[i]n short, local banks monitor firms, regional communities monitor local banks, the central bank monitors regions, and the public monitors the central bank through the political process" (2000: 157; Roemer 1993: 91; Bardhan 1993: 145; Putterman 1993: 162; Bardhan and Roemer 1993: 11).

Putterman contends that a particular weakness manifests in the last of these relationships: between the public (as principle) and the investment / public fund managers (as agents). The crux of his argument revolves around what he calls the 'nondecentralisability' of ownership itself under public ownership property rights. The claim is that the breakdown in monitoring and supervision of the 'people-state' / 'principle-agency' relationship filters down from the top and allows soft incentive and soft monitoring to continue at the lower levels of fund management and, in turn, finally to enterprise management itself. These soft interactions revolve around relations of political accountability, and not the harsh exit device of competitive markets. "There are limits both on the public's *ability* to evaluate bureaucratic and government performance and on its *motivation* to engage in the research activity necessary to such evaluation" (Putterman 1993: 159). Assessment is difficult because evaluation targets are numerous and there is much alternative and counterfactual information to consider. Motivation to monitor agent performance is weak because there is not much to be gained for the monitors; citizens are not able to use private information to construct their 'customised portfolios' containing the outcome of previous search efforts. Putterman's worry is that the incentives for individuals to seek out financially promising projects, and consequently to avoid waste and mismanagement, will not be satisfactorily achieved by a bureaucracy. As the public fund managers will not be adequately monitored, public ownership schemes are unlikely to secure sufficient financial accountability on management. The concern is that if this public-state agency problem cannot be solved as well as the analogous *owner-manger* relationship is by market mediation, the public ownership market economy will remain inefficient (Putterman 1993: 156–9, 166–7; Howard 2000: 156–7; Bardhan and Roemer 1993: 11).

This is the agency problem affiliated to the soft budget constraint. In the critical evaluation that follows, three contentious issues will be considered. In the first place, it is shown how Howard's response to Putterman indicates why NED can at least partly counter this problem. Secondly, even though the difficulty, in principle, remains, it also affects systems of private ownership / investment. As a corollary, and leading into the third point, the argument is made that, if necessary, it is in the collective interest to exchange some degree of investment efficiency for the social benefits democratic investment planning is likely to bring. In light of these discussions, the conclusion is drawn that my scheme of public ownership is preferable to one in which private ownership prevails.

Constricting the Agency Problem

Howard argues that Putterman's concerns about the national level are inflated.[14] "Although it is true that the per capita funds will roll into communities regardless of the subsequent allocation, everyone in the regional community will have a stake in wise investment of these funds" (2000: 158). This is true of NED. An additional advantage is that funds will be distributed between the guilds. In the process of 'rolling-in' to regional and local communities, each guild will reallocate a basic standard of its share to local enterprises within its domain, according to its own democratic criteria. Not only will everyone 'have a stake in wise investment', but such interests are likely to be further enhanced as all those effected by wise / foolish investment decisions will be members of the same guild. There is an incentive for investment and management committees within each guild to avoid extravagant investment projects which show a significant risk of failing. As the consequences of an incompetent and financially insecure guild will eventually be felt by all its members, investment teams and managers of the various workplaces should have some motivation to secure a reasonable measure of economic efficiency. As the guilds now permit a degree of competition, there is a further point to press. Howard continues his response to Putterman. "The numerous local banks and enterprise groups will compete vigorously for these funds, and gross misallocations by fund managers can be sure to provoke public criticism and political challenge" (2000: 158). Recall that in NED, industries—including all the relevant enterprise groups—are vertically demarcated. Each guild will be responsible for regulating and monitoring competition within its own sphere. The force of Howard's observation in this context is more pertinent. Whilst huge mis-apportionments are likely 'to provoke public criticism and political challenge', they will eventuate within the poorly performing guild—where they can be openly discussed by those directly affected. As the range of goods produced and services offered is limited to each demarcated industry, the general knowledge of the various technologies and methods of production is likely to be reasonably prevalent. In the face of such a collective knowledge, seriously incompetent teams of investment fund officials and firm managers can expect to be more easily exposed than in a scheme in which enterprises compete on an undifferentiated basis.

The argument against public ownership is that regional communities or banks, when monitoring local banks and enterprises, would have little incentive to insist upon a hard budget constraint. Yet in NED the monitoring is carried out on a demarcated basis. Each guild has its own finance teams and reserves, or guild banks. When the regional guild committees are monitoring the local workplaces within their functional jurisdiction, careless investment decisions would ultimately affect every member of the guild. Not only would this include the members of the regional committees, but also the guild's fund managers. This does much to undermine the claim that as the incomes of community officials are not dependent upon the prosperity of the banks under their supervision, they will not be interested in supervising them attentively. In my scheme guild officials will take the place of community officials. These officials will be concerned to monitor their banks carefully, as the financial performance of the guild as a whole will affect every member, including themselves. So in contrast to undifferentiated schemes of public ownership, the incomes of guild officials are partly dependent upon the wise investment and performance of the bank belonging to their respective guilds. In response to Putterman's fear that there is a lack of motivation to monitor agent conduct, in NED there is much to be gained for the monitors. With adequate supervision of fund managers, this scheme can be expected to assure financial accountability. Vertically demarcating enterprises and grouping them together so they fall within the same functional domain also goes some way towards meeting Putterman's other concern regarding the public's inability to evaluate performance. Although this remains a demanding task, the alternative and counterfactual information which needs to be considered will obviously be restricted to each industrial sphere. Difficulties in evaluating targets should at least become more limpid, and hence more manageable. My contention is not that the agency problem will disappear, only that it can be restrained.

The Agency Problem in Private Property Regimes

The agency problem associated with the soft budget constraint is not only synonymous with schemes of public ownership of capital. With the political community as principle, the worry is that it will not have enough information to tell if an ailing firm is suffering through poor management or through other variables beyond its control. With owner-manager firms, this agency problem hardly exists. But moving beyond small-scale owner-entrepreneurial capitalism, larger enterprises within corporate capitalism are also confronted with an agency problem regarding management. In these large-scale capitalist firms, ownership and management is separate. "A large joint stock company is owned by a large number of shareholders; control is concentrated in the hands of senior executives. The shareholders constitute the principle and the executives the agent" (Kornai 1993: 51). In modern capitalism the planner-manager agency problem manifests in the 'stockholder-manager agency problem'. Managers are supposed to please their shareholders by attempting to maximise the firm's share value. However, they may wish to keep open an unprofitable division of the company to keep employees on, or they may prefer lavish expenditures that run counter to the stockholders interests of profit maximisation. As the bodies of shareholders are often so large, they are sure to encounter difficulties in monitoring their managers. So the agency problem (how to discipline managers to maximise profits) is also found in contemporary capitalist societies (Roemer 1993: 92; Bardhan 1993: 146).

Defenders of the private ownership market forces economy insist that capitalism is able to contain this agency problem. Weisskopf states that many finance economists believe capitalist property rights enforce discipline on enterprise managers. He reiterates their line of reasoning:

> If a firm is being poorly managed, the value of its shares on the stock market will fall and the firm will become an increasingly appealing target for a hostile take-over by new investors who have reason to believe that the installation of new management will improve firm performance (Weisskopf 1993: 130).

The claim here is that the stock market signals how present managers are performing, gives incentives for them to improve and provides a device for their substitution if they fail. The institution of the stock market is, so the argument goes, a disciplinary mechanism that solves the agency problem (Weisskopf 1993: 130; Roemer 1993: 92). It may not though be as efficient as it initially appears. Bardhan points out those corporate take-overs are usually drawn-out, wasteful affairs. Buyout premiums are usually much higher than market price (on average, 50 percent in American take-overs), which for Bardhan "illustrates how much value corporate managers can destroy before they face a serious threat of disturbance"; furthermore, "[e]ven in the take-over process there is a basic asymmetry of information: managers are more informed about the source of a firm's problems than outside buyers" (Bardhan 1993: 146–7), which presumably decreases the likelihood of their dismissal. It seems that all complex economies, whether their property rights are publicly or privately owned (or a combination of the two), are to some extent hindered by the soft budget constraint agency problem. Although NED does not have a stock market to continually evaluate managerial performance, this is not a great omission. This leads nicely into the third issue, the trade-off between investment efficiency and the collective social advantages our scheme of public ownership is likely to advance.

Efficiency of What?

Putterman's argument suggests that schemes of social ownership of capital are necessarily inferior to those of private ownership. As we have just seen, this is not the case. It is nevertheless possible in principle that NED may not continually meet the conventional capitalist efficiency criteria. But if, as Putterman recognises, it can realise otherwise unobtainable goals, it could still be termed efficient in the wider sense. It would then be in the collective interest to allow some loss in investment efficiency in part exchange. Weisskopf summarises the socialist objectives that have developed from the multifaceted critique of capitalism, two of which are especially pertinent. Firstly, as capitalism distributes income, wealth and power unequally, a greater equality in the means to secure material welfare is demanded. This is not only expedient in itself, but also to help secure equality of participation in democratic politics. Secondly, in response to capitalism's lack of opportunity for economic self-governance, socialists have stressed the need to extend democratic principles from the political sphere to the economic arena. It is precisely these goals that lay at the heart of NED. The benefits include the direction of resources towards fulfilling social ends that are often (usually!) ignored by private ownership, securing a more equal distribution of economic power, and, crucially, by preventing wealth being concentrated in a few hands, it is a mechanism for realising some kind of democratic proficiency over economic affairs. Scepticism remains though as to whether public ownership is a prerequisite for the realisation of these benefits. Putterman argues that taxation, transfer and subsidy programmes can correct market failures without recourse to public ownership schemes. It is true that social democracies do make good use of redistributive taxation policies to improve the material welfare of the least well-off. This is one reason why they have proved popular with reformist socialists. It is also why POD has attracted socialist interest. It should be noted though, as Roemer does, that such measures are premised upon legislation, which can be amended or withdrawn. Taxes are a matter of legislation, which can change as political opinion does; they are politically unstable. In contrast, NED seeks redistribution through a more fundamental change in property rights, which is not so easily revoked. This is one of the key differences between social democracy and guild socialism. The former, upholding private ownership, is plagued by problems of periodical capital flight; the latter is not (Putterman 1993: 166; Weisskopf 1993: 120–3; Roemer 1993: 90).

There is an additional point on the usage of efficiency criteria. Briefly, efficiency to Cole does not mean capitalist efficiency—which he sees as protecting mediocrity and destroying native genius—but efficiency premised upon individual initiative, differences and distinctiveness. "Efficiency", he writes, "we are just beginning to learn is only in part a matter of machinery and up-to-date equipment: it is far more a matter of human attitude and temperament" (1921b: 4). Not surprisingly, Cole avoids the traditional capitalist ideals of industrial and economic efficiency. Rather, he redefines the issue. The key to efficiency is self-government, and if a system (including its democratically planned investment policy) is not based on self-government, it cannot be efficient. The obsession and preoccupation with efficiency, he infers, relates to an occupational hazard of the bureaucrat. It is evident that alternative criteria for efficiency have been adopted. For Cole, an economic system can only be regarded as efficient if it secures for individuals the opportunity to develop their unique talents, and it can only do this if it is decentralised and self-governing. In contrast, Putterman seems to have in mind the yardstick that efficient production and distribution techniques are those that can turn out high quantities of goods for the lowest possible costs. This notion of efficiency is similar to the Western preoccupation with the growth syndrome, which, whether capitalist or state socialist, has inflicted the most devastating humanitarian and ecological damage. These growth and efficiency values account for many of our contemporary urban and environmental problems. The assumption that they should take priority has to be rejected. Following Cole's example, political life must be ranked over and above the conventional capitalist efficiency criteria (1972: 156–7; Houseman 1979: 81–2).

Summary

These are the critical issues involved in democratic investment planning. So is it necessary to maintain a system of private ownership? The message in this chapter is that it is not. My conclusion is that socialists, and indeed Rawlsian liberals, should opt for a public ownership scheme in which democratic investment planning is incorporated. It is unlikely that such a model would eliminate the agency problem comprehensively. As Howard acknowledges, weak incentives to insist upon hard budget constraints are likely to continue, at least to some extent (2000: 158). I do believe though that the issue does not render public ownership initiatives superfluous, but quite the opposite.

Conclusion

An exposition of Cole's democratically planned economy, the likely problems involved and the manner in which they may be overcome has been the central concern of this chapter. I have addressed the most immediate factors that he fails to consider adequately and introduced structural mechanisms which help fill the gaps left by these omissions. It was suggested that Cole's basic economic proposals have the potential to allocate goods and resources in a way that overcomes both the dangers of command planning and the theoretical flaws which tend to impair market socialism. Centralised command planning was swiftly rejected. The main reason cited was that it is not democratic. These one-party systems also tend to frustrate dynamics within civil society. Critics have pointed out that in these regimes, political and social power is treated without difference, as is state-sanctioned propaganda and freely formed public opinion. The ugly result is that economic, political and cultural affairs all come to be monopolised by the bureaucratic apparatus of the party. Such totalitarian command states, in the process of absorbing civil society into state structures, seek to obliterate it. Although this is an ideal-typical description (social movements and independent citizens initiatives may to some extent have troubled these regimes), the problem is clear enough:

> Under the one-party systems, civil society is always on the verge of extinction. Attempts to establish it from below are inherently risky and dangerous and threatened from all sides by the Party official, psychiatrist, soldier, secret agent or vigilante (Keane 1988: 5).

Attempts to unify the state and civil society from above by centralised command planning, orchestrated by the (single) party, have been disastrous (Keane 1988: 2–5). They have also denigrated socialism's credibility.

Unlike centralised command planning, NED's planning is mostly decentralised, horizontal and based around democratic interactions between locally organised bodies of citizens—or between citizens' demarcated interests, to be more precise. A degree of democratic centralised planning will however exist where necessary. The objections to command planning—its hierarchy based upon superior and subordinate relationships, its lack of opportunity for producers and consumers to participate in economic decision making, its repression of individual freedom, its disregard for consumer satisfaction and the epistemological critique that information cannot be transmitted to a central authority quickly or efficiently—become largely extraneous. So the political economy of NED is constituted through political structures of democratic planning; it will also make good use of a controlled market criterion. In contrast to ideal-typical market socialism, co-operation will not be substituted with undifferentiated competitive markets. In NED markets are demarcated, curtailed and subordinated to democratic planning. I have attempted to synthesize what is best from co-operation and competition. This is realised through the introduction of a controlled intra-guild competitive ethic in which the guilds will be permitted to distribute a percentage of their profits to their workforces based on a standard of performance. Indeed, it is NED's pluralist mediation of state and civil society that can make the best use of planning and markets. For Cole there is no question about the ideological dimension to the liberal separation of politics and economics. Insofar, he follows the young Marx in pointing out that if capitalists and workers can both be citizens, there is a serious problem with existing forms of citizenship. Yet he is also adamantly against the Soviet and Fabian attempt to fuse politics and economics. This chapter has shown how I have used Cole's insights to inform my institutional design, whilst remaining true to the general spirit of his thought. Part three of the following chapter adds further comment on the benefits the political arrangements in NED are likely to bring, i.e., that they are indispensable to the basic structure of the good society articulated by justice as fairness. And so, the debate with Rawls may now begin.

Notes

1 When the guilds engage in determining cost prices, Cole is adamant that the sum of maintaining their workers 'at a reasonable standard of life' has to be taken into account. The continuous maintenance of workers must include unemployment pay at the standard rate. This, for Cole, is a legitimate cost of production. He also claims that as prices are not fixed by the market, but through joint agreement (what Cole calls use-value), the guild system abolishes profiteering. The individual's pay is determined by his or her guild, rather than what can be obtained through market processes. The idea is that individuals are no longer treated as commodities (n.d.: 8; 1921a: 5).

2 These will be noted in the next section, 'The Plan-Market Controversy'.

3 Devine adds that in his scheme, market forces would not determine such cases. They would be regionally and nationally planned in accordance with socially determined priorities (Devine 1988: 214).

4 Italics mine.

5 A point fully recognised by Rawls (1971: 277).

6 Socialists have also argued that as unregulated markets only render indications in response to monetary demands, they distort the economy upwards towards satisfying the personal desires of the wealthy (Ticktin 1998: 74). Albert and Hahnel add that "since market demand is measured in quantity of dollars spent which in turn determines what is produced, in market economies members of different classes exert disproportionate influence on production. Thus, there is nothing democratic about 'consumer sovereignty' when there is an unequal distribution of wealth" (Albert and Hahnel 1991: 70).

7 This particular feature of Schweickart's scheme has important consequences for local control over communities. Under capitalism, labour is subservient to capital; workers must either follow capital or entice it to come to them. Workers, as well as regions, can be played off against each other. This is not so in his scheme. "Not only will local firms not run away, but fresh capital will not avoid the region. The tax-generated investment fund will be apportioned to regions per capita; regions will not compete for funds" (Schweickart 1993: 145). Local banks will not usually support distant projects. This will enable communities to assert more control over their environments (Schweickart 1993: 145, 255).

8 Community banks will have a cooperative nature. Their governing councils will be made up of representatives from their own work forces, from the community planning agency and from the firms affiliated to it (Schweickart 1993: 75).

9 In light of developments in economic theory since Cole's guild period, MaCain proposes that guild socialism be 'revised in the direction of market socialism' (MaCain 2001: C1). It is interesting that although Cole was not in favour of workers getting paid in proportion to output (1920: 14), he has been referenced by a market socialist as a forerunner of producer co-operatives (Estrin 1989: 169).

10 Hirst argues that the acceptance of the market-dominated economy also means the acceptance of "the private domination of hierarchically directed unaccountable agencies with great economic and political power" (1990: 71). As he sees it, deregulated markets are not free; they are politically beneficial to large corporations. Such corporations can compete with each other on a somewhat equal footing, whereas smaller firms and individuals have little choice but to accept the outcome of their competitions. The market, therefore, cannot be thought of as a neutral social mechanism in which all participants compete equally. On the contrary, the key markets are dominated by small and privileged groups (Hirst 1990: 71–2).

11 MaCain believes that material incentives are the least evil means of preserving effort over long periods (MaCain 2001: C1). This addresses the concern that guild "members will not be able to profit by any accidental superior productivity of their industry, since a judicious system of fixing prices or appropriating any possible surplus will maintain a uniform level" (Reynard 1920: 326). With the introduction of a sanctioned material incentive, the critique that "[j]ust as the individual

Guildsman is assumed to be without the vulgar instinct to grab, so a universal predilection for steady work—irrespective of reward—seems to be taken for granted" (Reynard 1920: 326) is countered.

12 This institutional feature is readily adaptable to the guild idea. Roemer and Bardhan hint as much themselves. They explain that "[i]t will be desirable for members of a corporate group to be technologically somewhat interrelated" (Bardhan and Roemer 1992: 109). This is for three main reasons: a) firms will share knowledge concerning each other's production, b) there is likely to be an overlap in previous research and development programmes and c) the main (guild) banks will be able to specialise in fairly constricted technological areas (Bardhan and Roemer 1992: 109).

13 See Bardhan and Roemer 1992: 107–9.

14 Howard claims that "Putterman's objection would have more weight for a scheme in which investment allocations to individual enterprises was made by a central bureaucracy rather than a regional or local community" (Howard 2000: 158). Indeed, we have seen that in NED decentralised decision making is, especially in the case of the co-operative council, indispensable.

CHAPTER FOUR

From Property-Owning Democracy to Property-Controlling Democracy

Having established the institutional contours of NED, the task of this chapter is to show why, when compared indirectly to POD, it is the just society. In justice as fairness, the basic structure is chosen through the method of pure procedural justice. To briefly recap, a just constitution incorporates a just procedure aimed to secure a just outcome. The two principles represent an 'independent criterion' for the procedure, the framing of a just constitution, and the outcome, just legislation. As we saw in Chapter One, this is the Rawlsian method of procedural justice. If the circumstances and the procedure are both just, then so must be the following distributions, irrespective of what they are. There is not an independent criterion for judging a singule distribution. Particular distributions must be seen as part of the wider scheme of co-operation from which they emerge. The original position is designed so that the basic structure is chosen under procedural conditions that everyone can regard as fair. Following this method, Rawls states that the regime—private property, socialist or the many various intermediate forms—which can satisfy the principles of justice cannot be settled in advance:

> The theory of justice . . .can . . . set out in a schematic way the outlines of a just economic system that admits of several variations. The political judgement in any given case will then turn on which variation is most likely to work out best in practice. A conception of justice is a necessary part of any such political assessment, but it is not sufficient (1971: 274).

He adds that justice as fairness "tries to set out guidelines for how the decision can reasonably be approached" (2001: 139); and that "on many questions of social and economic policy we must fall back upon a notion of quasi-pure procedural justice" (1971: 201). In choosing between POD and liberal socialism, Rawls recognises that information from historical circumstances, political thought 'and much else' will need to be considered. This is to supplement pure procedural justice. Using the schema of quasi-pure procedural justice, and making good use of the theoretical and factual information Rawls permits, the method of *developing* my argument is not so much to directly compare NED with POD, although some comparisons throughout will be unavoidable, especially in regards to the least well-off in both schemes *after* the four-stage sequence has been worked through. Rather, it will be firstly to highlight the difficulties POD will encounter when it tries to implement the principles of justice, and secondly to illustrate how these problems are either non-applicable or overcome when the two principles are embedded within the basic structure of NED. The two principles will, to the greatest possible extent, remain an independent criterion; they will serve as a medium of interaction, so to speak.

I will consider both the state and the commune in POD and NED respectively. In order to determine which constitutional convention is more suited to realise the two principles of justice, both are subject to critical scrutiny. Rawls believes the fundamental question about justice can be settled in the original position. I am not disputing this. My problem is with the modern-liberal institutions which are supposed to be capable of sustaining both the fair value of the basic political liberties and a fair equality of opportunity, and to maximise the material conditions of the least well-off. It will be shown why Rawls' redistributive state, due to the inevitable economic antagonisms his economy amplifies, will find these tasks hugely problematic. One of the earliest and best-known critics of the liberal state was Karl Marx. His powerful argument that the sovereignty of the modern state is somewhat illusory is of lasting value. To Marx, as the state defends the private ownership of the means of production, it is socio-economic relations which for the most part remain sovereign. This critique is introduced and expanded upon. It is then shown why, through an engagement with the commentary on justice as fairness from the academic left, it is particularly telling when applied to POD. Rawls is aware of the threat posed to justice as fairness by a small property-owning class commanding the power to effectively control the legislature, and introduces institutional measures to contain it. I will argue, however, that POD is ill-equipped to cope with the powerful economic forces his market economy initiates. In class-divided societies like POD, the two principles are internally inconsistent. By way of contrast, in the more egalitarian NED, there is no inherent contradiction. The dynamic takes a different organisational form in my scheme. Despite being significantly revised, NED remains informed by Cole's libertarian socialism. Cole set himself the demanding task of constructing a theoretically sound political pluralist alternative to state sovereignty. It will be seen that he largely succeeded. In what follows, the argument that NED embodies an institutional setting which contains a genuine alternative to sovereign power is made. The need for ultimate control, whether overt or covert, by either a body resembling the modern state or a small yet dominant economic class, is not a prerequisite for the democratically planned decentralised economy sketched. As the objections to Cole's scheme from critics who question its political pluralism have a direct relation to NED, I am, I think, obliged to theorise a response. In doing so, it is shown that the substance and volume of sovereignty is favourably re-defined. Despite NED's lack of central planning and its role for a curtailed market, more issues fall within the scope of democratic decision making, only now in civil society, than in POD. From this point it is shown why the constitution of NED represents a significantly superior starting point by which the two principles can be accommodated.

The argument in this chapter is divided into three parts. In the first part it is shown why POD will find it intolerably difficult to sustain the two principles. The second part demonstrates why the constitution in NED provides a theoretically sound context in which to embody both principles. Then in the third part, adopting the four-stage sequence, the two principles are applied to the basic structure of NED, and in the process it is demonstrated how the difficulties encountered in POD discussed in part one are transcended. The conclusion drawn is that this leaves the least well-off in NED in a far superior position than their counterparts in POD. The three parts are 'The State and Sovereignty in Rawlsian Liberalism', 'The Commune and Sovereignty in New Economic Democracy', and 'The Realisation of the Two Principles of Justice'. To begin, I would like to show how the Rawlsian method of quasi-pure procedural justice is used to establish NED as the just society.

The Four-Stage Sequence Revisited

It was explained in Chapter One that Rawls sketches a four-stage sequence to highlight the link between the two principles and a just constitution. To briefly recap, the principles of justice are firstly established in the original position. Secondly, the contractees are made aware of the general economic and political features of their society; they use this information to choose the political constitution that will assure the rights and liberties of the first principle. At the third stage, legislatures, with particular knowledge of their society but not themselves, frame laws which will determine just economic and social policies. At the fourth stage, in which the veil of ignorance has now been completely lifted, rules and laws are applied by administrators and the judiciary. The first principle is applied at the constitutional convention, the second principle at the legislative stage.

Employing the procedure of the four-stage sequence provides the means by which the advancement of my argument is premised. In explaining his scheme, Rawls reasons that "[b]y moving back and forth between the stages of the constitutional convention and the legislature, the best constitution is found" (1971: 198). For my purposes the movement will proceed roughly as follows. At the first stage, the two principles are chosen exactly as they are in justice as fairness. Although I shall add to the list of basic political liberties, there is no call to dispute their ordering. At the second stage, Rawls presumes only that the chosen political structure will be 'some form of constitutional democracy' (1971: 197–8). Again, there is no need to contend this assumption. But here my argument is bolder: the assertion is that the just constitutional democracy is a revised libertarian socialist commune system. Then at the third stage, the guilds—in consultation with the consumer councils, and together with the communes—are introduced as the legislating bodies. In NED, although there is a plurality of functionally demarcated legislatures, there is only one judiciary, who, in the final stage, will interpret the laws in much the same way Rawls suggests. This, however, is not the finalised order. NED is a society that has transcended the state–civil society paradigm. My civil society has been re-politicised through a thorough democratisation of its basic economic institutions. Political power does not rest solely in the hands of our pluralized state. Therefore, the initial inference that only the communes will form the political convention, the guilds not appearing until the third stage, cannot be satisfactory. For Rawls, "[p]olitical power is always coercive power applied by the state and its apparatus of enforcement" (2001: 40). But in NED it also rests with and is applied by the guilds. When this is combined with the understanding that the communes are constituted through electives from the guilds and consumer / civil councils, it becomes clear that the guilds are integral to the political system. As such, they must be instituted at the second stage, the constitutional convention. It follows that the same logic must also apply to the consumer and civil councils. This demand is reinforced by the knowledge that, due to market externalities, consumption is quite often anything but an individual act. And as NED includes consumer interests within the remit of citizenship rights, the consumer and civil councils must also be acknowledged at the constitutional stage. So, by moving 'back and forth' between the second and third stages as Rawls permits, I arrive at NED's basic constitution. In my thesis the political arrangement, the democratic convention, consists of the commune structure, the guilds, and the consumer and civil councils.

Care should be taken though not to confuse the Rawlsian method. Consider the entry into the four-stage sequence of productive property. As we have seen, Rawls recognises that the equal basic liberties central to a constitutional regime are certain to clash. The priority of the first principle ensures that a basic liberty can only be constrained in the interests of the other basic liberties and not, for example, for the sake of economic advantage. So although no basic liberty is absolute in the finally adjusted scheme, they are equally secured for all citizens. If there are too many basic liberties, which Rawls refers to as 'truly essential liberties', their specification into a unified scheme spelling out their 'range of application' is likely to prove unmanageable. As such, Rawls proposes a criterion of significance to determine when a particular right or liberty is fundamental.[1] They are to guarantee, equally, the social conditions indispensable for the development of the two moral powers inherent in all citizens (1993: 335–6). The capacity for a sense of justice demands the equal political liberties required to apply the two principles to the basic structure. The capacity for a conception of the good entails the powers of practical reason, which can only exist through liberty of conscience, freedom of association, freedom of speech, etc. So for Rawls, a liberty is more significant if it is essentially involved in, or a more necessary institutional means to protect, the exercise of either of the two moral powers. "The more significant liberties mark out the central range of application of a particular basic liberty; and in cases of conflict we look for a way to accommodate the more significant liberties within the central range of each"

(2001: 113). Rawls includes in the remit of basic rights the holding and use of personal property. A material basis allows for personal independence and a feeling of self-respect, which, he insists, are both vital for the development of the two moral powers (1993: 318–20). But interestingly he does not take as basic the right to private property in the means of production, or the equal right to participate in their control. Neither private nor social ownership of productive property is to count as a basic right "because they are not necessary for the adequate development and full exercise of the moral powers, and so are not an essential social basis of self-respect" (2001: 114). Rights to various forms of productive property may still be justified, but further specification must be made at the legislative stage, and on the premise that the basic rights and liberties of the first principle are fully respected. Justice as fairness is a public political conception, which for Rawls means it must not prejudge, in terms of the fundamental constitution, the ownership of the means to produce. His hope is that this will be endorsed by what he calls an 'overlapping consensus'[2] (1993: 327–9, 337–9; 2001: 111–5).

I think Rawls is wrong on this issue. A genuine opportunity to realise a sense of justice and fulfil personal conceptions of the good most certainly requires a non-statist scheme of community *ownership* of the means of production—a system in which productive resources are under the *control* of social co-operative labour. Only a politico-economic arrangement like this can provide for personal independence and the social basis of self-respect. The reasons why were indicated in the previous chapter, and will become clearer as this chapter unfolds. I will confirm why in the concluding passage.[3] But for now I will meet Rawls on his own grounds. The guilds—together with the consumer and civil councils, and the commune system—are included at the constitutional convention as the realisation of the basic rights and liberties of the first principle require them. As we saw in Chapter Three, the guilds are the institutions that will regulate their own markets. Following Rawls' logic, I will assume they could, should the situation demand, accommodate both private and social control of productive resources. As such, they cannot be excluded from part two of the four-stage sequence on the grounds that they prejudge private or social property in the means of production. Their inclusion at the legislative stage is, for now, justified by reference to the political rights and liberties of the first principle.

1. The State and Sovereignty in Rawlsian Liberalism

A Critique of the Liberal State

Liberal democratic theory has attempted to sanction state sovereignty whilst simultaneously placing restrictions upon its power. The state needs a monopoly of coercive power to protect trade and commerce, law and order, national defence, etc. This force could, however, potentially undermine the political and social freedoms of the individual. Liberal democracy sought to overcome this problem through the innovation of one of its most basic institutional arrangements: representative democracy. Individuals are free to pursue their own material objectives while the state supposedly upholds the general interest, thereby ensuring the greatest happiness for as many people as possible. It is the combination of two institutions, the democratic constitutional state and the free market, which, from the liberal democratic perspective, guarantees authority without sacrificing liberty. This is liberal democracy's response to the potential threat sovereign power poses to individual freedom (Hirst 1989: 81–2; Held 1989: 48–9). Although Rawls' redistributive liberalism upholds a social democratic mixed economy, it accepts these two institutions implicitly.

Marx was not at all convinced by liberalism's 'solution'. The liberal fight against tyranny and for political equality was, he concedes, a significant advance towards human emancipation (Marx 1975: 221). However, due to the internal dynamics central to its economy, capitalism inevitably generates immense inequalities which themselves drastically limit real freedom. The liberating potential of political equality is, Marx insists, hugely restricted by class inequalities. In the liberal democratic tradition, the state may represent the public interest rather than private concerns. But for Marx, the opposition between public / general and private / particular interests is mainly illusory. To presume that the state can defend the former is to suppose that classes do not exist, one class does not exploit another, there are no conflicts of interest between classes and class differences have no impact on economic and political life. In treating everyone equally, in particular the defence of individuals' property rights, the state's neutrality simply generates partial effects—it sanctions and supports the privileges of those who own property. This ensures that the real source of power, private ownership of productive forces, is 'depoliticised', i.e., it is not held to be a proper subject of politics. The outcome of treating the economy as non-political is that the huge gulf between owners and non-owners of the means of production is seen as the result of free contract, and regarded as no concern of the state. By defending private property though, the state cannot remain neutral in regards to property ownership. For Marx the state is not an independent set of institutions operating above society, and it is not a public power defending the general interest. On the contrary, it is thoroughly implanted in socio-economic relations and deeply connected to particular class interests (Marx 1975: 221–3, 229; Held 1989: 33, 48–9).

In his early writings Marx insists that it is not the state which underlies the socio-economic order, it is the other way round. The notion that the state is sovereign is regarded as a fallacy. Political power can more adequately be explained through an analysis of socio-economic relations. It then becomes apparent that *in class societies* the state is not the organ through which the common public interest can be realised. Orthodox Marxism views the state as a class instrument co-ordinating a class-divided society in favour of the ruling class. On the occasions when Marx recognises the state's bureaucratic institutions may take dimensions and develop sources of power not directly controlled by the dominant class,[4] and thereby retain some independent power, he still regards the state as a conservative force. Even in these exceptional periods, this arbiter state's independence from capital on economic matters is weakened by its dependence on the accumulation of capital for its revenue. Economic organisations create the wealth from which the state apparatus is financed. The state, clearly, is wholly dependent upon the resources which stem from the organisation of profitable production, taxation and capital markets. Capitalists control resources which they may withdraw or redirect as they see fit. The state bureaucracy is thereby compelled to sanction and support capitalist predominance in economic matters. Insofar, those in state power have an interest in preserving the vitality of a market forces economy. Marx confirms that in this sense the state cannot avoid its dependence upon the class who collectively own productive processes. For the sake of stability, state policies need to be compatible with the objectives of the owners of the means of production. Capitalists therefore do not necessarily have to transmit their preferences to state officials directly. State policy in a capitalist society is determined by the government's first concern to protect the development of the economic base whilst coercively preserving social stability. So for Marx, state agencies are inevitably entangled in the encounters of civil society. The state is viewed as an extension of civil society, maintaining the existing socio-economic set-up for the enrichment of certain interests only. In the long-term, these particular interests are those of the capitalist class (Marx 1970: 44–6, 50–1; 1975: 230; Dunleavy and O'Leary 1987: 210–1, 231, 243; Held 1989: 33–7).

On the whole, Marx's combined writings on the state indicate that state intervention in capitalist societies will be decidedly reactionary. Government administrative structures are shaped in ways which support capital accumulation, irrespective of both the degree of capitalist control of the state and the intensity of class antagonisms. If intervention obstructs capital accumulation, then it also threatens the state's material basis. The certain outcome is that state policies must be favourable to capitalist relations of production. This ensures that a dominant economic class may actually *rule*, even though it does not directly *govern*; it can determine the political agenda irrespective of whether it is officially represented in government.

Marx's analysis of the modern state's general economic dependence on the capitalist mode of production, which thereby restricts its movement and intervening capacity, retains its penetrative force. In his libertarian socialist writings, Cole does not refer directly to Marx, but his reflections on the modern liberal state mirror Marx's polemic. He also insists that the state 'faithfully' reflects the socio-economic structure. Political power expresses social power, which in capitalism is inevitably economic. He stresses that "economic power is the key to political power, and that those who control the means of production are able, by means of that control, to dominate the State", and that "no Government dares to run seriously counter to the wishes and interests of the great economic magnates" (1972: 5). Cole's contention is that whatever the forms of state organisation, its true character is determined not from within, but by the 'interplay of economic forces'. So for Cole, as with Marx, capitalist power 'stands behind the state'. Others too have drawn attention to this phenomenon. Dunleavy and O'Leary (1987) point out that the freedom of large powerful corporations to organise their production process as their wishes dictate restricts the options open to elected governments. It is, they argue, an exercise of power which limits what citizens can and cannot express through the constitutional democratic channel. Although large firms are still compelled to address external controls like market regulation and consumer demand, they only apply to end-products:

> A whole chain of decision-making inside corporations—about how to organise the productive process, where to make investments, how many people to employ, etc.—all these decisions are not directly controlled by markets but vest discretionary power in the hands of corporate executives (Dunleavy and O'Leary 1987: 294).

These executives can, if they wish, withhold resources and refuse to co-operate with government policy-making. As this has a direct influence on the electoral, government agents will prioritise business interests, in which case consideration for business profitability is reflected in all major policy-making deliberations (1972: 4–6; Dunleavy and O'Leary 1987: 293–4).

Rawls' Response

It is open to the Rawlsian liberal to respond in two ways to Marx's class-state analysis. Firstly, by denying it is correct, and secondly, by refuting the charge that POD will engender social classes as Marxists usually understand them. In regards to the former, Rawls, perhaps strangely for a liberal, does not wish to make any such denial. On the contrary, his own renunciation of capitalism has much in common with Marx's. As we saw in Chapter One, Rawls rejects capitalism as it cannot sustain the two principles of justice. It does not respect the idea of reciprocity, and it fails to secure the fair value of the equal political liberties. He affirms that the ownership of the means of production in capitalist society inevitably accumulates in the hands of a small class who dominate the economy and thereby indirectly exert a disproportionate influence upon political life. So for Rawls, as for Marx, economic inequalities in capitalist society inexorably undermine political equalities. However, Rawls insists that POD has the background institutions capable of averting the concentration of wealth and capital. The recognition is that monopolies have to be prevented from controlling productive resources. To guarantee the equal value of the basic liberties, POD must keep the ownership of the means of production widely dispersed (1971: 225–6; 1993: 327–8; 2001: 137–40). It is then the second line of defence that Rawls takes up.

In his (disappointingly brief) response to Marx's critique of liberalism, Rawls notes that Marx would object to POD on the grounds that it generates political and economic forces which are detrimental to its ideal description, and that a regime with the private ownership of productive assets cannot possibly realise the two principles. And Rawls' next line is: "This is a major difficulty and must be faced" (2001: 178). It is, therefore, a real shame that his response, which amounts to little more than two pages, is so insufficiently scant. He could not have thought the difficulty that major, or his reaction would have been far more detailed, as it is in his repudiation of utilitarianism. Nevertheless, he does write:

> To the objection that the political rights and liberties of a constitutional regime are merely formal, we reply that, by the fair value of the political liberties (working with the other principles of justice) all citizens, whatever their social position, may be assured a fair opportunity to exert political influence (2001: 177).

As this constitutes the key part of Rawls' (lack of) reply, let us take a closer look at how all citizens are to be 'assured a fair opportunity to exert political influence'. Political liberties enable citizens to take part in public life. He asserts that "justice as fairness treats the political liberties in a special way. We include in the first principle of justice a proviso that the equal political liberties—and *only* these liberties—are to be guaranteed their fair value" (2001: 149). Political liberties are to be sufficiently equal so that all citizens, irrespective of economic position, have the same chance to stand for public office, take part in elections, 'and the like'. Rawls suggests that this may be realised through reforms like the public funding of elections and limitations on campaign donations, equal access to media, regulations on the freedom of speech, etc. The key aim is to ensure legislators and political actors are "independent of large concentrations of private economic and social power in a private-property democracy, and of government control and bureaucratic power in a liberal socialist regime" (2001: 150). His hope is that this will 'further the conditions of deliberate democracy'. Guaranteeing the fair value of political liberties will, he insists, secure an equality of access to a public facility arranged to serve political purposes (1993: 328). The public forum is established by constitutional rules which determine the access to positions of political power. The idea is that the claims of all citizens are treated fairly by the 'political process as a public facility'. Without this warranty, the wealthier are liable to form cartels and exclude the less wealthy, and it cannot be assumed "that the inequalities permitted by the difference principle will be sufficiently small to prevent this" (1993: 328: 2001: 148–51).

Re-Clarification

It is then reforms in the public facility that, Rawls hopes, will maintain the equal value of political liberties, sustain the independence of legislatures, and assure all citizens an equal opportunity to influence political life. This is a spirited attempt to contain what is probably the most tenacious problem in market forces economies. However, as the following analysis will indicate, Marx's critique of the modern liberal state still has particular damaging implications when applied to Rawls' scheme. The inequalities required to satisfy the reciprocal, compensatory and incentive facets of the difference principle ensure that large accumulations of capital in private hands cannot be averted. Under these circumstances, the equal access to a public forum required to guarantee the fair value of the basic liberties of the first principle cannot be assured. In short, the economic inequalities demanded by the dictates of the difference principle will unquestionably undermine the basic liberties of the first principle. To validate this claim, the following sections engage with the body of literature produced by the academic left. Rawls has been both fiercely critiqued and passionately defended by commentators who are socialists of some description. The breadth and depth of these discussions are considerable. It will therefore be instructive to briefly reiterate the precise details of the argument I am making. Rawls' propositions—a framework to establish a system of justice that is fair, the original position and the veil of ignorance, the ordering of the two principles, the difference principle and the components of social primary goods—are accepted virtually in their entirety. As such, issue is taken with the socialists who reject these elements of Rawls' theory. At the other end of the scale, the socialists—mostly left-of-centre moderates who defend Rawls' conclusion that the key institutions of modern liberalism can be just—are also rejected. In my argument, Rawls' premises are not only defended, but fully endorsed—it is his social liberalism that is repudiated; disagreement is taken with the socialists who reject Rawls' premises and, albeit for different reasons, with the social democratic socialists who defend his liberalism.

The Contradictory Problem in Rawlsian Liberalism

Debates on a theory of justice within the academic left have included the key question: 'does a theory of justice impose class-divisions upon society?'. In order to show that it does, and that class-alliances will doubtlessly frustrate the realisation of equal political influence, this contention will now be addressed. Miller (1989) claims that if the Marxian account of social conflict holds weight, commitments to uphold the difference principle cannot arise from the original position. The problematic feature of the difference principle, Miller identifies, is that it will have no appeal to the parties who will occupy the best-off positions in society. His argument is that market economy societies have: a) no institutional arrangement which is acceptable to both the best-off and worst-off classes, and b) the best-off class is also a ruling class. In regard to the former, Miller points out that Marx held that there is not a social contract in which the best-off and worst-off classes will comply. The second notion is, as specified above, classic Marxist social theory. It stresses that the interests of the best-off / ruling class are served by ideological frameworks and by all major institutions. So when the veil of ignorance is lifted, the difference principle could not be enforced. Where societies in the circumstances of justice have any of these features, Miller insists, the ability to uphold the difference principle would not emerge from the original position (Miller 1989: 209–12).

Rawls claims that parties in the original position are able to stick to their agreement in actual circumstances, the 'constraints of commitments'. Miller argues that this reasoning "cannot produce a rational agreement to realise the difference principle . . . if the difference principle is subject to the same defect of potential intolerability that Rawls ascribes to utilitarianism" (1989: 214). This is especially so where the best-off find it intolerable to sacrifice advantages to compensate the worst-off. Parties in the original position would foresee the possibility of being in the best-off class, and realise that their interests are not compatible with Rawls' standard of social justice:

> On a Marxist view it would not be uniquely rational in the original position to commit oneself to help realise the difference principle. . . . For he [sic] must take into account the possibility that he is in fact a member of the best-off group in a highly non egalitarian society. And in terms of the needs and desires characteristic of such groups it matters a great deal whether one has wealth, power, and status (Miller 1989: 220).

So if Marxist social theory is correct, parties in the original position are likely to anticipate that once the veil of ignorance is lifted and they return to society, those who find themselves in a dominant exploiting class will realise the difference principle would be intolerable for them (Miller 1989: 213–21).

The argument is that parties in the original position will not be able to form a social contract, as they will foresee an inability to accept the social changes it requires. Miller is right that in class-divided societies there are substantial problems in fulfilling the strict demands of the difference principle. It does not, however, follow that no commitment to reducing economic inequalities can emerge from the original position. The argument that the Marxian analysis of social conflict is accurate does not have to involve the claim that parties in the original position cannot commit to the difference principle. It simply means they are compelled to reject the societies in which income from private property guarantees class-divisions, class-antagonisms, class-hostilities, etc. In the original position, Rawls insists that every possible eventuality is considered until a satisfactory agreement is reached in accord with the difference principle. Miller, on the other hand, is arguing that this is not possible, as they would have to consider their actions if they ended up in an exploiting dominant ruling class, the likelihood being that they would foresee that it would be impossible to stick to the consequences of the difference principle. To realise Rawls' principle requires a lessening of the divide between the best and worst-off. The wealth, power and status of those better off would need to be continually reduced. Although Rawls would counter that Miller has overlooked the value of reciprocity, the probability is that there will be limits to how much the dominant upper class could accept. But whilst this admittedly rules out POD, it does not imply that the difference principle cannot be the key organisational feature of an alternative classless society.

As an indictment of liberal capitalism, though, Miller's polemic is significant. POD removes certain questions from the public sphere, in particular a range of economic issues. But as we have seen, the problem is that if the electorate is supposed to be sovereign, there cannot be a small wealthy class capable of wielding power greater than elected officials. In a real democracy, the electorate is unobstructed by a privileged wealthy class. POD, however, will be characterised by precisely this kind of minority class. Property income guarantees inequalities are not just unavoidable, but also considerable. Rawls, to reiterate, is troubled by this (1993: 377–8). He recognises that institutions which adhere to equality of opportunity "are put in jeopardy when inequalities of wealth exceed a certain limit, and political liberty likewise tends to lose its value, and representative government to become such in appearance only" (1971: 278). To compensate, he allows for some economic matters to fall within the political agenda; indeed, the difference principle demands it. The distributive branch has the unenviable task of ensuring inequalities do not 'exceed a certain limit'. Here the government is heavily involved in the economy of POD. But capital will, as it has always done, protect its interests; and due to its strategic economic position, the government is obliged to respond favourably.

There remains then an unresolved tension, what may be called the 'contradictory problem'. On the one hand, the state has to assume a redistributive function, probably quite considerable, to satisfy the requirements of the difference principle. In point of fact, Rawls' principles of justice necessitate this. Yet on the other hand, given that concentrations of wealth exert disproportionate political influence, the state cannot make this involvement too extensive, as it cannot risk seriously threatening the long-term interests of capital. It is possible that symmetry of sorts can be struck, but given the inevitable economic antagonisms, it is precariously balanced. In ambiguous cases, i.e., those in which it is difficult to foresee whether certain policies will improve the material conditions of the least well-off, the dilemma for elected officials is whether to approve those proposals that require more state intervention, and be certain to implement the difference principle, or to approve those that require less state action, and be sure to avoid repelling capital. The latter is the probable outcome. Investor confidence is vital for economic stability, and this includes POD. If those with capital interpret government policies as detrimental to their interests, they can refuse to invest. The effects of withdrawal of investment will be devastating in Rawls' market economy. The inevitable economic slump will guarantee political instability. Rawls' government will therefore be compelled to prioritise business interests, in much the same way the state does in capitalist societies. It is certain that this will render the realisation of the demands of the difference principle problematic, to say the least.

Furthermore, POD needs growth for stability. But as Schweickart points out, growth can be unbalanced and is plagued by externalities. Rawls is alert to these problems. The transfer and distributive branches will redistribute the required degree of income, and the allocative branch will correct "the more obvious departures from efficiency caused by the failure of prices to measure accurately social benefits and costs" (1971: 276). Nevertheless, inequalities are unlikely to be reduced to any great extent, for labour is still subordinated to capital. If workers cannot attract capital, they must uproot and move to where it is. Regions can be pitted against each other. Rawls' scheme has no mechanism for democratically deciding investment rates, nor where they may be directed. The market does this, and then government intervention corrects the resulting imbalances. Yet here the tension noted above simply resurfaces. In private investment regimes government solutions must be on a national scale, otherwise capital will quickly flee the more tightly regulated regions. But large-scale intervention is to invite a hostile reaction from those with resources to invest. Again, it is difficult to see how the specifications of the difference principle can be satisfied (Schweickart 1993: 254–6). Given these dynamics in the liberal state, Rawls' optimism that reforms in the public facility will be robust enough to secure the equal value of political liberties is looking increasingly difficult to substantiate.

Addressing a Socialist Defence

Not all socialists agree with the argument I am making. DiQuattro (1983) defends Rawls from his left critics. He argues that justice as fairness is basically compatible with socialist ideas of social justice. By drawing out the egalitarian consequences of the difference principle, he attempts to show that justice as fairness is not compatible with class-divided societies conceived in Marxian terms. Rawls does mention the varying life prospects of those in different social classes, but these are viewed by reference to a share of primary social goods. Rawls calls his classes 'relevant social positions', each one representing different levels of well being. There is any number of classes, each one distinguished by occupation, wealth and income differentials (1971: 91–8). As we have seen, this scheme supposedly involves a widespread ownership of the means of production. The idea is that although land and capital are not equally held, they are broadly distributed. Divisions will not, Rawls hopes, be so great that a small class will be in a position to control productive resources (1971: 87, 280). DiQuattro, following Rawls, infers that in POD, differences in income, wealth and power are likely to remain, but capitalist class divisions will not. "There is no small class that, because it monopolizes ownership and control of the means of production, can extort a surplus from a working class owning nothing productive but its power to labour" (DiQuattro 1983: 52–7).

This argument is dependent upon two highly dubious claims: a) that the difference principle is, when employed in a market forces economy, able to guarantee the quasi-egalitarian distribution indispensable to the sustainability of the fair value of political liberties, and b) that the widespread ownership of the means of production can be maintained in a market forces economy. Without either, a 'fair opportunity to exert political influence' is unlikely to be assured. In regards to the former, left critics have inquired as to what degree of economic inequality the difference principle will actually permit, and, critically, it has been shown that there is no guarantee that they would be minimal:

> We have a community in which there are no significant social divisions. Income, wealth, and other advantages are equal to within a few percentages. There is only one way to modify the society to produce a different distribution. On the new distribution, five percent of the people would have ten times their previous incomes, and everyone else would have one percent more than his previous income (Crocker 1977: 265–6).

In this example the difference principle dictates that the latter distribution is just. Here justice as fairness would demand a highly non-egalitarian method of distribution. However, drafting a socialist defence of Rawls, Amdur (1980) argues that the difference principle is not the only fix on financial inequalities. He draws attention to the additional considerations Rawls recommends to reduce the inequalities that would otherwise be compatible with the difference principle. Along with the fair value of political liberties are a fair equality of opportunity and the social bases of self-respect. Rawls insists that those with similar talents must "have the same prospects of success regardless of their initial place in the social system, that is, irrespective of the income class into which they are born" (1971: 73). In order to ensure that social class does not affect the expectations of those with similar skills, Rawls proposes that resources be ploughed into the educational institutions in disadvantaged areas. In regard to the social bases of self-respect, which is considered to be a fundamental primary good (1993: 318), Rawls recognises that a "person's lesser position as measured by the index of objective primary goods may be as great as to wound his self-respect" (1971: 546). So beyond a certain point, inequalities sanctioned by the difference principle are likely to impose a loss of self-respect. The original contractees will, consequently, insist that inequalities must not be permitted once they are large enough to threaten the self-respect of the worst-off. Without self-respect, Rawls believes the other primary goods will be seriously de-valued. It is, he insists, irrational to sacrifice self-respect in the hope of securing an increase in other primary goods (Amdur 1980: 325–6).

The problem here though is that whether the emphasis is on political liberties, fair equality of opportunity or the social bases of self-respect, Rawls does not specify precisely the degree to which inequality becomes detrimental to these requirements, nor does he indicate how this question may be addressed. He merely states that they are threatened when inequalities of income and wealth 'exceed a certain limit' (1971: 278; 1993: 328). Amdur stresses that if self-respect depends partly on relative position, egalitarian consequences must follow. "If it could be shown that all inequalities of wealth and income have grave consequences for the self-respect of the least advantaged, then Rawls's theory would require complete economic equality" (1980: 326, 329). Yet if this is so, the contradictory problem resurfaces: the social bases for self-respect are wholly at odds with the compensatory facet of the difference principle. It is also in contradiction with Rawls' argument that inequalities serve an incentive purpose. Person 'A' can argue that inequalities in income and wealth must through legislative regulation be reduced, probably quite radically, to protect the three additional considerations. Or, alternatively, person 'B' may prefer to restrict planning and institutionalise inequalities so that incentives and compensation for socially necessary labour are provided for. But these tendencies clearly pull in opposite directions. It is unlikely a lasting balance can be struck. It seems more probable that one will subordinate the other. Ultimately, in a market forces economy, we cannot have it both ways.

Turning to the second questionable claim, the sustainability of the widespread ownership of productive assets, in Rawls' mixed economy, enterprises compete to supply consumers with goods. Due to the limited expenditure of buyers and the restricted scope of markets, not all sellers can be successful, at least not in equal measures. Those that do thrive, with their increased revenue to re-invest, are in a superior position to assert their influence on the next round of bargaining. It is not just making a profit that matters; it is the maximisation of profit. As explained in Chapter Three, capital has a self-expanding tendency, it is money used to invest in order to make more money. The insatiable obsession with growth ensures that expansion into new markets becomes irresistible. Likewise, dropping the selling price of finished articles in order to drive out competitors and capture the given market makes practical good sense in the unrelenting pursuit to accumulate ever-increasing profit margins. Admittedly, the process may be delayed with the various state interventions Rawls proposes, but the claim that markets tend to produce winners and losers is indisputable. Those who do not prosper often have little choice but to sell their cost-ineffective resources to the highest bidder, which is of course those with the means to re-direct them, the market winners. The most viable option for the former is usually to return to wage-labour. The certainty is that these dynamics continue until a small financial elite quickly establishes itself as a minority ruling class. This now looks suspiciously like a capitalist class-division. Whether Rawls calls his economic categories relevant social positions, rather than social classes, does not alter this.

This is essentially the view of Macpherson (1973). He suggests that POD is 'a liberal-democratic capitalist welfare state'. His argument is that Rawls' two principles of justice assess the "various distributions of rights and income *only within a class-divided society*" (Macpherson 1973: 89), and that the inevitability of class divisions undermines the ability of these principles to carry out their prescribed roles. The first principle demands equality of liberty and opportunity, yet the second principle is designed to indicate the cases where class inequalities in life-prospects are justified. Rawls maintains that in a market society, classes distinguished by income and wealth inequalities are congruous with equality in liberty and personal rights. Macpherson denies this. In POD, income inequality is necessary to ensure the incentives efficient production needs. Welfare-state transfer payments have to be restricted to the extent that one class remains better off than others. It is here that Macpherson questions Rawls' 'capitalist economic rationality'. Rawls "does not see that the class inequality in his market system is bound to be inequality of power as well as of income, that it allows one class to dominate another" (Macpherson 1973: 92). Rawls is aware of the problem posed to equality of liberty and opportunity by large concentrations of wealth, which inevitably leads to large concentrations of power, and has his governmental institutions to restrict them. But the limits imposed would still allow class differences in life-prospects. The problem is a theory of justice which fails to see that in competitive markets in which capital and labour are owned separately, any capital, concentrated or otherwise, is a controlling power which impedes upon the other. Macpherson refers to this as the 'extractive power' inherent in capitalism, in which those with capital demean the developmental powers of the non-owners. His argument is that Rawls' two principles of justice are internally inconsistent. The first principle needs continuous income transfers from the most well-off to the least well-off to prevent large accumulations of private capital. Yet regarding the second principle, as there is still the need to provide incentives, transfers and interferences must not be large enough to undermine economic efficiency. The former does not coincide with the latter:

> If a limit on transfers and interferences low enough to comply with the second principle could be high enough to prevent the concentration of capital from exceeding *its* limit, namely the point at which accumulations of private capital become 'concentrations of power detrimental of liberty and equality of opportunity' (which limit is required by the first principle), then his two principles would be consistent. But it is impossible to find a limit on transfers and interferences low enough to do the one thing and high enough to do the other (Macpherson 1973: 93).

In accordance with the second principle, some limits on transfers and interferences are required. But then if so, the accumulation of private capital inimical to equality of liberty and opportunity will not be averted. For any concentration, Macpherson concludes, is detrimental (Macpherson 1973: 88–93).

There is a convincing impetus to this critique, and it overlaps somewhat with the contradictory problem that confronts the state in POD. A word of clarity though: when Macpherson highlights the internal inconsistency of the two principles, it is when they are working, or not, in a private capital regime. When they are employed in a socially regulated system, with a communal control of the means of production, Rawls' principles of justice will be neither contradictory nor inconsistent. But as we have seen, although Rawls rejects capitalism, he does not abandon private property in productive resources, private investment or competitive markets. And in this society, it cannot follow that class conflict and class antagonisms somehow miraculously abate. The assumption that in class terms power, domination and exploitation will be sufficiently contained demands a giant leap of faith. It is far more likely that POD will divide rigidly along class lines. Despite the egalitarian assumptions of the difference principle, limitations on redistribution are by definition imposed. Greater returns are not permitted purely on the basis of the best-off benefiting the worst-off. Rewards are not only through this disproportionate contribution criterion. Those who contribute more to the common good deserve a larger share themselves. This is to compensate for the greater costs encountered in the fulfilment of their socially necessary labour. Incentives are deemed to be just because they align with the compensatory facet of the difference principle (1971: 101–2, 315). This highlights why it would not be fair to establish an equal incomes policy. Certain individuals should receive more because their contribution towards realising consumer demand involves sacrifice. Large economic inequalities are therefore fundamental to POD. Income from property ownership is conditional, but it remains hugely unequal. It is naïve to suppose that class antagonisms will simply vanish in these conditions. The role of the state is equally problematic. In Rawls' mixed economy it is the state which limits inequalities; the market is relied upon only where it corresponds to just principles. The state, via its policies of taxation and redistributive payments, along with its provision of public goods, takes preference over the market. Likewise, the maintenance of a widespread and relative egalitarian ownership of the means of production requires not just excessive but continuous state intervention. We have seen how unrealistic it is to expect the state to effect egalitarian measures on any permanent basis. To conclude, class relations as Marxists have traditionally envisaged them will, it seems, be a permanent feature of POD. And under these circumstances, Rawls' insistence that all citizens in POD will be assured an equal opportunity to influence political life has to be rejected.

Capitalism in Essence

There is though some substance to DiQuattro's and Amdur's defences of Rawls. It is true that Rawls seeks to modify capitalism quite considerably. Rawls regards the well-ordered society the theory of justice dictates as a social co-operative union. The difference principle demands that those in the most advantaged stratum enhance the common good by improving the conditions of the least advantaged. This mutual benefit principle seeks to reward social obligation. Unlike market principles of distribution, in which social fortune, pure luck, natural capacity, etc., are all determining variables, the distribution sanctioned by the difference principle is conditional. The prosperous must improve the well-being of those with less good fortune. Simultaneously, the greater rewards of the former represent compensation for the cost of carrying out their social obligation. As distribution is not determined simply by natural and social contingencies, the difference principle restricts the range of differentials. Rewards that cannot be shown to be related to performing a social function are simply not allowed. This will, to some extent, restrain the power of those who procure their wealth by simply owning the instruments of production. In this respect Rawls is right: POD is distinguishable from laissez-faire and welfare-state capitalist systems (1971: 72, 75, 101–2, 112; 2001: 138–40; DiQuattro 1983: 57–9, 66–9). There is much to admire in Rawls' laudable attempt to moderate capitalism, and it can be appreciated why socialists like DiQuattro and Amdur are attracted to it. There are considerable differences between ideal-typical capitalism and POD. Institutions in the former do not pass the Rawlsian qualification. Capitalists can maintain powerful positions irrespective of either the productive service they offer or the contribution made to improving the conditions of the least advantaged. Simply owning capital need not realise either requirement. The difference principle, in particular its reciprocity value, rules out capitalism as unjust. Capitalism permits huge inequalities and rewards natural and social fortune, whether or not a useful social function is discharged. It is for these reasons that Rawls, in *Theory*, refrains from using the term capitalism, and explicitly rejects it in *Restatement*.

The problem though is not the commendable endeavour to temper capitalism; it is that the institutions essential to it—private ownership of productive resources, competitive markets and wage-labour—are all retained in Rawls' economy. Although it is supposedly distributed widely, private property remains central; the market, along with the state, is still the mechanism for the distribution of goods and resources, and wage-labour is precisely what it has always been: a wage paid to non-owners of the means of production in exchange for their labour. Operating within these institutions, the owners of capital (capitalists, in other words) may finance the redistribution required to improve the material conditions of the least well-off without seriously threatening their privileged positions. Indeed, they can provide their useful social function without reducing inequalities in any drastic way. On this point, Nielsen (1978) suggests that whilst the position of the worse-off may be improved in absolute terms, this cannot compensate for the weakening of their predicament in relative terms. Exploitation persists because the inequalities considered necessary to provide incentives determine vastly deviating life prospects when the different strata people come from is taken into account (Nielson: 198). This is essentially correct. In POD distribution is arranged politically via the principles of justice. Even if an unmodified capitalism is deemed unjust in terms of the difference principle, the market is still indispensable as a distributive mechanism. It is hard to see how capitalist market incentives would not be dominant. Rawls insists that economic inequalities require justification and are hence conditional. But they, and the power relations that inevitably follow, are still an indispensable feature of the economy he sketches. Even after state intervention, there will still be marked variations in the life prospects of those in different classes.[5] The equality of opportunity needed if everyone is to be given the chance to fulfil their potentials is denied, as is any realistic chance for the majority of small-holders / producers to retain, on a permanent and secure base, their modest share of the means of production.

Summary

When Rawls declares that essential to a well-ordered society is a fair system of social co-operation, he does not mean simply socially co-ordinated activity, which could emanate from a central authority. Rather, he means when it is publicly recognised and accepted by all citizens. The fair terms of social co-operation stipulate the ideas of reciprocity and mutuality. There is a mutual and public recognition that the basic structure satisfies the two principles (1993: 16; 2001: 121–4). In a well-ordered society, the publicly endorsed principles of justice provide a mutually acknowledged standard from which claims on the basic structure can be assessed. All who contribute are to benefit by a publicly recognised standard. The principles of the fair terms of co-operation will be honoured by reasonable citizens, even when this requires subordinating their personal understandings of the good. This is couched in terms of the reasonable presupposing the rational (1993: 50–2; 2001: 5–7). But in light of the preceding analysis, it is doubtful that the rational will remain subject to the reasonable. Rawls supposes, indirectly, that POD has answers to Marx's critique that the liberal state is a shield behind which capitalist power thrives; that state intervention in market economies is certain to be reactionary as the state cannot jeopardize the long-term interests of capital. He might not put it in these exact terms, but his argument that capitalism, due to its inevitable concentrations of wealth, cannot sustain the fair value of political liberties is clear enough. Rawls argues that in contrast to capitalism, the constitutional rules in POD will guarantee an equal access to the public facility. The widespread ownership of productive assets will ensure legislatures an independence from the influence of concentrated private capital. As a corollary, an equal opportunity for all citizens to exert political influence is protected. A public and mutual acknowledgement that these are the fair terms of co-operation means all reasonable citizens are quite prepared to place to one side the pursuit of their own conceptions of the good, the rational, when a well-ordered society demands it.

The problem though is that the scope for state action is, informally but no less rigorously, restrained. On the one hand, the difference principle demands redistributive interventions, possibly quite considerable, yet due to capital's strategic advantage, they can only be relatively minimal as the state cannot imperil investor confidence. Yet on the other hand, to provide for the incentives that efficient production require, the difference principle dictates limits on transfers and interferences. But if so, the market can only be modified and regulated up to a certain point; it cannot realistically prevent the entrenchment of a small yet dominant financial class. Either way, the contradiction cannot be fully resolved. It is therefore doubtful that the widespread ownership of productive assets can be maintained. The difficulty is that the production of private goods and a market system of distribution are essential for the realisation of the compensatory and reciprocity aspects of the difference principle. But income derived from property-ownership assures that inequalities are not only unavoidable, but also substantial. The outcome is that one class will quickly come to hold more power than the others. We saw that in this predicament, the electorate cannot realistically be regarded as sovereign. This I referred to as the contradictory problem. Rawls is right that capitalism cannot be considered a just system. But as POD retains capitalism's key institutions, he does not move beyond what Macpherson calls a 'capitalist economic rationality'. In Rawls' competitive markets, as labour and capital are separately owned, the latter becomes a domineering power. When the two principles are employed in this economy, they do seem to be internally inconsistent for the reasons I have gone into. It is unclear how POD can solve this dilemma. The inequalities dynamic is not only at odds with the additional requirements of equality of opportunity and the social bases of self-respect, which call for a more thorough equal incomes policy, it also debilitates Rawls' insistence that an equal access to the political forum is assured in POD. Again, it is indistinct how the basic liberties of the first principle can be secured. The ideas of reciprocity and mutuality that specify the fair terms of social co-operation, publicly recognised and accepted by all citizens, are highly unlikely to emerge in these circumstances. POD, therefore, with its sovereign capitalist class, cannot be considered well ordered.

2. The Commune and Sovereignty in New Economic Democracy

The first thing to note is that NED is far more egalitarian than POD. In the latter, private wealth can be invested and used to create more wealth. Not so in the former; there will seldom be any idle rich because all incomes will be earned, and there will be far less disparity between both the guilds and the intra-guild co-operatives. In a wage-labour enterprise, the incomes of senior management are justified to a tiny group of individuals. In the guild co-operatives management incomes, like everyone else's, are justified to the workforce. This represents a vastly superior starting point by which the two principles can be satisfied. All incomes are salaried and subject to democratic adjudication. In POD income-generating property is the key source of huge accumulations of individual wealth. In NED not only are there no capitalists, there are no interest payments to private individuals. As a non-statist scheme of communal ownership, there are no objective economic classes distinguished through ownership / non-ownership of the means of production. As such, Marx's critique of the liberal state is extraneous. There is however a quite different contentious issue to consider: can NED sustain its political pluralism? The critique considered below is in relation to Cole's libertarian socialism. Although NED has qualified this scheme, it retains a (minimised) role for the commune system. Therefore, mounting a response to this objection does, in effect, constitute a defence of NED.

Really Pluralist

As Cole no longer sees a role for the modern state (1920b: 43), there is a supposedly stateless administration. Controversy reigns though as to whether his final model actually signifies this. It is claimed that the national commune is merely another political leviathan, and hence a reinvention of the modern sovereign state. Noting that Cole opposes the principle of state sovereignty, Elliott (1925) observes that he nevertheless retains a body politic that is granted the final power of adjustment. This body, Elliott insists, bears a striking similarity to what others call a state:

> The present parliament of England is not constituted in just the way that Mr. Cole would have his national 'commune' chosen; but it occupies exactly the place that the highest of the hierarchy of communes does in his theory of the 'new state' (Elliott 1925: 484).

So for Elliott the word 'commune' is but a pseudo-name for the kind of sovereign parliament lambasted by Cole (Elliott 1925: 483–4). This concern regarding Cole's political pluralism is fairly representative of the general feeling amongst his critics.[6] These objections are far from immaterial. Cole's commune is to be entrusted with considerable constitutional powers. It is also to have the last say when it comes to settling conflicts, which may to some degree deviate from his argument that the principle of state sovereignty is indefensible. However, there are seven key factors which, once recapitulated and where necessary reconsidered, demonstrate that the sovereignty of the commune cannot be equated with the kind of ideal typical sovereign state which controls all authority and is unlimited in its exercise. As the latter three are amongst the most salient features of NED, they are considered more extensively.

The Democratic and Pluralist Economy

The communes' role is essentially one of co-ordination. They will not, in contrast to the modern state, be afflicted with the unenviable task of preventing competing private interests from tearing the social fabric asunder. At the national level, although the national commune would adjudicate producer and consumer interests, it would have nothing like the authority sovereign states have to intervene in all areas of citizens' lives. Political life will alter drastically once the democratised economy NED pictures is installed. Consumer and producer interests are divided, producers are interested in the process of production—freedom at work, etc.—whilst consumers are concerned with quality, quantity and the prices of goods and services provided. There is a demarcation of interests: the producers are collectively sovereign over work conditions, and the consumers are sovereign over the goods produced. So while the guilds try to adjust supply to meet demand, the multitude of consumers' interests will legitimately determine the quality and quantity of production and matters connected to distribution. By establishing the means for dialogue between producers and consumers, democratic participation beyond the political sphere is enhanced. Cole, as we have seen, also insists that the greatest amount of civil interests should be represented (1920b: 38, 60, 88–97).

Cole is adamant that it is only by allowing our partial wills full expression, and not allowing them to be subordinated through an appeal to a general will, that democracy can be realised. For this to be possible, there must be suitable public spaces structurally secured so that producers, consumers and community representatives are guaranteed sufficient means for consultation. Here the community has genuine control over what is produced. The need for political institutions—the local, regional and national communes—is to co-ordinate producer, consumer and community interests. Once the essential features of Cole's democratic and pluralistic economy are established, the agenda of the political body will be radically transformed. The qualifications introduced into Cole's libertarian socialist economy do not in any sense affect the accuracy of this assertion. On the contrary, they enhance the democratisation of the economic sphere. It is true that there is now a limited role for a curtailed market in NED, but dialogue is still a key feature. The subordinated market, it will be recalled, may only allocate the goods required to satisfy consumer wants. The products essential for the fulfilment of basic needs, along with the distribution of new investment, will be determined by decentralised and inclusive structures of participation and democratic planning. There is still a necessity for appropriate public spaces. Furthermore, as competition is contained and regulated within each particular guild, the communes will not be called upon to mediate competing private interests. Private savers will be prevented from becoming private investors, so NED will not, unlike POD, be burdened by huge inequalities in wealth. The introduction of my revisions, which are designed to approximate an egalitarian economy, will not alter this.[7]

The Bottom-Up Approach to System Building

In Cole's thesis libertarian socialism is above all a theory of citizenship, of how active participation can determine common ends. He stresses that citizenship values must be achievable within groups. Whether it is by inter- or intra-group participation, individuals are to participate at different levels of political life. To begin with, in small groups; their representatives then form regional committees that are the political agencies at the next level of association. In these successive levels, the multiplicities of interests (or wills) are expressed under two general headings: functional and territorial (the old 'general' citizen no longer exists). The workplace and the town ward are the self-governing spheres that are of first importance to individuals. Upon this there are institutional structures that express a more general and larger level of interest. First there is the municipal, then the regional, and finally the national level; the co-ordinating function of politics is needed at these three major levels. Briefly, representatives from the functional and territorial constituencies form the communal, or government authority. Authority positions are not filled from above, but from below. Although there are still vertical lines of authority, the general idea is that the government system must be as decentralised as possible. Each level is to assume only the minimum amount of responsibility deemed unsuitable to the level below. Furthermore, the vertical lines are *ascending* and not *descending*; the higher levels are to be kept directly accountable to the lower levels from which they are elected (1920b: 117–38; Vernon 1980: xxii–xxx, xxxviii–xxxix). It is the middle tiers that communicate with the local and national levels, so it is those whose predominating function is developing responsibilities. NED is best understood as a theory of decentralisation (1920b: 60–1, 101, 136). Central government has fairly restricted powers, bound above all to the matter of co-ordination; and here it is constrained by the representation of regional, local and professional interests. The federal and decentralised government is limited in its control over localised units. In this respect, the constitution of the local, regional and national communes is at odds with the doctrine of state sovereignty.

The Reconstruction of the State

Cole is attached to the idea of community, and his lengthy quest to find its correct organisational expression is at the heart of his system-building. His community is placed firmly in the ethics of decentralisation and a radical participatory democracy, and it is in this setting that the state has to take its place. It is the variety of inter-related functional bodies that enables community expression, and as it stands, the modern state cannot relate to this. So for Cole a complex organisational structure is required to accommodate a diffused sovereignty. As Wright (1979) points out, it is not so much a question of abolishing the state, but of reforming it. For bodies of community controls are still needed, even in Cole's radical proposals. Along similar lines, MaCain (2001) specifies that although "the commune may be described as a state, its functions are the minimal ones of coordination and arbitration among the major functional groups in society, and thus it may be thought of as a natural and minimal state" (2001: B7). And for Vernon (1980), if there is a state, "the most reasonable conclusion is that the concept applies not to the national commune or to any institution alone but to the whole communal structure at its three principal levels taken together" (1980: xliv). To this Vernon adds that "the feature of the state that is missing is its character as a focus or site for *political* contestation" (1980: li). Whether or not NED is a thoroughly stateless society, one thing is clear: too much has changed to permit the simplistic response that the communal structure is synonymous with an ideal typical sovereign state (1920b: 119–21; Wright 1979: 48–9).

The Restriction of the Appeal Court

Although the communes are to have the final word on conflicts that are *brought before them*, their arbitration is limited to precisely that, those that are *brought before them*. The functional bodies are empowered with significant policy-making powers that the communes, set by statute, cannot intrude upon. All the time matters are settled between the functional bodies; they have no constitutional powers of arbitrary intervention. Far from commanding the authority to intervene at will, they may only operate within their own demarcated limits. The commune's control over the functional organisations within their jurisdictions is formally restricted. If these statutory limitations do not quite spell the end of sovereignty, they come about as close as is practically possible (1920b: 128).[8]

Bureaucracy and Functional Democracy

In NED there is not a small class of private individuals who, if they wish, can withdraw their investment. But will there be another powerful class, a government bureaucracy perhaps? Schweickart declares that a stable civil service wielding power equal to elected representatives is a possibility in any society. He acknowledges that his scheme has no immunity here, and because the economic antagonisms in POD call for state intervention, it too requires a large civil service. So which is worse—a privileged business class or a privileged civil service? For Schweickart, "the real choice is between a government bureaucracy without a privileged capitalist class and a government bureaucracy with a privileged capitalist class. No contemporary economy can do without a government bureaucracy of some sort" (1993: 215). Although he does not deny that his model of economic democracy has a state bureaucracy, he is keen to add that as it cannot instil an investment strike, it is differentiated from the capitalist class. The claim is that the bureaucracy loses much of its privilege.

Fair enough. But I do not think the issue should be restricted to state bureaucracy. Although it is true that no contemporary economy can function without a 'bureaucracy of some sort', there is no reason why it has to be a state bureaucracy. I am indebted to Schweickart for his superb scheme of democratic investment planning. In the process of incorporating it into NED, however, it has been functionally demarcated. It is worth labouring this point, as it distinguishes my scheme from his. Every guild, and the IGC, has its own mini civil service and, inevitably, its own bureaucracy. Bureaucracy has been stripped from the state and reinstalled in a politically organised civil society. As investment decisions have been 'guildised', state (commune) bureaucracy is restricted to the minimum. NED has no sovereign state, but it does have an IGC—in consultation with the two consumer councils—to determine new investment. So what are the advantages of disconnecting, then dividing, the state's bureaucracy, and re-establishing it in other bodies? Although it cannot be assumed that some of the problems commonly associated with the bureaucracy of the sovereign state will simply vanish, important distinctions can be made. It is likely that individuals are less threatened by smaller intermediate bureaucracies than by a formidable state apparatus. Their powers, their scope of action and the range of issues falling within their jurisdiction are all restricted. The main difference though is probably in regards to democracy. This will become clear by taking a closer look at Cole's constitutional proposals.

He insists that it is only through a model of co-ordinated functional representation that real democracy can be achieved. Cole is not attacking the representation concept itself, rather he criticises the principle that in one act an individual can be represented in their entirety. He seeks a more adequate expression of community will than is at present offered by geographical representation. He wishes to replace the current misuse of the representative principle with an elaborate representational model that ensures that people are represented in terms of their multiple functional loyalties. A condition of the functional principle is that industrial democracy is held responsible to the community. Industrial rights are not unconditional; the community grants them if a service is well rendered, and terminates them when it is not. These rights are therefore correlative to function. In this sense the functional principle is a provision for ensuring the guilds do not operate merely for their own benefit, but are responsive to community interests. Rather than grant property owners absolute rights over their holdings, Cole would permit them only in regard to the rendering of a useful service. Following Cole, NED grants no individual or group an unconditional license to administer their activities solely as they please. Reservations can be introduced through the consumer councils to ensure the preservation of the public interest. The general intention is that it will not be possible for any guild to profit whilst disregarding the common good. For commentators such as Carpenter (1922), this is a particular strength of guild socialism. Through the functional principle, although private rights in industry are not abolished, they are nevertheless exercised in accordance with the sanction of the community. It is this 'correlative functional principle of responsibility to the community' that ensures the guilds will not have such wide-ranging and self-contained interests that they can defy community sanctions. As such, they are prevented from developing into mini-sovereign 'statelets'. Sovereignty—and this is the pivotal point—is to remain in the space existing between the interconnecting webs of self-governing associations that together constitute the community. Cole is adamant that democracy must not be limited to parliamentary politics, but it must not end in industry either, as in his hands it is a theory of social organisation (1972: 7–15; 1920b: 12; Carpenter 1922: 301–5; Wright 1979: 58–9).

Cole does though accept that when it is impossible for all members of an association to deliberate together, problems of governance are likely to emerge.

Such associations are compelled to assign a degree of power to certain members, and to establish a 'representative legislative assembly'. In these more complex associations, the executive committee generally remains separate from the legislature, and is confined to implementing its decisions. The difficulty is that whenever people act together, they inevitably develop a sense of community. The flip side is that representative committees, as well as rank-and-file members of associations, will generate this community essence. The presence of a degree of committee loyalty will affect how committee members perform, however well intended, their duty to the other members. The members' will is liable to be twisted as it passes through the intermediary of the representatives. Cole calls the tendency for representatives to substitute their wills for those they are supposed to be representing 'perversion', a degree of which he admits is inevitable. Although these dangers are less applicable with functional representation, they do not vanish completely. Nevertheless, whilst the representative group cannot claim to represent its members as 'centres of consciousness', it can still approximately represent that part of themselves that they 'put into associated effort'. Functional representation accepts some distortion as inevitable, but not to the extent that organisational democracy is jeopardised. Although citizens cannot be represented in general terms as individuals (for individuals, fundamentally speaking, cannot be *re*-presented), a representative can nevertheless represent a common viewpoint that a group of individuals hold in relation to a particular and specific social purpose. This democratic principle applies not only to individuals as citizens, but to any domain in which they co-operate to perform a social function or share a common social interest. So, "real democracy is to be found, not in a single omnicompetent representative assembly, but in a system of co-ordinated functional representative bodies" (1920a: 104–8, 118–23, 185–7; 1920b: 33–4).

For Cole, the main problem of exercising democratic control over representatives in the modern state is that it is not possible to counsel or criticise them in any meaningful way. The difficulty is that electors are not collectively active throughout their representatives' tenure of office. But as functional associations have a permanent being, functional democracy overcomes this obstacle. The idea is that in functional democracy, elected officials will not be delegates but representatives, acting mainly upon criticism and advice from an instructive and active constituency, rather than through definite instructions. Cole remains optimistic about the likely successes of this system, not least because the electors have some knowledge about the job the representative has been chosen to do:

> A functional association . . . is concerned with doing a definite job, and its officers are also concerned with getting that definite job done. The member is connected with the association because its business is his business, and he is therefore able far more intelligently to initiate and criticise action in relation to it (1920a: 114).

Provided methods are secured whereby the represented can constantly instruct, counsel, criticise and advise their representatives, the tendency to misrepresent wills can be averted. To be effective, communications must be persistent and sustainable. As such, they are clearly more amenable and responsive to full-time organisations like those of the workplace. I have argued elsewhere, drawing from empirical inquiries into producer co-operatives, that, with certain structural innovations, the guilds will be robust enough to resist oligarchic tendencies.[9] It is noteworthy that even Weber, the chief proponent of bureaucratic inevitability, did not deny that the groups most likely to resist bureaucratic control are those "who are still in possession of their own means of subsistence" (Weber 1990: 13). Weber mentions the peasantry; I would add to this NED's guilds.

Rawls expresses a concern that a socially regulated system, under the guidance of 'agreements reached by industrial associations', such as NED, is sure to develop a bureaucracy to control economic activity (1971: 281; 1993: 328). But if some kind of bureaucracy is inevitable in all contemporary economies, and POD is no exception, then the immediate goal is to devise a scheme in which any drawbacks are abbreviated to the greatest possible extent. The demarcated bureaucracies in NED's pluralist economy will at least be more democratic than the bureaucracy in an extensive state, irrespective of the absence or presence of a capitalist class. Through the devolution of functions, the power of centralised bureaucracy is restricted, and the dissemination of authority from the state to a democratised civil realm represents a significant step towards the realisation of NED's pluralist state.

Legislation

My discussion would be incomplete without addressing the cardinal issue of NED's legal proposals. Cole attacks the principle of a constitutionally unchallengeable state power embodying unlimited legislative sovereignty in a hierarchy of authority. He seeks to replace the centralised sovereign state with a social order in which power and administration is disseminated to the functionally autonomous and self-governing associations. He proposes that at the head of the national commune there will be a 'Constituent Assembly and the constitutional legislature of Guild democracy'. This will be the most powerful and comprehensive legislating body within guild socialist society. The guilds though are also to have their own legislative and administrative functions (1920b: 149–51; Hirst 1989: 2–6). This section demonstrates the plausibility of Cole's pluralist legality.

The most detailed critique of Cole's legalism is still K.C. Hsiao's *Political Pluralism* (1927). Hsiao notes, correctly, that Cole attempts to divide legislative power between several independent bodies so that the constitutional apparatus may be used to balance powers between diverse functions or organised interests, and prevent any from becoming supreme. In response, he argues that without a 'definitely established constitutional authority', i.e. a sovereign parliament, conflicts between disputing bodies may end in deadlock. Society would then be forced to settle federal conflicts on a non-constitutional basis. Prolonged attempts at compromise mean losses to all, and innumerable political conventions are expensive expedients. Without there being a written constitution, some disputes would be impossible to settle, and so a federalism with no constitutional sovereignty is inconceivable. Hsiao's scepticism is in regard to what he sees as the pluralists 'anti-legalism'. The division of the constitution into independent organs will, he insists, present insuperable problems. He notes that Cole acknowledged, even if only by implication, the difficulty of demarcating the numerous functional legislative spheres and attempted to overcome this with his supreme court (which came to be called the 'Constitutional Committee of the National Commune'), a court that is to settle cases of impasse. Hsiao claims that every time Cole's supreme court has to step in to settle unresolved disputes between the diverse bodies, the pluralistic state moves closer to monism. As such, the denial of legal sovereignty contains a contradiction: it is not logically possible to have two or more sets of laws. For law to be fundamental in controlling and restricting citizens' behaviour, it not only must be consistent, but must also derive from a single source in a legislature that overrides all others (Hsiao 1927: 42–4).

The disagreement between Cole and Hsiao comes down to this. In Cole's scheme, although there is only one judiciary, there will be various sets of laws. Legal sovereignty will not be concentrated solely in one body. In contrast, Hsiao contents that as it is logically impossible to have two or more sets of laws, they can only be passed by a supreme legislature that commands legal sovereignty.

In reply to Hsiao's polemic, Hirst states that it "is specious, since pluralism never argued against a legal order. To suppose it did is to identify all legal regulation with the full consequences of the doctrine of sovereignty" (1989: 29). To be sure, Cole does not take issue with the claim that regulation is essential. On the contrary, he insists that social affairs are clearly in need of organisation and co-ordination, hence his elaborate system building. Hirst acknowledges that there may be problems with Cole's arrangements of a congress that represents the various functional bodies and his supreme court. For example, the ad hoc adjudications of this court would in all probability frustrate co-ordination, producing anomalies that would result in more ad hoc decision making, and so on. However, to identify this problem in Cole's reasoning is "to accept the need for formally codified law and settled judicial procedures, not to wallow in the excesses of the doctrine of sovereignty" (Hirst 1989: 28–9). These judicial procedures are an integral part of Cole's theory. The general picture is one of a coordinated pluralist order in which the autonomous legislating functional bodies are aware of the legal boundaries of their jurisdictions. Clearly a balance is needed. A guild should patently not have the constitutional power to imprison an individual for minor offences. Or as Cole states, "[o]bviously a Guild cannot put a man to death" (1919: 1). When a case is tried in court that falls within the province of a guild, it is tried by the legislation initiated by that guild (or, if the situation dictates, the guild congress). When it is a more serious offence, the legal status of which falls beyond the extremities of the guild legislatures, then it is tried in accordance with the national constitutional legislature. On the proviso that the legal boundaries of the guild's dominion are unambiguously set by statute, the problem of interpretation for the judiciary will be no worse than in any legal system. In regard to their translation, it hardly matters which legislative body the laws are passed by. In contrast to Hsiao's logic, there is no reason to assume that the dichotomy of legislative power 'is always liable to lead to conflicts of jurisdiction'. Appeals to a 'definitely established constitutional authority superior to the disputing bodies' are not the only prerequisite for a codified legal order.

Hirst confirms that the pluralist state would be a minimal one, whose principle aim is to create and sustain the conditions for independent associations to exist and develop by means of their own internal deliberations. This state would be constituted so that no single agency could command a 'plenitude of power'. Associations would be consulted in the legislation process. The pluralist state may have primacy in rule making, but it can only operate within its own demarcated constitutional limits. As it would use its legal primacy to establish its fundamental goal, a pluralist socio-political order, it will have little in common with the classic theory of sovereignty. But this does not imply that the pluralist state is incompatible with a legal order. The key theme to Hirst's response to Hsiao is that the political theory of pluralism has no inherent objection to the necessity of a systematic legal system. As such, Hsiao's charge that pluralist political theory contains an anti-legalism is erroneous (Hirst 1989: 29–30; 1990: 17, 76). However, it is true that the national constitutional legislature is by far the largest and most powerful legislating body. It is a public order power implementing a legal system which regulates the interaction of functional bodies. It is also to have the final say on the interpretation of the laws it has passed. It will be separated from, and superior to, the other legislating associations. As this is imperative to the preservation of a legal order, there is perhaps some substance to Hsiao's claim that Cole's supreme court may not invariably 'fit into the pluralistic system' as readily as Cole proclaims. But it is equally clear that the substance and volume of sovereignty has been re-delineated. On the stipulation that the particular legislating bodies do not circumvent or overstep their legal precincts, NED's national legislating assembly will not hold the legal power to overrule the laws they pass. This is the crucial distinction between NED's and the sovereign states' legislatures: the latter is omnipotent, the former is not. Although a legal order has to command primacy in its own domain, the state need not contain an unchangeable 'plenitude of power and legislative omnicompetence'. A pluralist state will sustain a legal order, but it "will claim legislative sovereignty *within its own constitutional limits and objectives*, that is where the difference lies, for it is these limits and objectives which redefine the content of sovereignty" (Hirst 1990: 77).

To reiterate, NED has no inherent objection to a codified system of legal regulation. Its legal order will embody and sustain the conditions for a plurality of independent legislating associations to exist simultaneously. The implication is that the absence of a concentration of legal sovereignty in one body is not synonymous with the rejection of a legal order. NED's legal system will not, in terms of its jurisprudence, concede extensive admissions towards the sovereign state.

Consumer Councils

So far I have been discussing how NED's re-politicised civil society will operate in the absence of a sovereign state. Although mention has been made of the consultation role of the two consumer councils in relation to the guilds, the emphasis has been more on the latter. As the former are constitution bodies legally empowered to block certain products or reject given methods of production—that is, they are central to NED's anti-sovereignty—a more comprehensive account of their role is obligatory. As well as the functions Cole ascribes to them, there are three other key ways in which the two consumer councils will fulfil their task. Firstly, they will expose and eradicate market externalities, secondly, they will gauge public opinion on the business of investment and thirdly, they will provide an extra-market mechanism through which all members of society, not just the well-off, can express their opinions on the course of future production.

The first is a crucial task. Externalities, as Schweickart points out, 'render certain market transactions non-optimal'. Market transactions often affect more people than those initially exchanging. When this happens, the market fails to indicate a true description of costs and benefits. An often cited example is pollution. If various technologies generate a similar productive output, but the technology that causes less harm to the natural environment is more expensive, there is no incentive for producers to adopt it. By itself the market neither promotes low-impact polluting technologies nor restricts those which cause higher levels of pollution. It is the same with consumption. If enough people use 'bio-accumulative' household products, eventually the aftermath will be felt by everyone. In contrast to one of liberalism's most central claims, consumption is not always a purely private matter (Schweickart 1993: 136–7). NED has the institutional arrangements suitable for addressing this problem. The consumer councils will seek to discover and publicise information on the causes and consequences of externalities. In this respect they are a precondition for the exposure and eradication of the negative effects of market transactions. As the consumer councils have the same objective as the guild democratic investment fund legislatures, these two bodies will work closely together. The role of the former is to bring externalities to light and inform the latter, who will then take them into account when awarding grants. That is, after externalities have been exposed, the producer co-operatives who have taken steps to minimise them will be appraised favourably by those responsible for conferring finance for new investment.

In the second place, whilst the market may be thought of as a quasi-democratic process which serves as a medium to record consumer preferences, it cannot account for conjectures on rates of investment in the absence of purchases. For items bought, the market registers societal tastes. But where money is saved, judgements are not being expressed as to how much investment society should make, and in what direction it should be channelled. The consumer councils are in an ideal position to undertake market research and gauge public opinion. Again they will work closely with the investment fund bodies. It is the responsibility of the national guild investment fund legislatures to take the major contentious issues—the development or curtailment of nuclear energy, for example—into account when determining future investment. But on the smaller community level, the consumer councils will work alongside the local guild investment to fund legislatures. They can even serve to provide a system of checks and balances. Here their role will be to gather and circulate the information that may serve to constrain the dangers of secrecy. The desire to make decision making as transparent a process as possible informed Cole's attempts to institutionalise dialogue. It also informs mine.

In the third place, the consumer councils will provide a structural mechanism in which all members of society, irrespective of the prerogatives of personal wealth, can participate in determining the direction of future production. This function compensates for one of the main weaknesses of markets. In order for consumers to express their preferences through the market mechanism, they obviously need money. The more money, the more preferences can be expressed; the less money, the fewer preferences can be expressed. The result is that production in a market forces economy is geared towards serving the expensive tastes of the wealthy. The defender of POD could respond that this objection stems from the assumption that money is unfairly distributed. If income distribution is fair, and Rawls does of course conclude that in POD it is precisely that, does this not solve the problem?[10] I would say only partly. The dynamic between economic inequalities and the determination of future production is still considerable. Despite the prescriptions of the difference principle, the market forces economy in POD still permits—in fact it demands—significant concentrations of wealth, and therefore power. The result is that those with greater means to consume largely dictate the course of future production. Rawls' proposed system of taxation and subsidies can presumably offer some kind of protection from the market winners exerting an excessive influence in this regard. But if justice is to be equated with fairness, then fairness must extend to the extra-market mechanisms in which plans for future production are subject to genuine democratic regulation. And this is better done from below, by the functional institutions of NED, rather than from above, by the state in POD. The analysis of Rawls' formidable state in part one of this chapter testifies to this. A society in which the poorest are structurally restricted in their capacity to determine future production, regardless of the fairness of the initial income distribution, cannot be considered fair.

Summary

These seven factors indicate that Cole's scheme, and by implication NED, is not a 'perfect example of a monistic state'. He is therefore entitled to claim that the political institution he visualises to unite the guilds and councils, the commune, cannot be equated with the doctrine of state sovereignty. As one critic acknowledges:

> Mr. Cole . . . gives to his co-ordinating body, the commune, a distinctly federal character as representing not immediately the members of his community, but rather the various functional organisations in which they are grouped, and thus *gives it in spite of the coercive power which he ascribes to it, a certain pluralistic cast,* without, however, destroying its ultimate unity (Ellis 1923: 595).[11]

Indeed, the communal structure (state) and the producer / civic guilds and consumer / civic councils (civil society) not only interpenetrate, but are, to a large extent, analogous. As the communes' powers are formally restricted, they cannot dominate the self-governing associations of civil society, who themselves have an active role in determining social life. The NED commune is internally divided, not between state and civil society in ways that preserve inequality and hierarchy, but between the productive, consumptive and civic interests. So the claims that the commune represents a sovereign state, a new leviathan, a political monism, the present parliament of England, etc., are perhaps not as well founded as they may initially appear. And to the degree that such statements could be defended, exorbitant definitions of monism and pluralism would need to be accepted. To be sure, NED's communal structure and the sovereign state of modernity are incompatible bedfellows. Likewise, the economic system in NED does not harbour the kind of sovereignty Marx identified with liberal democracies. NED is a scheme of non-statist public ownership. Its economic policy is on behalf of and determined by the community as a whole, rather than the state, an economically powerful class or particular industries or services. The idea is that neither the communes nor organised labour are in a position to exploit the community in the way the capitalist class will be able to exploit, with the state's tacit approval, both the community and the workforce in POD. My contention is that between the political arrangements of NED and POD, it is the former that holds, in terms of constituting the more appropriate starting point from which to begin to implement Rawlsian principles of justice, the ascendancy.

3. The Realisation of the Two Principles of Justice

Let us begin by concisely re-summarising the four-stage schema. Both principles of justice are assigned to the basic structure, but the first principle applies directly to the constitutional essentials. The second principle is employed only after the first principle has been secured. The first role of the basic structure, which involves the exercise of political power, secures the equal basic liberties and forms a just constitutional regime. The second role accords with the second principle, and concerns the background institutions which provide social and economic justice (1993: 229). The veil of ignorance is gradually lifted as the four-stage sequence unfolds. Rawls specifies the availability of knowledge by distinguishing three broad groups of facts: a) the key components of social, political and economic theories, b) the general social, political and economic facts about society and c) particular pieces of information about individuals, their natural talents, position and status, interests and beliefs, etc. In the original position, along with the instruction that the circumstances of justice apply, only the first group of facts are made available. The course of history, and what types of societies currently exist, are unknown. In the next two stages, public facts about their society, although not personal particularities, are accessible to the contractors. The supply of information is, at every stage, increased so that the two principles can be applied. "The notion of the rational and impartial application of principles defines the kind of knowledge that is admissible" (1971: 200). At the final stage, the veil of ignorance is lifted completely. The four-stage device then guides the framing of a just constitution. It extends the notion of the original position, setting out a specific series; each stage inheriting the constraints endorsed at the previous sequences, and as the implementation of principles requires. To re-confirm, the distinction between the two principles is drawn because a) they are applied at different stages and accord with the two co-ordinate roles of the basic structure b), establishing the constitutional essentials is more urgent c), it is easier to see if they are realised and d) it is less difficult to reach agreement about what they should be. (1971: 200; 1993: 230; 2001: 49).

The Constitutional Convention

At the second stage of the four-stage succession, where delegates sketch the contours of a system detailing government power and the rights of citizenship, they will choose the political constitution of NED. They now have a general knowledge of social theory, and they are aware of the economic infrastructure and the political climate of their society. The just procedure must ensure that the constitution embodies the equal liberties of the first principle. NED's basic structure is constituted by the commune system, the guilds, and the consumer and civil councils. In POD the fair value of equal political liberties cannot be assured because economic inequalities will be large enough to allow a small powerful class to exert undue influence on the legislature. As they can effectively control the political process, the constitutional convention would have failed. Rawls is right to insist that inequalities must be regulated so they do not concentrate to the degree that an equal opportunity to influence political life is undermined. He is also right that the best way to do this is with a widespread dispersion of the means of production. It is though a mistake to assume POD can accomplish either. By way of contrast, the present concern is to show how the basic structure of NED upholds the fair value of equal political liberties by restricting inequalities in the way Rawls demands. The value of substituting wage-labour and private ownership of productive assets with co-operative labour and communal ownership will, following Rawls' logic, be explained in the next section, the legislating stage.

The Commune System

Cole had no doubts that the functional organisation of society harbours an 'indispensable safeguard of personal liberty' (1920b: 158). In his discussion on liberty, he suggests that theories of sovereignty invite tyranny because they contain the argument that not just *all* individuals, but the *whole* of individuals, can be included in a single organisation. Alternatively, in a functionally organised society, individuals belong to a variety of associations, each of which may only claim that part of the individual which relates to its social function. In diametrical opposition to the doctrine of state sovereignty, the functional theory asserts that associations may only partially 'express and extend' individuals' wills. Associations can never 'exhaust' individuals. Cole is keen to press this point: a functionally organised society is far less likely to submit to tyrannical rule than one characterised by state sovereignty because functional associations are more truly representative and thereby more able to preserve liberty (1920a: 179, 191). One need only take the most cursory glance at the entrenched oligarchic tendencies of democracy in Western Europe and North America, and the despotism of the former dictatorships in the USSR and Eastern Europe, to see that Cole, in terms of sovereignty and the state, is absolutely correct. In the absence of a sovereign state, the collective ownership of firms and the public investment fund in NED allows a tighter degree of collective control. Crucially, the gap between owners and workers will be largely abolished, without recourse to Rawls' formidable state. As there are no significant class divides, the national commune can express the common interest. A distinction of sorts will remain between state and civil society, but the process towards unification is given great impetus.

Rawls' government is far more extensive than the national commune in NED. Liberalism has traditionally been concerned to defend the minimal state. Although all liberals agree the state must protect individual freedom, they disagree about what this entails. Rawls is not a libertarian liberal. The libertarian doctrine, he stresses, does not amalgamate liberty and equality, and lacks a sufficient criterion of reciprocity. Rather, it endorses 'a network of private agreements'. Insofar, it treats the state as a private association, and thus cannot be regarded as a *social* contract theory. Therefore, "quite naturally it has no place for a special theory of justice for the basic structure" (1993: 265). The Rawlsian state, by way of contrast, does more than protect autonomy, provide public goods and safeguard property rights. It involves securing compliance with the just principles of the basic structure which give rise to a fair system of co-operation (1993: 262–5). Indeed, POD incorporates more than a 'nightwatchman state'; the redistributive requirements of the difference principle demand significant state involvement in the private sphere. If the commune system in NED is a state, it is a minimal one. It does not have the constitutional powers the Rawlsian state has. It may intervene in cases of impasse or on other financial matters like the funding of the consumer and civic councils. But as it is formally prevented from intervention for redistributive purposes—this being a matter for the guilds and the IGC—it poses less threat to liberty. Hirst contents that although associational socialist society is not a stateless social order, it is not compatible with a centralised, bureaucratic and omnicompetent state. A state like this concentrates decision making and administration, and is at odds with the principle upon which associationalism is founded. A hierarchically organised state, directed from a single centre, cannot be democratically managed. Rather, a "society of democratic associations requires a state which not only shares the attributes of civil society, that is, pluralism and democratic self-management, but to a degree merges with it" (Hirst 1990: 76). It is my contention that this body politic is the one that would be chosen in the constitutional convention.

The Guilds and the Consumer / Civic Councils

In contrast to market socialism, despite sharing the concern for workers' control, co-operation in NED will not be replaced solely by competition. As the price mechanism does have informational and motivational benefits, my scheme will retain a controlled functionally demarcated market economy, but this will not be its primary organising principle. NED prioritises democratic planning over market considerations. The provision of a non-market mechanism is required to compensate for the areas where markets perform badly, namely the disregard of the needs of the poor. Price setting of 'need' goods through deliberations between organised interests is one of the key features of NED's democratised economic sphere. The institutionalisation of an inclusive system which grants all citizens, including the poorest, the right and opportunity to have their say about what is produced is, in the manner in which it proposes to increase participation and dialogue, a key process towards the re-politicising of civil society. Rather than the guilds preparing budgets for all their economic dealings, this only needs to be done in relation to the production of certain goods. In regards to citizens' basic needs, the guilds and consumer councils will determine the just price, taking into account considerations about the use of cross-subsidies, in much the same way Cole proposes. Without these measures to help invoke the communitarian spirit, worker's co-operatives, driven by the market dynamic of competition, are likely to become as egoistic, self-centred and selfish as capitalist enterprises—and moreover, so are the firms Rawls is ready to allow. The problem with the latter, though, is that vast inequalities in income and wealth, and consequently power, would continue to inhibit the fair value of the equal political liberties. But as a limited degree of competition is needed to inspire motivation, generate innovation and prevent technological stagnation, NED has been theorised so that it represents a genuine alternative to the extremes of co-operation and competition.

Instead of incorporating marked public and private domains, NED is characterised by a pluralized public sphere and a re-democratised civil sphere which respects private interests. Unlike POD, as my subordinated market will only allocate certain goods and resources, leaving new investment to be determined by the decentralised planning process, it will not determine the scope and direction of future development. When this is coupled with the restriction of competition so that it falls within the relevant guild's jurisdiction, where it can be closely monitored, the capacity of what is left of the market forces economy to harbour the kind of inequalities capable of undermining the legal and political equalities of the first principle is curtailed. Capitalism is troubled by a lack of opportunity for economic self-governance. POD does not rule it out, but it does not prioritize it either. In contrast, NED makes it a prerogative. Rather than command over production being divided by an unequal distribution of economic power, which inevitably leads to control coming to rest with a small class of private individuals, NED qualifies property rights so that control is redistributed along egalitarian lines. Not only does it help organise the community politically, it prevents workplaces from reinvesting profits back into their firms in the hope of maximising profit margins. For theorists like Marx and Cole, the state cannot realise democracy if private interest and unaccountable power dominate civil society; and as is now clear, Rawls' own critique is also along these lines (1993: 360). Functionally demarcated democratic investment planning not only attempts to make financial power accountable by subjecting it to public adjudication, it also seeks to reduce the possibility that private interest can determine the flow of capital, and, therefore, the overall direction of the economy. Preventing wealth concentrating in the hands of a few powerful individuals, and thereby equalising the distribution of economic power, is, as Rawls rightly insists, indispensable to the consummation of the first principle.

To reiterate, as competition is contained within each guild, sectional self-interest will not undermine the communitarian spirit; as goods produced through market considerations are subordinated to those provided to satisfy needs, the market loses its privileged place, and as profits cannot be extracted by reinvestment into new projects, private savers are prevented from becoming private investors. As such, there is not the dichotomy between owners and non-owners of wealth that results from property ownership. In relation to the equal political liberties of the first principle, citizens will not have so much that they can dominate others, or so little that they can be dominated. In NED's politico-economic system, property rights are largely egalitarian. Individuals cannot be eclipsed in the way non-owners of private property are in capitalist societies,—and, it would seem, in POD. It is these limits on economic inequalities that help preserve, or at least restrict encroachment upon, the fair value of the equal political liberties. They consequently help sanction the equality of participation in politics Rawls justly demands.

The Third Stage

At the legislative stage, which equates to the second principle, proposed bills are judged by legislators who still have no knowledge of particularities. In this stage attention is no longer directly focused on the pre-established basic liberties of the first principle, only insofar as care needs to be taken not to violate them. Economic and social policies must sanction a fair equality of opportunity and maximise the conditions of the worst-off, within the constraints of the constitutional convention. Rawls notes that it is more difficult to assess whether the second principle is being applied appropriately. The economic and social information made available is far more complex and gives a larger cause for reasoned disagreement than at the second stage. This difficulty will not disappear in NED, but due to the more restricted scope of the functionally demarcated legislating bodies, the material considered will be less extensive than that confronting the Rawlsian state. The problem will not be solved, but it will be minimised. This will help in the choice of both labour relations and rights to productive property. It is at this stage that Rawls believes it suitable to determine between private or social ownership of the means of production. This section will show that co-operative labour and communal ownership, rather than wage labour and private ownership, is the most appropriate institutional arrangement to satisfy both parts of the second principle. NED's functionally demarcated markets are distinct from Rawls' undifferentiated markets. The background institutions are not a sovereign state and a market forces economy as they are in POD; they are a pluralized state and a politically organised civil society. The communes and the guild—with the consumer and civil councils holding, as usual, the right to consult and the power of veto—are the legislating bodies responsible for ensuring that both parts of the second principle are fulfilled. The taxation and cross-subsidiaries needed to satisfy equality of opportunity and the difference principle will be co-ordinated within each guild, and also between them. The IGC will, therefore, be the co-ordinating body; the commune, as a final court of appeal, will act only in cases of impasse. It is within this basic structure that economic democracy will be installed.

Fair Equality of Opportunity

The first principle, equality of rights and liberties, relates directly to equality of citizenship. The second principle proposes an equality of opportunity. The difference between the two is that political equality is hardly controversial, but what equality of opportunity involves, and how to sustain it, certainly is. Rawls insists that fair equality of opportunity demands that those with equal talents and an equal determination to apply them must enjoy the same chances of success, irrespective of their class background. This requires an equality of education and checks on economic inequalities. A fair equality of opportunity is undermined when considerable wealth and property accumulates within a small group of individuals. Even with political equality established, inequalities of wealth and power have enormous effects upon the chances for competitors to succeed. Competitive advantages are clearly attached to other variables than citizenship. A genuine equality of opportunity can only exist if, as with legal and political equalities, background impedances to fair competition are also removed. Rather than asserting that goods be distributed in a way that guarantees all group members obtain a proportional share, Rawls would introduce institutional mechanisms to ensure that group membership is not advantageous to individuals' prospects for success. So for Rawls, the realisation of equal opportunity requires measures aimed at neutralising the effects of organisational influence. This view of equal opportunity assumes it is possible to identify the group membership which can assist or harbour competitions for power and primary goods. However, as Levine points out, although Rawls does insist that inequalities in income and wealth must be prevented from affecting individuals' opportunities, he does not elaborate upon the issue to any great extent (2001: 10, 53; Levine 2002: 187–9).

By way of contrast, in my analysis of the political structures in NED, it has been shown that these tasks fall to the guilds. The obstructions to fair competition are more likely to surface in the full-time professional organisations that are run along democratic lines. Each guild will be responsible for managing competition within its domain. The bodies at either the local or regional levels are in an ideal position to identify how group memberships effect competition between the intra-guild co-operatives. A policy of open books, widespread circulation of information, equal access to new technologies, etc. will inspire a visibility in regulation. For Rawls, to ensure a fair equality of opportunity:

> A free market system must be set within a framework of political and legal institutions that adjust the long-run trend of economic forces so as to prevent excessive concentrations of property and wealth, especially those likely to lead to political domination (2001: 44).

As part of the process of background procedural justice, the basic structure is the social framework that will 'adjust the long-run trend of economic forces'. Due to their restricted scope of applicability and aided by their public decision making, functionally demarcated institutions are likely to find this a less daunting task. Likewise, the decentralised and democratic planning of new investment in our basic structure will also help guard against secrecy. The intra-guild co-operatives will compete for new investment grants. In doing so they may appeal to their past record in creating employment, utilising safe technologies, efficiency in production, etc. The guild banks will also hold their reserves; the idea is that an overall transparency will emerge. It is these kinds of institutional mechanisms, which will be used to prevent the monopolies Rawls rightly fears, that are optimal in preventing certain group memberships from gaining domination. They will ensure that any remaining competitive advantages will not be so wide-ranging that they can seriously jeopardize equality of opportunity.

The Difference Principle

Those at the bottom of the economic hierarchy in POD have the transfer branch of the state to improve their condition. But in a class-divided society like Rawls', the state's dependence upon the success of business profitability, and the continuous and extensive redistribution required by the demands of the difference principle, guarantee that capital-state tensions will be intense. NED is better equipped to uphold the difference principle. The provision for the least well-off is more extensive. Their fundamental interests are separated and located in functionally demarcated organisations. To reiterate, their interests as producers are represented in their respective guilds, and their interests as consumers in the two consumer councils. In NED there is not the tension between the requested state action and the equal necessity of protecting the interests of private investors that plagues POD. With no sovereign state and no sovereign capitalist class, this obstacle to the fulfilment of the difference principle is extraneous. NED is a scheme of social governance, and without a formidable government to oversee economic relations, the guilds will assume accountability for their poorest members, unobstructed by an outside agency whose room for manoeuvre is restricted by the economic power of a small minority class. The benefits of being a member of a guild co-operative revolve around the possession of extensive democratic rights, the receipt of a salary, as opposed to wage-labour, and full employment rights. The external agency in NED is the IGC. As the body which is responsible for setting down guidelines for guild practice, it will determine the policies that will maximise the material conditions of the least well-off. Although this body has authority, in contrast to the liberal state it is not a mask behind which capitalist power thrives. There are considerable implications that follow from this. In NED production to satisfy basic needs is the first priority. Here inter-guild operating cross-subsidies may be required. In terms of the goods that are not produced for a use-value, i.e., those that satisfy wants rather than needs, the guild co-operatives are at liberty to profit through market performing criteria. In both avenues of production, whether it is to reimburse a co-operative for below cost production—which will at times be the case with 'need production'—or whether it is to mediate intra-guild competition—which will be the case with 'want production'—each guild is responsible for its own financial efficiency. As they plan their regulations, the guilds are ideally suited to take the difference principle into consideration. This point is crucial. NED is far more egalitarian than POD, and it does not permit income from property-ownership. But in accordance with the efficiency, reciprocity and compensatory facets of the difference principle, it will reward hard work by sanctioning a degree of economic inequalities. Yet if income differentiations are required for incentive purposes, then the Mondragon example offers an empirical insight into how minimum they can still be. Mondragon is a system of 180 co-operatives encompassing approximately 20,000 workers in the Basque region of Spain. In these workplace democracies the ratio between the highest- and the lowest-paid salaries seldom exceeds 4.5–1. This has proven enough to secure efficiency (Schweickart 1993: 65, 199). Following this fine example, NED will, for reasons that Rawls considers imperative, allow some variation of income.

In addition Rawls stresses that it is difficult to ascertain whether the difference principle is realised. The "matters are nearly always open to wide differences of reasonable opinion; they rest on complicated inferences and intuitive judgments that require us to assess complex social and economic information about topics poorly understood" (1993: 229). Often all that can be determined is that laws and policies are 'not clearly unjust'. "The application of the difference principle in a precise way normally requires more information than we can expect to have" (1971: 199). But it is possible, drawing from judgements based upon "speculative political and economic doctrines and upon social theory generally" (1971: 199), to regulate markets in such a way that the task becomes as least problematic as possible. This is precisely what NED does. Due to the limited range of application of functionally demarcated organisations, the complex economic information will, although still extensive, be restricted in scope. Placing the responsibility of carrying through the dictates of the difference principle into the hands of functional bodies is likely to be a much less ambiguous process than when a redistributive state attempts the same on a far larger and undifferentiated basis. The problem of assessing complex social and economic information will not of course disappear, but it will at least be attenuated. As such, the complex task of identifying and eliminating the inequalities that do not maximise the conditions of the least well-off will be made easier.

This is by no means all. For Rawls, increasingly amounts of primary goods, as 'necessary means' to the fulfilment of life plans, are desired by all self-interested rational individuals. Rational individuals are therefore 'maximisers'. Rationality is understood in a 'narrow sense': in economic terms it implies 'taking the most effective means to given ends' (1971: 14, 93). Further on he asserts that a just society does not necessarily require 'a high material standard of life'. What citizens "want is meaningful work in free association with others, these associations regulating their relations to one another within a framework of just basic institutions. To achieve this state of things great wealth is not required" (1971: 290).[12] Too much personal wealth is now said to be a 'positive hindrance', 'a meaningless distraction' and a 'temptation to indulgence and emptiness'. In addition Rawls mentions the dynamic captured in his 'Aristotelian principle'. Here individuals are viewed as essentially 'doers', exercising and enjoying their capacities; they are not seen simply in consumerist terms (1971: 426; Macpherson 1973a: 342). Rawls is acknowledging the basic *consumerist* concern with primary goods, and the *productive* desire for meaningful work—interests inherent in all citizens. As will now be clear, their demarcated representation in organisational terms is one of the cornerstones upon which the entire political fabric of NED rests.

In their capacities as producers, Rawls is indicating that people have keen interests in using and developing their skills; in much the same way Marx emphasised in his notion of 'species-being', essential to which is creative and joyful labour.[13] The claim that worker controlled co-operatives can enable the pursuit of these attributes in a way wage-labour enterprises cannot rival is an essential component of the libertarian left critique of capitalist markets. Although POD permits a right to property in productive assets, it is not basic to the first principle. I believe this to be a fault in justice as fairness; I also find Rawls' attitude towards workplace democracies somewhat dismissive. This is all the more bizarre when the importance he attaches to them is considered. Addressing, briefly, Marx's critique of liberalism, Rawls notes that Marx would object "that our account of the institutions of property-owning democracy has not considered the importance of democracy in the workplace and in shaping the general course of the economy. This is . . . a major difficulty" (2001: 178). Whilst the declaration that worker-managed firms, operating within a competitive economy, are 'fully compatible with property-owning democracy' is made, the only real elaboration is the suggestion that producer co-operatives may be granted subsidies to establish themselves. The advantages of doing so "could be justified in terms of the political values expressed by justice as fairness" (2001: 178). Despite the huge implications to his theory, particularly in regard to what may pass as a just institution, no further comment is offered. For such a systematic and thorough theorist, his reluctance to explore the relation of justice as fairness to workplace democracies is, on my reading, far too brief. Questions such as "would worker-managed firms be more likely to encourage the democratic political virtues needed for a constitutional regime to endure?" call, Rawls confirms, for 'careful examination' as—and the very next line is striking—the "long-run prospects of a just constitutional regime may depend on them" (2001: 178–9). How very odd then that he should simply declare, "I shall not pursue these questions. I have no idea of the answers" (2001: 178). Here ends Rawls' discussion on democracy in the workplace! Had he devoted more time to this 'major difficulty', he would have seen that a system of workplace democracies, as articulated in NED, is indispensable to the realisation of the difference principle—as it is to the two principles in their entirety.

Turning now to the necessity of representing citizens' interests as consumers, the needs of the worst-off are self-determined and provided for in NED in a manner that, I suggest, goes way beyond POD. The idea of consulting the worst-off about what they themselves regard as necessary to fulfil their needs is that they can actively help determine what items are produced before the process of production takes place. Personal wealth is not the sole factor in the communication of 'market votes'. Not only does 'need production' take priority over 'want production', it expresses the idea that consumer representation is treated as an invaluable and inalienable right of citizenship. The effects on the well-being of the least well-off are likely to be considerable. Self-respect and an appreciation of one's own worth is regarded by Rawls in *Theory* as the first primary good (1971: 396), and in *PL* as of 'fundamental importance' (1993: 318). As such, "the parties in the original position would wish to avoid at almost any cost the social conditions that undermine self-respect" (1971: 440). In terms of fulfilling their interests as consumers, rather than relying upon the prerogatives of private wealth and state redistribution as Rawlsian liberalism does, citizens in NED have firstly the consumer councils, and secondly the guild regulated markets, to cater for their needs and wants, respectively. By providing the opportunity for all citizens to stake their claim on both, the preservation of a sense of self-worth is more realistically assured. The implementation of a more egalitarian scheme for the determination of future production, one that is not dependent upon personal fortune, can only enhance the self-respect of the least well-off. Any society that cannot compare with NED on these grounds must contain the social conditions that, logically, must be avoided 'at almost any cost'. This is, after all, a rational extension of the maximin principle—a failure to maximise self-respect is, on these terms, tantamount to undermining it. The difference principle asserts that inequalities are just only if they maximise the position of the worst-off. Note the word maximise. A 'trickle down' effect, be it constant or occasional, on its own does not satisfy this principle. The point is the worst-off must have their condition improved as much as is possible (Swift 2001: 26–7). To maximise—not just improve, but *maximise*—the conditions of the least well-off, consumer councils are indispensable.[14]

Respecting Economic Liberties

The politico-economic arrangements with which NED aims to implement both sections of the second principle have now been established. Although at this third stage the fair value of the equal political liberties are not being directly addressed, a serious invalidation of liberties understood in an economic sense would, no doubt, have serious implications for the basic liberties of the first principle. There is then cause to show that economic liberties have not been undermined. In NED the private sphere has been democratised and re-politicised, and this transformation raises key questions concerning economic liberties: 'are they limited by co-operative labour?' and 'are they restricted by directives to produce for basic needs before wants?'. To take the former question, it should first of all be noted that certain liberties cherished by liberalism will remain. Individuals are free to seek and change work as they see fit, either within or between guilds; the freedom of movement and of association are as absolute as they are in POD. They are also at liberty to respond to market signals, in their capacities both as producers and consumers. It is true though that as NED will not allow certain market practices, individuals cannot make money just through ownership. Guild co-operatives cannot offer interest payments to private individuals or groups in exchange for their investment capital; neither are they at liberty to employ wage-labour. Guilds can accommodate numerous sole traders and small firms within their ranks, but once they expand beyond a certain size, they must comply with the co-operative nature of guild production. A restriction on some specific liberty, however, is exactly that, it does not amount to an attack on liberty as such. On the contrary, the changes introduced should do much to increase the general arrangement of liberty. Particular economic liberties may be compromised so that the best overall arrangement is finalised. A specific economic liberty, though, can only be moderated for the sake of other basic economic liberties, and never to further the self-interests of particular groups. The final arrangement is to apply equally to all citizens. This is, after all, an extension of Rawls' logic. In relation to the first principle, he grants no priority to liberty per se, nor is any single liberty held in precedence. "No basic liberty is absolute, since these liberties may conflict in particular cases and their claims must be adjusted to fit into one coherent scheme of liberties" (2001: 104). Any adjustments must be made so that the liberties more central to the two moral powers are compatible. Applying his reasoning to economic liberties, no matter that, strictly speaking, they are not directly equated with the first principle, does no harm. Even if, following Rawls, their equal value cannot be guaranteed in the way they can with the basic political liberties, greater urgency is given to their approximation.

Those who equate capitalism with liberty, and deny the link between socialism and liberty, often do so by uniting capitalism and the market. But the objection to capitalism from socialists like Schweickart is in regards to wage-labour and the private ownership of productive resources:

> . . . the relationship of private ownership of the means of production and wage labour to liberty is so problematic that restricting private ownership so as to eliminate both wage labour and interest should enhance, not detract from, society's overall system of liberty (Schweickart 1993: 194).

To the extent that NED is a scheme of communal ownership in which wage-labour has no, or very little, role, Schweickart's sagacity on the enhancement of liberty can be fully endorsed. To the extent that NED's curtailed markets are tightly regulated by functional bodies and subordinated to the processes of democratic planning, which determines production for need, the liberal critic may still not be satisfied. Liberty, the objection is likely to be, is violated when employment contracts are overly regulated. Political intervention in the form of a minimum wage is one thing, but insisting upon the full package of democratic rights in the workplace, and all that it entails, is a vastly more radical proposition. It is true that in NED, as there is no private ownership of the means of production, it is not possible for one class of individuals to profit from the labour of non-owners. But these restrictions on liberty for the few must be balanced against the way liberty for the majority is enhanced in workplace democracies. As Cole observes, "[t]he best guarantee of personal liberty that can exist is in the existence, in each form of association, of an alert democracy, keenly critical of every attempt of the elected person . . . to pass beyond his [sic] representative function" (1920a: 191). Even Roberto Michels, the paradigm theorist of oligarchic tendencies and arguably the most feared critic of democracy, conceded that the organisations which are most likely to sustain democratic decision making are workplace democracies (1999: 162). In wage-labour enterprises workers have no choice but to follow the owner / manager's will, at least if they are to stay employed. This is not the case in NED's guild co-operatives; the only will here is the collective's, in which all members enjoy equal democratic rights. Not only are subjective freedoms protected, the worst-off are able to determine their own plight in a way wage-labour cannot rival. It is difficult to dispute the conclusion that with no input into investment decisions and company policies, the liberty of wage-labourers is at best minimum (Schweickart 1993: 186–90, 250).

In regards to the issue of producing to satisfy basic needs, it is true that the two consumer councils are legally empowered organisations. They have the constitutional right to insist that the guilds produce the 'need goods', arrived at through decentralised planning, before they produce the 'want commodities', arrived at through market criteria. The most immediate objection is likely to be that liberty is transgressed when producers are not free to respond to consumer indicated market demand. This is only true up to a point. Once need goods have been produced in satisfactory quantities, the guild co-operatives are at liberty to respond to market signals as and when they freely choose. It should be noted that workplaces in any system are never at liberty to produce whatever takes their fancy. In market economies their choices are restricted by market signals which, as we have seen, in a society with a significant unequal distribution of wealth, not all sections of consumers are represented adequately. In state socialist regimes there is little or no choice: production is determined through central planners. This approach may satisfy needs, but usually at the expense of producer liberty and consumer choice. In both cases producers are at the mercy of 'outside' forces. Neither system is ideal. In NED, whether producers respond to disorganised consumer demand, via markets, or to organised consumer demand, via democratic councils, they are in either case responding to external influences. One is market driven, the other is council driven. Granted that there is more room to experiment with the former, which is one reason why NED retains a role for markets; the real issue is that the opportunity to maximise profit is likely to be lower with the latter. However in extreme cases, i.e., where certain groups are continually producing for use-value rather than through the profit motive, it would seem just to regard them as forming part of the least well-off. This may require relaxing the objective index of primary goods. In accordance with the dictates of the difference principle, redistribution would then become mandatory. If the 'disproportionate need' production occurs between collectives *within* a guild, it is for that guild to determine how it implements the difference principle and compensates the effected collectives. How it does this is its own business. If the disproportionate need production takes place *between* the guilds—for example, the agriculture guild may be required to produce predominantly more to meet needs than any other guild—then the redistributive function will fall to the IGC. In either case, the potential disadvantage in regard to lack of opportunity to produce in accordance with market-expressed wants, and any resulting loss in profit-maximisation occurred, will be reimbursed. In NED the difference principle is realised through planning by the guilds, not the state. To conclude this sub-section, far from violating economic liberties, the politico-economic arrangements in NED should do much to reinforce them.

Summary

Working within the process of 'quasi-pure procedural justice', as Rawls calls it, and adopting the two principles as an 'independent criterion', I have argued in this section that the key basic structure of NED is capable of realising the principles of justice. Although Rawls states that which regimes can embody the two principles cannot be decided in advance, he does add that justice as fairness attempts to establish guidelines for how the choices can reasonably be approached. My argument has proceeded along these lines (no mention has been made to particular distributions as, keeping within the parameters of the Rawlsian method, I assume there is no ideal pattern of distribution that can be assessed in isolation from the scheme of co-operation from which it emanates). It has been demonstrated why NED's key institutions are equipped to satisfy the two principles, and, moreover, how it does this with less difficulty than POD.

Conclusion

This chapter has argued that the basic structure of NED—the commune system, the guilds, and the consumer and civic councils—are the key institutions which are more suited to realise the two principles of justice than the market forces economy and the redistributive state that constitute POD. It has been shown why the worst-off in NED will be better off than their counterparts in POD. As the argument made throughout has been fairly prolonged, this conclusion will not attempt to summarise the entire argument. But it will be useful to briefly reiterate three important factors that can be drawn from it. Firstly, justice as fairness demands a libertarian and democratic socialism such as NED. Secondly, when applied to NED, the two principles are neither contradictory nor internally inconsistent. In the third place, as co-operative labour and communal ownership of productive assets are indispensable to the satisfaction of the basic political liberties of the first principle, they should be introduced at the constitutional convention.

On the first issue, the institutional structures of income from private ownership and private investment strategies, wage-labour and the undemocratic character of the capitalist division of labour ensure capitalism cannot sustain the two principles. And Rawls, as we have seen, offers no defence of capitalism. Yet whilst he rejects capitalism unambiguously, liberal socialism, which for Rawls is socialism with markets, is defended as a possible candidate for the just society. He suggests that "the choice between a private-property economy and socialism is left open; from the standpoint of the theory of justice alone, various structures would appear to satisfy its principles" (1971: 258). Elsewhere he repeats that just principles would require a socialism of some description "if the stability of a well ordered society could be achieved in no other way" (1975: 546). Amdur offers some additional reflections:

> The principles of justice would require some sort of socialism if the self-respect of the worst off could be maintained in no other way, or if the fair value of liberty could be protected in no other way, or if fair equality of opportunity could be achieved in no other way (Amdur 1980: 333).

Amdur claims that as these propositions follow logically from Rawls' theory, justice as fairness can be used as an argument to support 'some sort of socialism', and he is, as the argument of this book indicates, entirely correct. It does seem likely that market socialism, with its substitution of private property and wage-labour with social ownership and co-operative labour—features it shares with NED—can go some way towards meeting the requirements of justice as fairness. But, to return to the earlier discussions, market socialism—now in contrast to NED—retains market-based exchange relations in which a regard for the plight of others is unlikely to emerge. And without the additional institution of democratic investment planning, they are bedevilled by the kind of inequalities Rawls is keen to avoid. Presumably the state in 'Rawlsian liberal socialism' would act in a similar way as it does in POD, but in societies which cannot realistically prevent large concentrations of wealth, we have seen how problematic it is to expect the state to fulfil the redistributive functions required by the principles of justice.

In regard to the second issue, NED is not simply another version of market socialism. It does have an important role for markets, but they are functionally demarcated, and regulated by the guilds. In any economy that has a role for markets, care needs to be taken to constrain inequalities. This, as Rawls frequently states, is essential for the realisation of the first principle. As we have seen, though, this problem is not easily contained in POD. In direct contrast, NED is not inflicted with intense class-divisions. As such, what I called the contradictory problem—the state has to provide extensive income transfers to satisfy the demands of the difference principle, yet transfers cannot be too extensive, as the state is also compelled not to jeopardise the long term interests of those with private wealth to invest—is inconsequential. In NED new investment is determined through the institution of democratic investment planning; as private savers are not private investors, there is not the need to prioritise the interests of a capitalist investment class. On the same issue, it can now be confirmed why the two principles, when applied to NED, will not be internally inconsistent in the way they are in POD. In the latter, the sustainability of the equal value of the political liberties of the first principle requires continuous state redistribution to keep economic inequalities within certain limits; yet the second principle asserts that inequalities must still be large enough to meet the compensatory facet of the difference principle, and to provide the incentives an efficient economy needs. NED is more egalitarian than POD. The key institutions of NED are, as we have repeatedly seen, arranged in such a way that huge economic inequalities will not exist. There is, consequently, not the need for political intervention to prevent large accumulations of private capital; the remaining diminutive and more tightly controlled inequalities can be left to regulate the difference principle without fear of violating the basic liberties of the first principle. This is hugely significant: under these conditions there is no internal contradiction between the principles of justice.

Finally, concerning the third issue, for Rawls political liberties are more fundamental than others. He does not include economic freedoms in the first principle: to own the instruments of production and enter into market contracts as one desires, to sell or exchange what one produces, and to inherit and give to anyone of one's choice. They may be justified, but this is a matter for the legislative (third) stage, and not the preceding constitutional convention. So for Rawls the liberties of citizenship are more basic than economic freedoms. In the introduction to this chapter I said that although Rawls' principles of justice will, in the interests of convenience, be respected, in the conclusion I would confirm why co-operative labour and a non-statist communal ownership of productive assets are so central to the satisfaction of the fair value of equal basic political liberties that they really need to be institutionalised at the constitutional convention. Given the analysis made throughout this chapter, the reasons for this are now, I think, quite clear. This is not to dispute the ordering of the two principles, but it is evident that democratic input into our economic lives, in our activities as both producers and as consumers, is an imperative prerequisite to a sense of personal independence and a social basis of self-respect. This is vital to the development of the two moral powers—capacities for a sense of justice and personal conceptions of the good—and therefore essential to the realisation of the basic political liberties. Others have made similar arguments. For example, Clark and Gintis (1978) argue that the concern with equal basic liberties demands an economy in which inclusive and democratic associations of workers are in command of productive processes. They insist that "to conform to Rawlsian principles, the democratic control of economic activities must be supplemented by mechanisms other than pure market coordination plus state redistribution" (1978: 303). Their contention is that the categories of political liberties must include the opportunity to participate in productive decision making. Far from enjoying equal liberties, workers in capitalism are under the command of the owners of the instruments of production, and as this chapter has shown, this will also be the case with POD. It follows that "the extension of democratic principles to the production process would have the effect of strengthening the system of total liberties, since the experience of equal participation in decision making strengthens individual commitment to principles of justice"

(1978: 312). A common, if keenly contested, objection to a democratic regulation of production is that it is economically wasteful.[15] But if liberty is taken to include participation in the productive sphere, as it must, then to forfeit liberty in the interests of efficiency would violate the ordering of the two principles. Equal basic liberties, it will be recalled, are ranked above economic efficiency (Clark and Gintis 1978: 312–4). From the preceding argument of this chapter, it should be clear why I endorse and substantiate this reasoning. To sustain the basic liberties of the first principle, production must be under communal *ownership*, and the *control* of the instruments of production placed in the hands of co-operative labour.

Notes

1 Rawls believes this corrects a defect in *Theory* (2001: 112).

2 The term 'overlapping consensus' is explained fully in Chapter Five, where it is analysed.

3 This idea will also be the subject of further discussion in Chapter Five, especially in its third section.

4 Most notably in texts like *The Critique* (1843) and *The Eighteenth Brumaire* (1851).

5 DiQuattro concedes this point (1983: 62).

6 Nicholls 1994: 48–9, 87–8; Ellis 1923: 585–6, 590–3; Elliott 1968: 188; Gray 1946: 454–5; Von Mises 1951: 261; Hsiao 1927: 122–3; Glass 1966: 44–5; and Ulam 1951: 90 all raise various similar objections.

7 Throughout his libertarian socialist period, Cole remained opposed to the idea that in the production of use commodities, profit motives might take precedence. He maintained that when the main object of production is the realisation of a profit, the resulting opposing policies will undermine the community spirit. This anti-social behaviour inevitably leads to the 'perversion of function' (1920a: 57–8). NED will be alert to the dangers of systematically prioritising profit-making purposes; the introduction of a *controlled* and *subordinated* profit-motivated sentiment will not, as the measures reiterated above illustrate, lead to the kind of opposition, confusion and conflict Cole rightly fears. (See 1920a: 50–61 for a fuller account of Cole's position.)

8 There is however some tension in Cole's thought here. If all the guild budgets are to go before the commune for ratification, as he suggests (1920b: 145), this would provide the opportunity for it to exert its influence upon the functional bodies almost at will. This charge, though, cannot be applied to NED, as the revisions introduced and analysed in Chapter Three indicate.

9 See the author's *G.D.H. Cole: Emancipatory Politics and Organisational Democracy* (2004), University of Sussex Department of Philosophy, Part Two.

10 Schweickart raise this issue, although not directly in relation to Rawls (Schweickart 1993: 86).

11 Italics mine.

12 Further on, Rawls re-emphasises that all citizens should have "at least one community of shared interests to which he belongs and where he finds his endeavours confirmed by his associates" (1971: 442).

13 See section three of the next chapter.

14 Rawls recognises that for markets to be efficient, "it is necessary for consumers to be well informed about both prices and the relevant features of available products" (1993: 364), and proposes that the legislature discourage superficial and misleading advertising (1993: 365). Given the above analysis on NED's guild regulated markets and consumer councils, together with the application of Marx's critique of the liberal state to POD, this task may be carried out with less difficulty in NED.

15 See section three of the following chapter for a discussion on this contention.

CHAPTER FIVE

Political Liberalism

It has now been shown how NED aims to democratise the economy, and its alternative political structures have also been analysed. As yet, though, little has been said about the cultural aspect of this scheme. This chapter readdresses the balance. Through a critical evaluation of Rawls' idea of political liberalism, an argument is developed that NED's cultural political structures are more suited to sustain what Rawls calls the 'common ground'. The task is, again, not to structure the chapter so that a direct comparison between political liberalism and NED is central throughout. Some comparison is of course unavoidable, but this is not how my argument proceeds. The method is similar to that of the previous chapter. Rawls' revised theory of justice as fairness is firstly introduced; particular attention is paid to the idea of an 'overlapping consensus', which is one of the key features of political liberalism. Critiques of Rawls' mature position are then addressed. From here I conclude that although he does place emphasis on the importance of community, in political liberalism the sustainability of the overlapping consensus is problematic. Attention then turns to the political structures in NED. We shall see how they provide the institutional setting within which the above difficulty can be overcome. To help explain, recall Cole's suggestions for how the civic services are to operate in a functionally demarcated society. Democratic self-governance, he said adamantly, must also apply directly to the non-economic civic sphere of social life. On the side of service provision, there will be education, drama and music guilds to serve one set of purposes, and health, medicine and sanitation guilds to attend to another. With regard to the interests of consumers, the former civic guilds will be regulated through consultation with the cultural councils, and in respects to the latter, the health councils. However, Western societies are now far more plural and multicultural than they were in the period in which Cole theorised his libertarian socialism, approximately 1914–20. The role of the civic services will therefore need to be more extensive. In NED they are the public spaces that constitute the forums in which deliberations over ideals of the good will be heard. As such, they are responsible for sustaining a vibrant and diverse cultural marketplace within which citizens are free to choose and revise their own preferences. In contrast to Rawls' political liberalism, NED has a re-politicised civil society, and it is not, initially, the responsibility of the state to uphold the overlapping consensus.

Nevertheless, in their capacities as final courts of appeal, the local, regional and national communes will, following the Rawlsian state, endorse a principle of neutrality to serve as the criteria by which cases of impasse will be resolved. The civic services will also adhere to a moderate neutrality ideal; it will though admit to a looser interpretation and allow for some non-coercive perfectionist measures. We will see that this is a prerequisite for the realisation of Rawls' second moral power. These terms are fully explained and elaborated upon as we proceed. Finally, as the conception of the political in NED is thicker than it is in POD, a response to the immediate objection that the basic structure of the former upholds a controversial conception of the good is essential. This discussion is quite involved, and is therefore introduced more fully at the time. The chapter is divided into three parts: 1) 'Rawls' Political Liberalism', 2) 'New Economic Democracy and Political Liberalism' and 3) 'Co-Operative Non-Alienating Labour and the Overlapping Consensus'.

1. Rawls' Political Liberalism

There are three parts to this section. The first, 'Rawls' Revisions', introduces his qualified argument that the liberalism justice as fairness articulates is a *political*, not a *comprehensive*, doctrine. It is shown why the idea of an overlapping consensus, which is arguably the most prominent innovation in *Political Liberalism*, is central to Rawls' mature liberalism. The most penetrating critiques of this ideal are addressed in the third part, 'Critiquing the Overlapping Consensus'. In order to pave the way to this review, I shall, in the second part, 'Addressing the Communitarian Critique', take note of the immediate objection that Rawls underestimates the relevance of community values. Although this contention holds some substance, I will outline why it is nevertheless exaggerated; this points ahead nicely to the critical discussions that follow.

Rawls' Revisions

It is in his later works (1993, 2001) that Rawls emphasises that his theory of justice is a political doctrine. He draws a distinction between this and comprehensive doctrines[1]—whether moral, religious, philosophical or metaphysical. Comprehensive conceptions stress the values, virtues and views which dictate *all* areas of human life (1993: 13). They are 'precisely articulated' schemes. In contrast, partial doctrines comprise only some non-political values and virtues, and are 'loosely articulated' schemes. Rawls now provides a public philosophy which falls short of being a comprehensive doctrine (1993: 154–8). There are three main features to a political conception of justice: a) its subject is *only* the basic structure of a constitutional democratic regime, and *not* other aspects of life in the 'background culture', b) it does not endorse any particular comprehensive doctrine and c) it is formulated through key intuitive ideas implicit in the public political culture of a democratic society (1993: 11–3, 376), i.e., the ideas of society as a fair system of cooperation, and citizens as free and equal (1993: 15–9). This political conception is more restricted in its application. For Rawls, a pluralism of doctrines is a permanent feature of modern democracies. A political conception of justice though, by drawing from the fundamental intuitive ideas held by the majority of citizens, can still initiate shared public support and thereby stability. It does not do this by designing a constitution in which rivalries between competing fractions are merely contained, a modus vivendi (1993: 147–8). Rather, it is secured via a profound agreement on the fundamentals of the basic structure of society. The objective is to find stability in a deeper social unity. A conception of justice can inform the structure of the modern democratic societies which safeguard a wide array of ideas of the good. This particular feature represents a reinterpretation of his initial theory. In *Theory* the conception settles disputes publicly, now it must do so even though people subscribe to different moral philosophies. To realise social unity, the goal is to secure the allegiance of free and equal moral citizens to the basic institutions of society. For Rawls, only a conception of justice which can command the support of an overlapping consensus can achieve this. The overlapping consensus of justice also rules out formulating 'comprehensive conceptions of political justice', as the institutions of the basic structure must be just in the eyes of the substantive majority of citizens. It needs to be a public standard (nearly) all can accept, but because of the fact of pluralism, no comprehensive doctrine can be the basis of a publicly acceptable political justice. The need, Rawls now affirms, is for a procedure to adjudicate between the competing claims of comprehensive doctrines. The task is to forge a stable agreement. The principles of justice do this not by renouncing competing comprehensive doctrines, but by subsuming them. In sum, justice as fairness is presented in *Theory* as (part of) a comprehensive moral doctrine; not so in *PL*, where it now becomes a free-standing political conception (1993: xliii; 2001: 26–7, 32–4; Kukathas and Pettit 1990: 134–8,142–3, 146–8: Dreben 2003: 320).

Rawls does not dispute that comprehensive doctrines are important; his point is that their views must coincide with a wider political conception of justice to which they are all partly related, and to which they agree from a common point of view (identical public reasons)[2] as well as from their own perspective (various non-public reasons) (1993: 217–8, 223–5; Larmore 2003: 377–80). In a well-ordered society, the basic institutions of justice are endangered when unreasonable comprehensive doctrines become too formidable. Embracing controversial claims will not attract widespread support. For Rawls other liberalisms, such as those of Kant and Mill, are general and comprehensive moral doctrines.[3] They are:

> . . . general in that they apply to a wide range of subjects, and comprehensive in that they include conceptions of what is of value in human life, ideals of personal virtue and character that are to inform our thought and conduct as a whole (1987: 6).

By way of contrast, Rawls does not attempt to articulate his liberalism in comprehensive terms; it is not dependant upon grand metaphysical or moral standpoints. Political liberalism values tolerance; the basic structure of society must be regulated through principles which do not presume particular notions of the good. Comprehensive doctrines are unlikely to converge; they are certain to disagree about their conceptions of the truth or right (1993: 94, 126). As such, stability becomes an immediate problem. This realisation caused Rawls to move away from the contractarianism presented in *Theory*.[4] He now affirms that a theory of justice should not be premised upon principles detrimental to a well-ordered society. Political liberalism is therefore not reliant upon those constitutes of comprehensive doctrines that initiate principled dispute. It is, to repeat, deliberately neutral in this regard. An overlapping consensus of comprehensive doctrines can generate encouragement for a liberal constitution by highlighting the values and beliefs that all reasonable comprehensive doctrines hold. Rawls' constitutional liberal democracy does not appeal to claims of truth for its justification; it appeals to, given the 'fact' of pluralism and the 'consequences of the burdens of judgement', a notion of 'reasonableness' (1993: 94). The task is to reveal where comprehensive doctrines overlap in regards to a liberal kernel, the non-acceptance of which Rawls considers unreasonable. Accentuating the overlapping consensus, he insists, can mobilise wholesale support for his liberal constitution. And this constitution comprises a well-ordered society. Rawls concludes that this approach can ensure political unity and a stable social order (1993: 135–43; 2001: 28–9, 32-4; Kukathas and Pettit 1990: 138–40; Levine 2002: 208–9, 211). These are the fundamental bases to Rawls' political liberalism. In order to set up the critical discussion of the third section, I will turn immediately to the communitarian critique, a critique that in some respects is inflated.

Addressing the Communitarian Critique

Communitarians believe that community should be treated at least on an even par with the concepts of liberty and equality. Writers like Michael Sandel, Michael Walzer, Alasdair MacIntyre and Charles Taylor have all developed their own theories, but they share an agreement that liberal theories of justice, like Rawls', pay insufficient attention to the value of community. There are, they claim, certain shared practices and social understandings citizens hold in common that are not adequately accounted for in the individualistic and abstract method by which liberal notions of rights and justice are articulated (Kymlicka 2002: 208–9; Miller 1989: 60–7). From the communitarian perspective, Rawls has been criticised for overlooking the importance of community, where community is typically contrasted with 'liberal individualism'. The critique is of a culture of individualism in which egoism and self-gratification are rampant. The lack of communal bonds, it is claimed, leads to social disintegration and a sense of meaninglessness and alienation. Central to Rawls' liberal theory is indeed a concern with the freedom and autonomy of individuals—the capacity to determine subjective conceptions of the good. It is also true that mutually disinterested parties in the original position choose their own values in a way detached from any community. Swift (2001), however, argues that liberals like Rawls who are concerned chiefly with individual well-being can still endorse a sense of community. In liberal individualism, a well-being premised upon the autonomy and freedom of individuals, *all* individuals matter. Self-interest is pursued to the extent that it remains compatible with others doing the same. It is not just concerned with self-gratification, but about recognising the rights of all autonomous agents to follow suit. Liberalism's moral idea is that everyone enjoys the freedom to choose their own lives. As such, liberalism need not endorse an unbounded pursuit of individual self-gratification, but can incorporate the notion that people respect the moral claims of their fellow citizens (Swift 2001: 134–40). There is nothing wrong with Rawls' desire to safeguard subjective autonomies like the freedom to choose particular conceptions of the good. As a libertarian society, NED will do the same. Cole too was keen to reconcile individual freedom with his unique brand of socialist planning (1958: 7, 26). It is right that all individuals matter equally, that the pursuit of self-interest remains compatible with others having an equal chance to do likewise and that mutual respect is incorporated into social interactions. The question though is how to sustain a community ethic robust enough to realise these moral claims. Perhaps the best way to demonstrate how Rawls' society can harbour some sense of community—and, crucially, why there is still a need to go beyond it—is by highlighting his support for a 'neutral' state.

The Rawlsian state is not procedurally neutral; the "principles of justice are substantive and express far more than procedural values, and so do its political conceptions of society and person" (1993: 192). Neither is the political conception neutral in terms of the *effect* of its policies; it cannot possibly predict how they will influence the appeal value of comprehensive doctrines. This for Rawls is a commonsense fact of political sociology. Rather, the state is neutral in terms of its *aims* (1993: 192–3). In *Political Liberalism* Rawls adopts the term 'reasonable pluralism'. He argues that it is not legitimate for the state to act upon subjective conceptions of what is valuable; if it did, it would be a sectarian state. To be communal the state should assign 'special priority' to the shared values of freedom, autonomy, equality and justice (1993: 161). The Rawlsian liberal will permit state action only when it can be justified through appeals to the common ground. Here citizens of a political community share a common identity of free and equal citizens, as modelled in the original position. To claim that justice comes before particular interests is to claim that citizenship identity—what people have in common—is more important than differentiated identities. So long as people are sufficiently constituted by their identities as citizens, the implication is that when such an identity clashes with particular identities, citizenship identity takes preference. If so, liberals need not deny the value of a shared communal identity. Rawls argues that the state should be an impartial umpire; it is illegitimate for the state to judge, even democratically, how citizens should live. This would violate the individual's right to be treated with equal respect (1993: 191–4). So what exactly are neutrality liberals like Rawls neutral about? They distinguish between a) the capacity of citizens to choose their own conceptions of the good, the second moral power, which they are *not* neutral about; and b) the chosen particular conceptions of the good, which they *are* neutral about. The state is restricted to providing the background in which freedom and autonomy are secured. Rawls acknowledges that his theory of justice does involve a conception of the political good. State action may be premised upon a 'thin' theory of the good, although it is still neutral due to the common ground held between citizens. What the state cannot do is support particular comprehensive doctrines. As we have just seen, Rawls believes there is an overlapping consensus on a sense of justice, and the political values of freedom (the capacity to form, revise and pursue a conception of the good) and equality (a capacity that applies equally to everyone, and is captured in the original position through the collective ignorance of personal talents and circumstances) (1993: 19). Through deliberations in the original position, this articulates into a theory of justice. It is a neutral theory, as it builds from a common ground, drawn from shared reasons, not from those where people reasonably disagree (1993: i–ii, 192–4; 2001: 153–7; Swift 2001: 146–8, 154–7).

Rawls' belief in self-determination, therefore, leads to an avocation of the neutral state. The state should uphold the capacity for all citizens to seek their own conceptions of the good. He is critical of the kind of state perfectionism which encourages particular views of the good. For Rawls, the state must not pre-judge the intrinsic value of particular conceptions. This is what he means when he claims that 'the self is prior to its ends'—our ends are subject to re-examination. Everyone has the right to question their understanding of the good. In this sense, *the right comes before the good* (1993: 173–6). Rawls distinguishes between 'all-purpose means', primary goods and the ends which can be sought with them (1993: 180, 188). The communitarian perfectionist state, on the other hand, takes a stand on the ends it thinks have value. Communitarians hold that the neutral state should be replaced with a 'politics of the common good'. It encourages conceptions of the good that adhere to standards in the larger community, and establishes a benchmark by which citizens' choices can be evaluated. Rawls does recognise that the kind of moderate state action that may further particular interests can be justified to a certain point. But such doctrines cannot influence the state on constitutional essentials and basic principles of justice; these must remain neutral. The Rawlsian state may fund museums, but its constitutional arrangements or conceptions of justice must not be founded within particular comprehensive doctrines. Rawls' political liberalism is communitarian in the sense that it is established upon a common neutral ground. It does have a theory of community, one that promotes a shared goal: the common good of a just society (Mulhall and Swift 2003: 468–9). As Swift concludes, a society whose members respect each other's autonomy, and who are willing to temper the pursuit of their own interests when their fellow citizens require it—i.e., by not opposing redistributive taxation—is a society with solidarity and community (2001: 153–4, 199–200; Swift 2001: 157, 162; Kymlicka 2002: 217–220, 225). Nevertheless, the structural device Rawls believes can sustain his community ethic, the overlapping consensus, is, as the next section will demonstrate, theoretically problematic.

Critiquing the Overlapping Consensus

Many, probably even most, fundamentalist groups dislike liberalism's notion of autonomy. Their fear is that if adherents are brought up as free and equal citizens, especially in regard to the revisability of ends which should be treated as beyond critique, their membership will decline. The key problem is how the liberal state responds to non-liberal groups who not only reject autonomy, but see it as detrimental to their way of life. If the value of autonomy is enforced, to the minority groups who do not implement liberal principles this will be perceived as intolerance. Rawls, however, is prepared to cater to the needs of illiberal groups. He recognises that not everyone views ends as revisable, and softens his commitment to autonomy accordingly. As political liberalism partially accommodates comprehensive views, it may be seen as a narrower version of communitarianism. In this respect, political liberalism is distinct from the liberalisms that uphold autonomy comprehensively. So although the rights to heresy and apostasy are, for Rawls, amongst the basic liberties society must protect, he modifies his position on the revisability of ends. The principle should still apply in a public sense, but it need not be enforced in our private affairs. Even if comprehensive doctrines do not openly endorse the notion of revisability, Rawls believes it will do them little harm as it is only exercised in a political context. Its application is limited to the public domain, what Rawls calls our 'higher-order' interests; it is not meant as a general account of the entire remit of all non-political opinions. It is still possible that in citizens' private lives, in the internal life of associations, the right of revision will not be prioritised (1993: 195–200; 2001: 183, 187–92; Kymlicka 2002: 228–36). Kymlicka puts it nicely when he writes that "one way to understand Rawls's 'political liberalism' is to say that, for Rawls, people can be communitarians in private life, and liberals in public life" (2002: 236).

Although Kymlicka calls Rawls' strategy in *PL* ingenious, he doubts it can be successful. Rawls stresses that the legal right of autonomy need not be exercised in private life. The right to revisability of course still stands, but it does not have to be enforced. In private life individuals can, if they wish, continue to treat their ends as non-revisable. The difficulty, however, is that even if revisability is not encouraged in private life, the liberal state still enables it. Rawls insists that everyone is made aware of their basic liberties. At the very minimum, this requires knowledge of the freedom to leave the sect, group or association. So for Kymlicka, political liberalism will have no appeal to, and may even offend, certain communitarian groups. The revisability principle in political liberalism has a political significance, but it is not restricted to citizens' public identities. Rawls claims the two moral powers are only invoked in political life. But the capacity for a sense of justice (the reasonable) is distinct from the capacity to choose and revise a conception of the good (the rational). The former is exercised in political life, and the latter relates to citizens' 'non-public identities', which includes their comprehensive identities. One evaluates public institutions, the other evaluates comprehensive doctrines. Kymlicka's critique is that Rawls exaggerates the distance between political and comprehensive liberalisms: "Rawls has not explained why people who are communitarians in private life should be liberals in political life" (2002: 240). In terms of apostasy, heresy, education and legality, opinions do not cohere. Certain communitarian groups will therefore be hostile to political liberalism. The overlapping consensus argument will have little appeal to them. "Rawls's attempt to reconcile the traditional liberal commitment to basic liberties with a communitarian conception of the self seems unsuccessful" (1993: 199; Kymlicka 2002: 236–41).

Kukathas and Pettit (1990) and Mulhall and Swift (2003) also draw attention to the likely conflict between the liberal faith and certain comprehensive views. The example cited is the devoutly religious sending their children to strict schools where they are isolated from various alternative views. As the Rawlsian state must ensure that its future citizens are not indoctrinated with a particular religious upbringing, it would be required to prescribe certain educational stipulations. Political liberalism demands that children's education include knowledge of their constitutional rights and liberty of conscience. All children should be taught to consider matters for themselves. In terms of their future role as co-operating citizens, Rawls confirms that education must also "encourage the political virtues so that they want to honour the fair terms of social cooperation in their relations with the rest of society" (1988: 267; 2001: 156–7). But if this is so, the state in justice as fairness will need to enforce certain values which are not radically dissimilar to those held in the comprehensive liberal doctrines Rawls supposedly rejects. In the Rawlsian thesis, if the state does uphold comprehensive liberal values, it becomes another sectarian doctrine. But to sustain the status of citizens understood as free and equal can—indeed at times does—require state intervention. And to the comprehensive doctrines hostile to the overlapping consensus, it is highly likely that Rawls' liberal political values will appear sectarian (Kukathas and Pettit 1990: 141; Mulhall and Swift 2003: 476–7; Swift 2001: 165).

It is unclear whether political liberalism can fully resolve these tensions. Although on behalf on Rawls, it is equally unclear that any socially divisive society can. Someone may object to the idea that ends are fixed and immune from revision, or someone else may agree that comprehensive groups should be beyond the enforcement of liberalism's individual freedoms. But it remains an intellectual cul-de-sac, so to speak. That is, Rawls does not treat autonomy in a comprehensive sense; he recognises that there is opposition to the autonomy of comprehensive liberalism. Endorsing it in a political sense would, he argues, be sectarian. Non-liberal minorities demand the right to retain the internal restrictions that subordinate individual rights, that certain key ends are non-revisable. But as political liberalism upholds the revisability principle explicitly, which is central to the second moral power and therefore a principle element of the overlapping consensus, it is unsympathetic to this request. Rawls of course is well aware of this contradiction. His conclusion is that intolerant non-liberal comprehensive doctrines are being 'unreasonable', that the consequences of educating children may need to be implemented 'often with regret', and that when the right to apply the revisability principle is perceived as an infringement, it is simply 'unfortunate' (1993: 200). Perhaps it is these things, and if, as Rawls claims, the majority of comprehensive doctrines are 'loosely articulated' rather than 'precisely articulated' schemes, then the threat the latter pose to stability may not be so great after all (2001: 193). But there are no guarantees of this, and even if the majority are only partially comprehensive, there are no assurances they will remain so. Nevertheless, Rawls is probably right that the idea of forging an overlapping consensus offers, in light of the permanent pluralism of modern liberal societies, the best hope of realising the stability essential to the good society. To do this, however, it will have to be articulated with greater substance than it receives in political liberalism. As explained above, Rawls' liberalism can harbour a sense of community, one that is premised upon respect for individual freedom. Here the state is a community in which citizens collectively realise a common good, where they share certain final ends: the just society (1993: 146). We have though now seen the dynamics that will frustrate citizens' perceptions of the common ground. So in terms of the two moral powers, if the distinction Rawls draws between the public and private is suspect, how can the overlapping consensus be clarified and strengthened in a way that offers a more realistic hope of reconciliation? I try to answer this question by theorising a thicker conception of the political, without simultaneously sacrificing the commitment to the values of liberal egalitarianism; precisely how is clarified below. Before continuing with this task, it is as well to take note of the following concern, as it is through formulating a response that my position is finalised.

Within the liberal setting, citizenship identity is supposed to be so deeply felt that people pursue their own conception of the good in a way that does not undermine justice. The identity of free and equal citizens takes preference over particularistic identities. It must also hold priority over economic self-interests; the wealthy must be prepared to sanction the redistribution taxation justice requires. Insofar, it matters that there is a common identity within the citizenry as a whole. But as explained above, the problem is the likely intensity of identification certain groups have towards their particular associations or communities. It is unlikely that liberal citizenship can, by itself, stimulate agents to act according to just principles. Appeals to an abstract notion of citizenship are inadequate for this task. There must be a more particularistic claim about the significance of distinct localities, and the need for more substantial bonds. The question then is: can the abstract liberal values of freedom, equality, etc. sustain a sense of collective identification strong enough to motivate citizens to fulfil their duties to each other? Certainly it is a possibility, even a probability, that for liberal community to function, for citizens to be prepared to curtail their self-interests in order to treat their fellows justly, their common identity needs to be far more robust than the rather tame 'citizen of the liberal state'. So in light of cultural diversity, how may a common identity emerge? How can the sense of solidarity needed to motivate citizens to collectively comply with the exacting principles of Rawls' redistributive liberalism be sustained? What can generate the interactions capable of countering the various social boundaries? Without these, citizens do not feel like members of their state, and identify more with local groupings. Swift captures the dilemma:

> The real issue is that the state or nation is already too diffuse and distant for people to feel a sense of belonging and fellow-feeling of the kind that will prevent them sliding into individualism of the wrong—alienated, egoistic—kind. . . . On this view, the redistributive state justified by appeal to the idea of common citizenship is not motivationally sustainable (2001: 174).

It is, I agree, true that the state is far too impersonal to halt the fragmentation of society into particular identities. Nation-state politics are simply too remote to stimulate the required interest. The solution is to return politics to its rightful place, a rejuvenation of local political communities. The prerequisite of which is, as articulated in NED, the establishment of associations smaller than the state yet large enough to generate a community spirit (Swift 2001: 168–77; Mulhall and Swift 2003: 478). This issue is taken up in the following two sections.

2. New Economic Democracy and Political Liberalism

This second part of the chapter establishes the relation between NED and the ideas central to political liberalism. I shall refer to two disputes, firstly with regard to those between the liberal egalitarianism and the communitarian positions, and secondly to a debate within the liberal perspective itself: the question of state neutrality and liberal perfectionism. The differences between them are often subtle, but they are significant. Briefly, Rawls has a 'thin' theory of the political—the state is only entitled to use its coercive power to sustain the two principles of justice, which in plural societies includes the overlapping consensus, and it cannot take sides on non-political comprehensive values. In direct contrast, the communitarian state upholds a 'thicker' conception of the political—it can implement coercive measures to advance a certain way of life, a politics of the common good. Although liberal perfectionism is on the liberal side of this continuum, it moves closer to the middle in as much as the liberal perfectionist state can adopt a non-coercive criterion by which to advance valuable ways of life. This is a rather oversimplified summary. The divides between communitarianism and egalitarian liberalism, and, within the latter, between neutrality and perfectionism, are not always as extreme or as clear as this; the following discussions will help shed light on these complexities. Nevertheless it does help one to picture, on a very general basis, the key areas of dispute. Through a critical appraisal of these contentions, it is shown how the political structural arrangements in NED are able to withstand and overcome the problems identified in the previous section. It will, I think, be instructive to briefly outline the fundamental propositions central to this argument. The role of the communes, as high-level sovereign appeal courts, is to act in cases of impasse. In adjudicating between unresolved political contestations that come before them, they will adhere to the neutrality ideal. Although they are obviously high-level public institutions, they are not the immediate spaces through which the political process unfolds. That is, they are not the designated forums in which initial evaluations of conceptions of the good take place. In NED these occur primarily in civil society, through the civic guilds and civic councils. These functional bodies, I propose, would also adopt a moderate neutrality principle, but their neutrality will admit to a looser interpretation. Articulating the principle of neutrality so that the civic services may non-coercively advance certain conceptions of the good does involve relaxing the neutrality ideal, but, as will be shown, it does not amount to violating it. The neutrality of the communes and the softer neutrality of the civic services can be theorised in a direction that eschews diametrical opposition; the difference is more in degree of emphasis, rather than in form. For this proposition to be plausible though the latter must constitute the public forum in which deliberations initially take place, and the former is understood as a sovereign appeal court, rather than an exclusive domain for political contestation. A vibrant cultural marketplace can be sustained within this structural arrangement, guaranteeing in a more satisfactory manner the fulfilment of Rawls' second moral power. There are three sections to this passage, 'Evaluations of the Good in Civil Society', 'Moderate Neutrality in the Civic Services' and 'Neutrality in the Commune System'.

Evaluations of the Good in Civil Society

This section contends that the appropriate domain in which to evaluate conceptions of the good is civil society. The argument is substantiated through an engagement with Kymlicka's commentary on the social thesis defended by Taylor (1985). Briefly, Taylor denies that individuals can be 'self-sufficient alone', i.e., that they can 'survive outside of society'. He is critical of these so-called 'atomist' perspectives, which endanger 'the "community" dimension of modern life'. Rather he argues that the 'full capacity of choice' is a potential that has to be developed and exercised in a communal context. This is not a hugely contested claim, and Rawls has no wish to dispute it. But for Taylor, the social thesis demands the rejection of liberal neutrality. He argues that the neutral state cannot sustain the social environment required for the exercise of self-determination. The capacity to choose and revise conceptions of the good are, his argument goes, suited only to a community constituted through a politics of the common good, and in such a community the state prioritises dominant notions of the good. Liberal neutrality, in Taylor's view, fails to provide the social conditions that individual autonomy requires (Taylor 1985: 189–91, 197; 1985b: 206; Kymlicka 2002: 245). Kymlicka critically appraises Taylor's social thesis, and in the process proposes some very interesting questions. Responding to Kymlicka's challenges will help make clear how the political structures in NED steer a requisite path between the liberal egalitarian and communitarian positions. Kymlicka discusses three aspects of the social thesis; I shall offer a summary and response to each in turn. This will serve to inform the discussions in the following two sections. The sub-sections of this passage are named in accordance with these three aspects. They are 'The Cultural Structure', 'Public Forums' and 'Political Legitimacy'.

The Cultural Structure

To make meaningful choices, citizens need meaningful options. But for communitarians and liberal perfectionists like Joseph Raz (1986), liberal neutrality cannot ensure the plural cultural structures which make these options available. If the liberal state intervened in the cultural marketplace to uphold diversity, it would in effect be promoting particular conceptions of the good. This is precisely what it claims it is not entitled to do. Yet without political interventions of any kind, as some, perhaps many, options will not be self-supporting, the cultural marketplace will be unable to sustain the social bases which support modern pluralism. His argument is that neutrality "would undermine the chances of survival of many cherished aspects of our culture"; so for Raz, "[s]upporting valuable forms of life is a social rather than an individual matter" (1986: 162). Liberal neutrality is, the argument goes, self-defeating.[5] In contrast, a non-neutral state is not in breach of its premises when it quite deliberately attempts to impose the quality of choices by actively promoting a sufficient range of conceptions of the good. But liberal neutrality also seeks to strengthen the quality of options available. The liberal freedoms of speech, movement, association, etc. enable groups to popularize their lifestyles. Unattractive ways of life will struggle to attract adherents. As people can freely choose between the various conceptions of the good, liberal society, its defenders insist, creates a vibrant cultural pluralism of notions of the good. So both liberal egalitarians and communitarians seek to provide a range of worthy options. The disagreement, Kymlicka observes, is in which domain the notion of perfectibility should be located. Should conceptions of the good be evaluated in civil society, or become a matter of state action? Indeed, "the dispute should perhaps be seen as a choice, not between perfectionism and neutrality, but between social perfectionism and state perfectionism—for the flip side of state neutrality is support for the role of perfectionist ideals in civil society" (Kymlicka 1989: 894–6; 2002: 246–8; Taylor 1985: 205–8).

If Kymlicka's insight is right, if state neutrality does involve 'perfectionist ideals in civil society', then it adds much credibility to the political arrangements of NED. Indeed, the position NED upholds is that conceptions of the good are best evaluated in civil society through designated public spaces that are much closer to the individual than the distant institutions of the liberal state. Operating in civil society, and beyond the reach of the state, the civic services can ensure the provision of an adequate range of options. This is not the business of the communes, who are not entitled to influence the flow of the cultural marketplace. Note, though, that in contrast to what Kymlicka calls the 'social perfectionism' of liberal state neutrality, the social evaluation in NED is also a political process. Understanding the civic services in this way, as political bodies, a problem otherwise unsolved in liberal neutrality can be overcome. Although the latter can, as mentioned above, ensure the survival of worthy options that gain popular support, it cannot do the same for those equally worthy options that do not attract sufficient numbers of adherents. Rawls acknowledges that in a just constitution, some comprehensive conceptions will not survive. "No society can include within itself all forms of life" (1993: 197). This does not mean the political conception is arbitrarily biased against them, because the just basic structure provides a fair opportunity for all conceptions to maintain themselves. It simply means they cannot be preserved within the basic structure that justice as fairness articulates. Rawls expresses regret about this: "we may often want to say that the passing of certain ways of life is to be lamented. It is too optimistic to say that only unworthy ways of life lose out in a just constitutional regime" (2001: 154–5). But there is a danger here that a passive policy will not just let one worthy conception perish; it may be the fate of many, so much so that the cultural fabric will, as we have just seen, come to offer only a very limited range from which free and equal citizens can choose.[6] This would seriously undermine the exercise of Rawls' second moral power. There is, it seems, tension between Rawls' neutrality principle and what he calls the rational.

Public Forums

In terms of the organised public spaces needed for the shared evaluation of conceptions of the good, communitarians generally argue that the state is the most appropriate arena. Rawls denies this, claiming that collective enquiry is best achieved through the 'principle of free association' (1971: 328–9). So liberal neutrality does see the need for the evaluation of different options, but stresses that it should be approached socially, rather than politically. Liberal neutrality assumes a trust in non-state forums, and a suspicion towards those in the state. Here Kymlicka points out that "just as critics of neutrality have failed to defend their faith in politics, so liberals have failed to defend their faith in non-state forums" (2002: 251). Each side has failed to be moved by the genuine merits of the other. Liberals are rightly suspicious of the communitarian claim that the social is the domain of the political, that the use of coercive state power is wholly unsuited for the kind of deliberations that should continue to occur in civil society. For their part, communitarians are correct when they claim that a free culture is too fragile to sustain itself, that the survival of a diverse culture cannot simply be assumed. So for Kymlicka, each side raises valid concerns against the other. He concludes that both liberals and communitarians must provide a more thorough analysis of the strengths and weaknesses in both the political (state) and the social (civil society) territories for evaluating conceptions of the good (Kymlicka 1989: 899; 2002: 250–2).

Accordingly, he makes the following appeal:

> . . . before invoking the state as the arena for evaluating conceptions of the good, we should first improve the forums in civil society for non-politicized debate, so as to ensure that all groups in society have genuinely free and equal access to the cultural marketplace that liberals value so highly (Kymlicka 2002: 251–2).

The institutions that constitute the basic structure of NED are well suited for this task. As will now be clear, NED does not have a ridged divide between state and civil society, which relates to the communitarian assumption that what is social in the liberal sense should be subject to the political. Yet the liberal fear that the state, with its coercive apparatus, is a poor setting for collective deliberation also carries much weight. On this issue Kymlicka is right: a more robust defence of the diversified culture in civil society would strengthen the non-statist position. This is precisely the kind of defence I am in the process of substantiating. The civic services are the apposite institutions to host deliberations on the good. As differentiated decentralised organisations, the burdens of judgements, although still formidable, will become more manageable, or at least less unmanageable. They are also subject to a tighter degree of democratic accountability than one could ever expect to install in the larger and more remote structures of the state. An overall transparency in the formation of policy, a closer contact between elected officials and rank-and-file membership and a more appropriate public forum in which to elicit inclusive participation indicates that they are far more suited to accommodate evaluations of the good. The civic services, therefore, constitute the forums in civil society Kymlicka rightly calls for. NED rejects the communitarian assumption that the state is the most appropriate arena for evaluating understandings of the good, and, simultaneously, it differs from liberal civil society in that it sanctions political debate in the civil sphere. Only in this way can all groups enjoy, as Kymlicka puts it, a 'genuinely free and equal access to the cultural marketplace'.

Political Legitimacy

Taylor argues that state neutrality fails to support a common good. Citizens will only accept the legitimacy of the state in the light of a shared way of life, which is 'seen as a supremely important good'. "The common form of life has a status... when it is a crucial element in the members' identity" (1985b: 213). Such a common good is weakened in state neutrality, as people choose their lifestyles independent of state influence. For Taylor, a liberal culture of individual rights presupposes 'a distance from community decision-making' (1985b: 211). This threatens the legitimacy of liberal democracies as citizens are required to make the sacrifices justice demands, yet they share increasingly less with their fellow citizens who benefit from these sacrifices. For Rawls though the burdens of justice will be tolerated by all citizens, even where conceptions of the good conflict, because there is a shared endorsement of the two principles of justice. "A political conception", he suggests, "helps us reach political agreement on at least the constitutional essentials and the basic questions of justice", which ensures that "political cooperation on the basis of mutual respect can be maintained" (1993: 105). In contrast, Taylor reasons that citizens will only respect each others' claims if they share understandings of the good. The maintenance of the communitarian common good could, however, effectively increase the exclusion of already marginalised groups. On some communitarian accounts, minority groups will be required to revise their ways of life so that they become compatible with dominant values. These groups typically do not have the power to resist the demands of the mainstream. This prompts Kymlicka to claim that "surely liberal neutrality has the great advantage of its potential inclusiveness, and its denial that subordinated groups must fit into the 'way of life' that has been defined by the dominant groups" (2002: 260). Nevertheless, he also stresses that political principles held in common go some way towards securing political unity, but on their own they are not enough. Citizens need to feel a sense of belonging and common identity to supplement the shared principles of justice. What exactly can do this, though, "is one of the great unresolved questions of contemporary political philosophy" (2002: 257). So, in terms of sustaining social unity and legitimacy, Kymlicka rejects both the liberal faith in shared principles of justice and the communitarian belief in the politics of the common good. Rather, society needs more than liberal principles, but not enough to constitute a particular conception of the good. "This is", he immediately adds, "an immensely difficult theoretical question" (Kymlicka 2002: 252–3, 259–61; Taylor 1985b: 211, 213).

Sketching the institutional contours of NED is, in effect, to formulate an answer to this question. In my opinion Rawls is right that citizens must be free to choose their conceptions of the good independently of state influence. A state endorsed common good is liable to subordinate minority interest. Yet the communitarian critique that the legitimacy of political liberalism is undermined as citizens will come to have less in common with each other is equally correct. Rawls' political principles are, as suggested in the previous section and directly above, by themselves insufficient to sustain a common identity and political unity. The political arrangements that sustain the overlapping consensus need to be far tighter, and more intensely felt, than they are in political liberalism. In this regard, the communitarian proposition that a shared notion of the good is required for political legitimacy carries some weight. In the discussions that follow, there will be recourse to consider further the sense in which NED adds substance, and by implication political legitimacy, to Rawls' common ground. In other words, the 'great unresolved' question will be addressed. By way of preliminary discussion, I would like to reiterate that Rawls' political liberalism does have a community ethic, even if it is not as prominent as communitarians generally desire. Likewise, in response to the communitarian argument that a conception of the good which happens to be communal in content and which treats social bonds as intrinsically valuable tends to be subordinated by liberals, it should be emphasised that Rawls' political liberalism does have a common good, and can accommodate these conceptions, at least partially. Liberal justice, understood as safeguarding the freedom and autonomy of individuals, is a common good (2001: 199–200). Furthermore, as it allows smaller groups to exist, political liberalism's 'potential inclusiveness' enhances this common good and hence a sense of community.

So the issue is not that Rawls' principles of justice do not elicit a sense of community; they do. The real problem is, given liberal egalitarianism's justified dislike of the state, how to construct non-state measures that may serve to realise more vibrant and deeply felt community relations without creating a leviathan. How to create a 'thicker' conception of the political that can enhance Rawls' overlapping consensus without oppressing minority interests. My answer to these demanding questions is to theorise a political civil society that circumscribes the role of the state to the greatest possible extent. In NED the political arrangements are structured on the key premise that the state is not, initially, the means by which people help each other. Its institutions are too removed for citizens to feel any kind of personal connection. As a distant body, the task of subjecting state procedures to democratic accountability is also hugely problematic. In Chapters Three and Four it was argued that a society which upholds the functional principle as its demarcating criterion, and in the process transcends the state–civil society divide, offers the best hope for democracy to survive in large modern societies. It is in this institutional setting that political principles can be more profoundly experienced; this precipitates a sense of belonging and social unity that makes the sacrifices justice entails more tolerable, without simultaneously giving rise to a potentially oppressive communitarian politics of the common good. Only in this way can the liberal principles of justice be enhanced without engendering a particular conception of the good life.

Moderate Neutrality in the Civic Services

The dispute between the neutrality and the perfectionist ideals is a debate that has become central to liberal theory. NED seeks to uphold the principle of liberty explicitly, and in common with the liberal doctrine, aims to establish the proper limits to which the state can apply its coercive power. The neutrality-perfectionist contention, therefore, has an immediate relevance to how NED's political structures are theorised. But in contrast to liberalism, NED has no rigid divide between the state and civil society. Inasmuch, the neutrality-perfectionism debate takes on a different form; the dynamics involved in a re-politicised civil society affect it profoundly. As such, this section reiterates and elaborated the position NED adopts. This is done through three sub-sections: 'Neutrality and Perfectionism', 'Controlling a Non-Coercive Perfectionism' and 'Functional Organisations and the Revisability Principle'. The first sub-section establishes the degree of overlap which exists between the two ideals, and, hence, why the adoption of certain non-coercive perfectionist measures need not violate a principle of moderate neutrality. This informs the discussion in the second sub-section, which is self-explanatory. Finally, the third sub-section stresses that the demarcated nature of functional organisations ensures that they are in the optimal position to sustain Rawls' second moral power.

Neutrality and Perfectionism

To reconfirm, the neutrality-perfectionism debate revolves around whether the state should, on the one hand, take no stand in regard to the various conceptions of the good, or, on the other hand, whether it should encourage valid conceptions and discourage those that are not. Proponents of neutrality like Rawls argue that the state must remain neutral in this regard, whereas all perfectionists agree that it is legitimate for the state to advance human excellence. The divide between the two though, especially within the liberal perspective, is not always clear. For example, the impression that non-perfectionist liberalism is premised upon perfectionist assumptions has a long history in critiques of neutrality:

> Critics claimed that proponents of state neutrality violate its own constraints by appealing to particular values, including the values of a liberal society. Democracy, a respect for individual rights, and a measure of social justice carry with them particular value commitments that are not neutral between all conceptions of the good (Wall and Klosko 2003: 14).

Liberal principles may not force citizens' choices, but, the critique goes, they predetermine the boundaries within which acceptable choices fall. On the other side of the debate, an immediate concern about the perfectionist state is that, as it will command excessive coercive power, individual freedom will be undermined. Proponents of 'liberal perfectionism', however, have responded that they also want to curtail state action, and that state coercion is an ineffective way to uphold a particular good—a position which is not wholly removed from the neutrality principle. Raz (1986), for example, claims that perfectionism is not incompatible with modern value pluralism. The state should establish the conditions in which its citizens pursue a host of activities, but it should not forcefully advance a sole understanding of the good. Ever since Raz claimed that perfectionist politics may be non-coercive, the lines between a neutral and a perfectionist state have become blurred. For Raz, perfectionist politics can be harmonised with some of the assertions that elicit support for the neutrality principle. The distinction can also be loosened for other reasons, too. Kymlicka (1989), an advocate of state neutrality, proposes that the application of short-term state intervention in an attempt to encourage people to sample worthy ways of life is not 'inherently unacceptable'. "Hence a comprehensive defence of neutrality may need to focus on a prior stage of state perfectionism" (1989: 902; Raz 1986: 398–9; Wall and Klosko 2003: 15–8).

If the neutrality principle can be moderated so that a richer and more diverse culture materialises, and in a way that does not drastically revise the basic structure justice as fairness articulates, then why not allow it? It seems strange to allow a valuable and worthwhile way of life to wither away by adhering rigidly to an ideological standpoint. I wish to propose then that the civic services be granted the power to assist certain options that are in need of support. So long as they apply this power evenly, i.e., not on an ad hoc basis but following an objective criterion, they can establish a diverse culture in which the second moral power can be exercised more fully, and without abandoning the general commitment to neutrality. This could be carried out in a way that negates the threat of majoritarian bias:

> One might . . . argue that state subsidies devoted to supporting worthy forms of life should be allocated on a consociational process where a decision is passed only if it is supported by all of the cultural communities. Were state subsidies for valuable forms of life to be allocated according to a principle of unanimity of two-thirds majority, a dominant group would only be able to allocate money to itself with the consent of a minority. Thus the minority will be able to bargain for funds for its way of life (Caney 1991: 476).

Although in NED state (commune) subsidies are managed by the civic services, this method serves as a useful guide to the funding of worthy pursuits. The 'pluralistic perfectionism' that Caney describes—"there is no single correct conception of the good and there are many worthy ways of living. It is the duty of the state to promote these various diverse ways of life" (1991: 467)—can, when the varied lifestyles are promoted non-coercively by political bodies in civil society, be seen as the middle ground between the extremes of neutrality and perfectionism.[7] It is on this position that the political arrangements in NED's civic services are modelled.

Controlling a Non-Coercive Perfectionism

The sustainability of a diverse cultural marketplace of ideals of the good, indispensable to the fulfilment of Rawls' second moral power, requires a loosening of the neutrality principle so that certain soft perfectionist methods can be taken advantage of. But if the principle of moderate neutrality upheld in the civic services is to include a monitored measure of non-coercive perfectionism, how exactly is it to be controlled? This question can be answered through a discussion of personal autonomy. Perfectionists like Raz (1986, 1996) stress that autonomy has value only if the available pursuits are worthwhile. When the state undermines undesirable options, it may limit citizen autonomy to some degree, but not their opportunity to conduct a *worthy* autonomous life. The benefit of outlawing Class A drugs must be weighed against the loss of the drug user's autonomy. But if autonomy is treated as *a good*, rather than *the good*, then restrictive measures may seem warranted. Criminalising worthless and dangerous options like drug use will not affect the chances of leading a valuable autonomous life. Perfectionist politics will deliberately attempt to steer people in the direction of worthy options and away from those it deems valueless. Clearly this affects citizens' relationships with their political societies. These relationships worry state neutralists like Rawls, who argue that the coercive power of the state must be equally justifiable to all citizens. Some perfectionists, however, share the concern that all citizens should feel as though they are full members of their societies. Raz belongs to this school of thought. "The existence within a political society of estranged groups, who do not identify with the state, or the nation, and regard the government as an alien, potentially hostile, government, is destabilizing" (1996: 124–5). Feeling a part of, and identifying with, a community is, for Raz, an 'essential ingredient in people's well-being' (Raz 1986: 378–81; 1996: 124–5; Wall and Klosko 2003:18–20).

For instance, if the state upheld Christianity on the belief that other religious sentiments are for some reason detrimental to the good life, advocates of the latter would find it difficult to relate to the state. The likelihood is that they would value their religion higher than their political identity and, as a consequence, they could not regard themselves as distinct members of the society in which they are governed, and as this is often seen as a key component of what it means to lead a good life, it is obstructed by the state's sectarian stance towards non-Christian religion. This argument should interest both the state perfectionist and the state neutralist. "If an otherwise valid perfectionist measure were to make it impossible for some citizens reasonably to view themselves as full members of their society, then the measure might be unjustified" (Wall and Klosko 2003: 20). As citizens have interests in not being marginalised or separated from their political societies, these, as Wall and Klosko suggest, can be called 'alienation costs'. "Policies that make it reasonable for some to view themselves as second-class citizens would have high alienation costs" (2003: 20). Here the perfectionist may recognize that there are often perfectionist grounds for constraining perfectionist political objectives. So the need to ensure that citizens are not alienated places limits upon the state's power to uphold the good. Liberal perfectionism, so understood, is not wholly at odds with state neutrality. Both positions harbour concerns that when state's attempts to advance the good are too intensive, the resulting alienation will undermine citizens' ability to conduct good lives (Wall and Klosko 2003: 20–1).

Theorising the political structures in NED in the way I have contributes to this discussion. The first thing to re-stress is that it is not the business of the communes to determine the movement of the cultural marketplace. This task falls to the civic services. As citizens are free to make their own choices, when the civic services prioritise certain options, they must still respect personal autonomy. This places limits upon their power. The civic guilds and civic councils are the public spaces in which the likelihood of policies marginalising citizens from their political society can be democratically assessed. On the grounds of moderate neutrality, their non-coercive perfectionist politics can be restricted. The differentiated functional bodies in the civic services will determine when a perfectionist policy is more likely to cause alienation costs.[8] In light of the unavoidable reference to complex material and factual information, they are more suited for this task than when the distant liberal state attempts the same on undifferentiated bases. In previous chapters I outlined the advantages of functionally demarcating key interests inherent in all citizens. Democratic accountability, transparency in political decision making and restricting the burdens of judgements were among those cited. The same can be said here.

Functional Organisations and the Revisability Principle

NED's non-state political forums provide for the exercise of Rawls' second moral power. This can be appreciated by taking another look at the representative ethic NED subscribes to. The totality of the functional organisations—the productive and civic guilds, and the two consumer and two civic councils—represent only a *certain aspect* of individuals' lives. This proposition informs my entire system building. NED does not make the fundamental mistake the mass political party system makes. Rather than assume *individuals* can be represented, it denies this emphatically. It is, from my perspective, only *interests* that can be represented. Differentiated organisations which are restricted to accommodating a certain set of demarcated interests cannot possibly be mistaken for comprehensive doctrines. Comprehensive doctrines are exactly that, comprehensive; the religious doctrines which present themselves as all-embracing bodies of knowledge and seek to directly influence all aspects of their followers' lives are examples of this. Functional organisations on the other hand are concerned with interests that are particular; they are deliberately and self-consciously limited in their scope of representation. A manufacturing guild, for example, will not seek to control what its associates do in their leisure. Likewise, a consumer council has no interest in how its members earn their living. Functional associations are not, so to speak, comprehensive. Inasmuch as they respect explicitly the freedom of their members to choose their own conception of the good, they can accommodate the values of liberal egalitarianism. In some respects this resembles Rawls' liberal state. As will now be clear, in cases of impasse between the functionally demarcated organisations, the communes will be required to adjudicate. As unresolved disputes are between bodies, neither of which are comprehensive doctrines, the commune's action will fall within the common ground articulated by Rawls. Both POD and NED are committed to defending the overlapping consensus. There is a mutual recognition that a comprehensive doctrine that intentionally and systematically denies its members access to choose their own conception of the good requires legitimate political intervention to assure their provision. NED differs from POD though in the respect that in the latter this task falls to the state and in the former it is entrusted to the interacting functional bodies.

An example will help clarify how the freedom to assert Rawls' second moral power may be preserved in the absence of a sovereign state. In the case of education, the education guild is responsible for providing the service, whereas the cultural council has the task of representing citizens in their capacity as students, of all types and ages. These two bodies will determine—as with the formation of all other policies in NED—through consultation the local, regional and national curriculum. There is, however, a potential difficulty with this structural arrangement. Although neither functional organisation is a comprehensive doctrine, if the educational institutions in a locality sought to introduce closed schemes of learning, i.e., where only one religious, political, ideological, etc., perspective is taught, and / or is held to be above critique, and if the corresponding cultural council failed to assert the necessary corrective, this would, in effect, be a step towards a comprehensive doctrine. In this instance the political structures in NED would have failed to sustain the revisability principle. Although such an event is highly unlikely, the problem in principle remains. How then might this problem be solved? In Chapter Three it was acknowledged that in some cases centralisation is not just necessary, it is desirable. The issue we are now discussing is another case in point. The insistence that the curriculum must incorporate courses and modules in which the right to question, criticise and oppose is regarded as absolute is a directive that must come from the national bodies of the inter-acting educational guilds and cultural councils. Although the localities will still have significant space in which to gauge the supply and demand of certain programmes, none will involve doctrines that are beyond critical scrutiny. In all cases open debate will be mandatory. The local branches of the guilds and councils will not be within their statutory rights to amend this aspect of NED's constitution. Admittedly, this will decree a measure of centralisation, but in the interests of sustaining the freedom to choose one's own conception of the good, it is excusable. So if this is how the civic services will operate, what is the precise role of the communes?

Neutrality in the Commune System

It is now clear what, in a political sense, falls outside the communes' constitutional boundaries. The first section in this passage established that civil society is the apposite arena in which to evaluate conceptions of the good. The previous section then argued that a moderate neutrality position is the appropriate standpoint from which the civic services will operate. This section continues this discussion. It is shown why a similar position is applicable to the commune system, only this time it is defined in narrower terms. It is important to reiterate that the difference between a moderate neutrality (in civil society) and neutrality (in the state) is more in degree of emphasis, rather than in form. This should not strike the reader as odd; NED has, after all, transcended the state–civil society dualism. The first of two sections, 'A Sophisticated Neutrality Principle', introduces Klosko's (2003) elaborate neutrality principle and explains why it is practically suited to the communes. The second section, 'Substantiating the Overlapping Consensus', confirms that Rawls' common ground is secured more thoroughly in NED.

A Sophisticated Neutrality Principle

It was argued in the second part of the previous chapter that although the substance of sovereignty has been redefined, the local, regional and national communes are, as high level co-ordinating bodies and final courts of appeal, still to exercise sovereign power in cases of impasse. I have now corroborated that they will adhere to a principle of neutrality in their deliberations. Given that there are problems with neutrality, in particular that when applied strictly it is in danger of ruling out too much, the question arises how the communes' decision making will proceed. Perhaps the most promising approach is to redefine the neutrality method by which arguments can be objectively assessed. This is essentially the approach of Klosko (2003). He adheres to an ideal of neutrality in which state action is permissible if it cannot be 'reasonably rejected'. His neutrality principle, therefore, establishes standards of argument that serve to justify state (commune) policies. To substantiate the notion of reasonable rejection, adequate standards of argument are needed, those that are reliable and publicly obtainable. Inasmuch, neutrality favours methods of argument and forms of reasoning that are generally accessible to the public and broadly adhered to. "Pride of place is therefore given to empirical science, common modes of logical inference, and other forms of arguments that are demonstrable and replicable" (Klosko 2003: 170). This is a similar position to Rawls' (1993: 223–7). The neutrality endorsed is a neutrality of justification; citizens should only be exposed to state coercion if the reasons for it are accepted by themselves. He is clear on what is to count as unreasonable. "The particular focus of neutrality is rejection of arguments because of their dependence on comprehensive views. A given value or mode of reasoning objectionably rests on a specific comprehensive view if it cannot be supported without reference to the latter" (Klosko 2003: 168). With this as his yardstick, Klosko addresses the question of whether neutrality disqualifies too much. Can any value claim be regarded as beyond reasonable rejection? His response is to establish the value claims that it is indeed reasonable to reject (Klosko 2003: 168–70).

Political life involves choosing between values that, however conceptualised, are usually in tension and can be compromised in different ways. Yet as long as they are non-sectarian, neutrality will allow them. Some controversies do not threaten neutrality if arguments from both sides can be substantiated through methods acceptable to many comprehensive doctrines. In some cases two competing claims will be equally neutral, and here democratic processes are required as the means by which choices are made. Indeed, establishing priorities between non-sectarian values is a key role of democracy. Justifying neutral policies requires the satisfaction of an adequacy criterion. As the fulfilment of a given value involves trade-offs with competing values, a sound argument is required to meet the 'justificatory burden'. There is often more than one conception of a value—those that are neutral, and those that are not. Klosko pictures a continuum, at one end are the non-controversial values, at the other are the values unique to comprehensive views:

> Neutrality, of course, requires that a given public policy be justified by values from the neutral side of the continuum. The adequacy requirement entails that the specific conception of the value in question should be sufficient to support the trade-offs it requires (Klosko 2003: 180).

Dichotomising neutral from non-neutral values is an awkward and complex task, and in addition, citizens will not agree about proposed trade-offs. So in this regard, democratic decision making procedures are essential (Klosko 2003: 177–80).

Klosko's argument makes good sense; in particular he demonstrates why the neutrality principle is inseparable from democracy. As such, when the communes in NED are required to adjudicate, they will implement his notion of reasonable rejection. They will refer to the modes of reasoning and a form of argument that are publicly accessible, and not on value claims that can only be supported by reference to comprehensive views. Their task is to distinguish sectarian from neutral values, and only allow the latter to inform their decisions. Through this method they will determine the cases in which any views have been treated harshly by the policies of the civic services. By restricting the range of values that proponents on both sides of a given contention can invoke, and by highlighting the kind of trade-offs accepted, the neutrality of the communes can give prominence to the nature of disputes. Klosko concludes that the neutrality principle will not settle conflicts, but it will place limits upon the considerations that can be reasonably introduced. This neutrality principle, I agree, offers a practical method by which a fair and open decision making procedure can advance. "In eliminating appeals to conceptions of the good and ruling out sectarian modes of reasoning, neutrality narrows the grounds of disagreement" (Klosko 2003: 178). All the time citizens invoke acceptable values, those that are not associated with particular comprehensive doctrines, neutrality provides a useful framework within which deliberations can take place (Klosko 2003: 178, 182). So in cases of impasse, the communes will retain the right to overrule an unjust proposal, or to send an issue back to the offending body for amendment. In this sense decision making in the communes, as in the civic services, will go some way to ensure the often complex issues of 'moderate neutrality' and 'soft perfectionism' are at least made more transparent, and this counts for much.

Finally, it may be objected that, in allowing the civic services to implement a controlled non-coercive perfectionist measure, NED cannot sustain the moderate neutrality ideal it claims to subscribe to. There is, the critic may insist, an awkward tension between the narrow neutrality of the commune system and the moderate neutrality of the civic services. It should be remembered, though, that they are ascribed different functions: the former is a sovereign appeal court and the latter is a designated public forum for political deliberation. It should also be noted that the existence of non-neutral values in civil society is precisely the reason why the need for a neutral state has been theorised.[9] Rawls too recognises that perfectionist ideals are important to the free internal life of communities, that they are in accordance with the 'principle of free association' (1971: 328–9, 543). Nevertheless, it is still possible that, as with all approaches which attempt to incorporate or synthesize neutral and perfectionist measures, a tension of sorts may remain. Wall and Klosko conclude that, despite the ambiguous overlaps between perfectionism and neutrality, they still depart. For example, "not every perfectionist measure brings with it significant alienation costs [explained above], and those measures that do may yield benefits that justify the costs" (2003: 18–21). I would only add that a blueprint for the good society that is finalised in every detail is likely to be dogmatic. Therefore, any tension is, hopefully, creative, and subject to amendment upon further analysis.

Substantiating the Overlapping Consensus

It can now be explained how the role of the neutral commune system in NED differs from the role of Rawls' neutral state. Like the state in Rawlsian society, it is illegitimate for the commune to self-consciously advance comprehensive conceptions of the good. Like the state in Rawlsian society, on the occasions when the commune is called to act, it must be justified by reference to the common ground, i.e. the values of freedom, equality and justice—and not to promote particular non-political values. Like the state in Rawlsian society, the communes, when their capacity as final courts of appeal is exercised, provide the backdrop in which freedom and justice are realised. And like the state in Rawlsian society, the commune's coercive power may be used only when those forced to comply regard it as just. So, there is much in common with these two body politics. In terms of legitimate state-commune action, both adhere to a thin theory of politics. The differences are in relation to the organisations called upon to secure justice. In NED the civil realm has been re-politicised. Citizenship identity is therefore potentially more comprehensive; what people have in common is treated more extensively. This, as will now be clear, is necessary to sufficiently constitute people's identities as citizens. In relation to the scope for commune action, the theory of politics is even thinner than Rawls' thin theory. Yet in relation to society as a whole, as NED has no rigid divide between state and civil society, the conception of the political is thicker. The general idea is to construct a thick theory which does not bring forth a formidable and intimidating state. In terms of distributive justice, the guilds and the IGC are responsible for satisfying the requirements of the difference principle. In regard to the freedom of citizens to frame and seek their own conceptions of the good, whether in their capacities as producer, consumer, education, health and cultural affairs, there are institutional bodies through which particular conceptions can be pursued. These are all rights of citizenship. By minimising the role of the commune to the greatest extent possible, and simultaneously enlarging the intermediate organisations like the economic and civic guilds, the two consumer councils and the cultural and health councils, politics is brought closer to the individual citizen. In this decentralised institutional setting, a community able to foster the liberal values Rawls defends is brought a significant step closer.

There is nothing wrong with liberal values, and Rawls is basically right to assert that their subordination is unreasonable. My argument is simply that they will be realised with less difficulty in NED. Following Rawls' example, NED will safeguard the opportunity for everyone to pursue their own idea of the good life. The difference is that in Rawlsian society it is the state that may legitimately intervene with the particular communities that do not respect the values of liberal individualism. In NED this task will not initially fall to the commune, but will be resolved through dialogue between the relevant functional bodies. In cases of impasse, when the commune is called to act, it will, like the Rawlsian state, be unsympathetic to certain particularistic communities. The comprehensive doctrines that regard themselves as complete and closed bodies of knowledge will not be treated with privilege. Although the religious devotee may be disappointed, articles of faith and dogmas can, along with deeply felt secular sentiments, be evaluated through the civic services. These constitutional institutions will not attempt to prevent associates from practising the way of life they freely choose. They will though have the lawful authority to uphold, with coercion if necessary, a person's right to query particular customs and traditions. In this respect I emulate Rawls explicitly.

To summarise, Rawls' political overlapping consensus makes practical good sense, and NED will implement it fully. More than this, the institutional arrangements in NED ensure that the common ground is reinforced, yet more easily sustained than in POD. NED augments the overlapping consensus through two structural innovations. Firstly, by installing non-alienating co-operative labour at the constitutional convention, and hence making it a basic right of the first principle, consumer interests also fall within the basic remit of citizenship rights, they are not determined through the prerogatives of personal wealth; and secondly, by politically charging civil society so that a culture that provides for the full exercise of the second moral power can be democratically sustained. As explained above, many worthy conceptions of the good are not self-supporting, and in the absence of political interventions of some kind, a depleted and impoverished cultural marketplace threatens the exercise of what Rawls calls the rational. To compensate, the civic services will, through the implementation of controlled non-coercive perfectionist measures, provide an adequate range of options. These two sets of political arrangements ensure that citizens have far more in common in NED than in POD. The question now becomes whether the thicker conception of the political in NED seriously violates the neutrality ideal. That is, does its substantiated conception of the political invoke what Rawls would regard as controversial comprehensive values?

3. Co-Operative Non-Alienating Labour and the Overlapping Consensus

In NED the overlapping consensus is reinforced, in conjunction with the political civic services just discussed, through the implementation of a democratised economy which incorporates non-alienating co-operative labour.[10] This is a key part of my conception of the political. As argued in the previous chapter, it is only through these institutional arrangements that Rawls' two principles of justice can be adequately satisfied. In a just society all, or nearly all, citizens will be producers or will provide a service, and, equally, all will obviously be consumers. NED democratises this relationship by providing structural spaces in which dialogue between the two demarcated interests is sanctioned. This is the fundamental criteria with which the scheme is formulated. The most immediate objection is likely to be that as this arrangement invokes values that require a comprehensive interpretation—that elevating non-alienating co-operative labour over alienating wage-labour, or indeed any other labour relations, betrays the neutrality ideal—NED is no longer compatible with a Rawlsian political conception of justice. And if not, NED's conception of 'the right' could justifiably be called into question. This is a far more complex question than it may initially appear, but the charge can, I think, be denied to a significant extent. If communication between producers and consumers is enough to constitute a comprehensive notion of the good, then all societies that have ever existed or are ever likely to, including political liberalism, are comprehensive, plain and simple. The charge must go further, it must assert that in prioritising the comprehensive values of co-operative and non-alienating labour, other conceptions of the good are unavoidably disadvantaged; if it did this, it would become controversial, and hence violate the neutrality principle articulated in the previous section. My task in this section is to construct a reply that accusations of this kind are mistaken.

In order to show why NED is sympathetic to the general spirit of Marx's early writing, whilst simultaneously softening the endorsement of the productive realm, Marx's critique of alienation and his notion of 'species-being' are introduced. It is then shown why Rawls' political liberalism would reject Marx's polemic on the grounds that it incorporates comprehensive values. Building upon this, the liberal objection that elevating non-alienated labour as the foremost human good subordinate leisure and consumptive values is then established. Finally, in responding to the latter two critiques, the argument that NED can answer these questions within a moderate neutrality framework is presented. There are four sections to this passage, 'Marx's Critique of Alienated Labour', 'Intrinsic and Instrumental Values', 'Non-Productive Values' and 'New Economic Democracy and Marxist-Humanism'.

Marx's Critique of Alienated Labour

Marx begins his discussion on alienated labour by declaring a 'fact' of political economy: in the process of creating wealth, workers are impoverished. Implicit here are the assumptions that labour is the source of all wealth, and that workers' wages will drop to mere subsistence level. These 'laws' of political economy are not directly willed by the workers they regulate. Thus workers cannot, he insists, be considered free. People are not masters controlling their own fates, but slaves to the economic infrastructure they have brought into existence. So the society of alienated labour has no autonomy. Rather, individuals' lives are determined unintentionally by the kind of collective activity which is structured by impersonal exchange relations. In *Economic and Philosophical Manuscripts* (EPM) (1844) and *Notes on James Mill* (1844), Marx argues that a person's subjectivity is a function of his or her relationship with external nature (essential to which is the means of production), and with others. It is this subjectivity which is alienated by wage-labour. Alienation from peoples' 'human essence' therefore means their subjectivity—in respects of their physical and intellectual energies, our work capacity—is removed from them. In this separation material objects are not just things, they become incorporated in the objectification of human subjectivity. The product of labour takes the shape of an alien object, which becomes a power independent of the producers, and then dominates them. In the actual process of producing, workers externalise basic human attributes, thereby objectifying humanity. Marx stresses that when people produce just to exchange, they do not relate to each others' objects as human beings because they themselves do not relate in a human way to those they produce. Workers exchange labour power for wages, and in the process alienate themselves from their producing activities and their products, including the exchange value of these products. Workers also become alienated from each other and from their own social being because they do not contribute in any significant or meaningful way to the planning of production. Consequently they do not come to identify with universal interests. So in 'estranged' (wage) labour, the labourer's essence is objectified and alienated. The key point in *EPM* is that the workers' estrangement is the separation of social relationships from themselves. Marx's argument is that workers transfer to something else (god, political state or in *Capital* the inhuman power of capital—all of which assume an independent entity) that which is essential to their nature, to control their own activities and hence initiate historical processes. It is important to add that for Marx the process of objectification may be positive or negative, depending on the particular social relations of production in which it occurs. He concludes that in order to realise a sense of species being, or communal creativity, there is a need to end the system of commodity exchange in a distant market (Marx 1975: 282–7, 295–303, 327–30; Colletti 1975: 50–2, 54; Levine 2002: 234–7).

Marx dislikes markets because commodity exchange in capitalist society alienates peoples' human existence from their essence, their own creative powers. His concept of work attempts to capture this essence, or species being. This term refers to how, in the appropriate productive process, peoples' creative and free activity, in co-operation with their fellows, could be given expression, and how genuine control over the process of self-creation can be sanctioned. People act as a species being when they produce for others in order to satisfy their needs, so consciously directing labour. In this process of creative self-activity, when they see others appreciating their products, they feel fulfilled. There is a conscious understanding of the needs of others. This, as Marx puts it, is to produce in a 'human manner' (Marx 1977: 121–2). Under the system of private property, producers give to others only for exchange. Such exchanges are conditional: individuals expect something in return. Here there is no personal use-value; that is, if a person produces something s/he does not want, it is only to get something else back. Alienated labour, so understood, is to produce something of no interest to oneself. Relations are based around private property owners, not as species being. Products are in private hands, the exchange is one of private properties. So although exchange (or interchange) *is* human species activity, all the time it takes place within the framework of private property it is alienated species-activity (Marx 1977: 114–8; McLellan 1986: 34).

Marx's concept of the alienated products of labour is, as McLellan (1971) explains, expressed in what Marx calls in *Capital* the 'fetishism of commodities'. Here Marx tries to demonstrate that in commodity societies, products generate an independent and anti-human power. As with alienation, the fetishism of commodities emerges when products are exchanged in an impersonal market. Peoples' values become largely centred on appearances, things and what they are worth. The problem with fetishism is that it does not recognise the social relations which created these appearances. Commodities, as independent things which have only achieved their status through complex social relations, are given values and then appear to interact with each other and with people, whereupon they seem to have a life of their own. The relations of producers to their own labour appears in their eyes as a social relation existing between products, and not between themselves. Relations between people secured through the act of exchange are hence *indirect*, and are channelled through *direct* relations to commodities:

> Since the producers do not come into social contact with each other until they exchange their products, the specific social character of each producer's labour does not show itself except in the act of exchange . . . the relations connecting the labour of one individual with that of the rest appear, not as direct social relations between individuals at work, but as what they really are . . . social relations between things (Marx 1977: 436–7).

Individuals remain separated from each other and from the general interest. The chief form of social relations is based around commodities, but this means that the real social processes, *including the manner in which labour is exploited*, remains concealed (Marx 1977: 435–6; McLellan 1971: xxxvii, xii; Howard 2000: 77–9).

In general, the statement that humans are alienated from their species life means that each person is alienated from others, and that likewise each other is alienated from human life. They are also alienated from the essence of humanity, from their species being. To recap, alienation, according to Marx, takes four forms: from the object of production, from fellow workmates, from themselves and thereby from humanity. The labour process is outside the control of the worker. Private property of the means of production is detrimental to the development of human beings' most distinctive capacities. Alienation entails that work becomes a means rather than an end, giving rise to the indifference of the labourer to the nature of his/her labour. Since its availability to the Western world from the 1930s, the young Marx's theory of alienation has been the subject of prolonged analysis. For my purposes, I will concentrate mainly on its status as a comprehensive doctrine. Indeed, a common interpretation is that it is an example of perfectionist reasoning (Arneson 1987: 520; Elster 1986: 97). Marxist-humanism would organise work relations in order to realise human excellences. The particular way of life encouraged is a free and creative productive sphere, in which self-realisation is achieved through co-operative labour. For Marxists, this ideal can be satisfied by socialising productive assets and eradicating wage-labour. Joyful creative labour is regarded as the fundamental end, the highest human want. The next section demonstrates why Rawls would consider this position to be incompatible with political liberalism.

Intrinsic and Instrumental Values

Rawls makes clear that the right and the good are complementary; a political conception of justice needs both. Just institutions and political virtues must sustain conceptions of the good that people regard as worthy. "In a phrase, the just draws the limit, the good shows the point" (2001: 141). Prioritising the right implies that only the conceptions of the good that are compatible with justice as fairness can be pursued. From here, Rawls draws a distinction between civic humanism and classical republicanism, stressing that justice as fairness is consistent with the latter but not the former. The first perspective stresses the intrinsic value of political participation, the second points to its instrumental reasons. The civic humanist position is that people are political beings whose inner nature is realised through participating democratically in political life:

> This participation is encouraged not merely as possibly necessary for the protection of basic liberties but because it is the privileged locus of our (complete) good. This makes it a comprehensive philosophical doctrine and as such incompatible with justice as fairness as a political conception of justice (2001: 142–3).

Rawls explains that the rejection of civic humanism does not carry with it the denial that engaging in political life is a good, even a 'great' good, only that it is not, for all citizens, the 'chief' or the 'sole' good. A significant number of people, possibly the majority, find political life uninteresting or onerous. The need for political participation is to ensure that the state respects the freedom of citizens to pursue happiness in their family, work and leisure lives. Political participation has, he insists, "a lesser place in the conceptions of the (complete) good of most citizens" (2001: 143). It is, unsurprisingly, the classical republican view that Rawls endorses. This position holds that citizens' participation is needed, not to express their human essence, but to help maintain democratic liberties. The instrumental virtues of political participation are valued because they help sustain the essentials of liberal democracy:

> The idea is that unless there is widespread participation in democratic politics by a vigorous and informed citizen body moved in good part by a concern for political justice and public good, even the best-designed political institutions will eventually fall into the hands of those who hunger for power and military glory, or pursue narrow class and economic interests, to the exclusion of almost everything else. (2001: 144).

The important point for Rawls is that as classical republicanism does not incorporate comprehensive values, it is fully compatible with justice as fairness, understood as a form of political liberalism (2001: 140–4). Although Rawls is discussing political values in the wider sense, rather than directly in terms of production as Marx does, it is evident why he would regard Marx's appeal that productive relations must be arranged in order to give full realisation to our species-being as incompatible with justice as fairness; it is, as Rawls would correctly insist, a comprehensive philosophical anthropology.

Non-Productive Values

Kymlicka raises a similar point in relation to non-productive values. He begins though by affirming the attractiveness of creative labour. The degradation of labour that many workers in capitalism are subjected to is, he declares, 'abhorrent'. Yet although he stresses that creative labour *is* preferable to alienated labour, there are, he adds, other values, like pleasure in leisure and consumption, that appeal to people. Work of some kind is needed to fund them, and 'all else being equal', we would like it to be meaningful. But, he insists, 'all else is not equal'. Dull, repetitive and boring labour may produce more items in a shorter space of time than creative labour. If so, the latter is simply more time-consuming, and therefore conflicts with the desired leisure and consumptive values. "The question, then, is not whether I prefer unalienated labour to alienated labour, but whether I prefer leisure so much that I would accept alienated labour in order to acquire it" (Kymlicka 2002: 192). Along the same lines, many people get immense pleasure from their capacities as consumers. "Agreeing to perform alienated labour in return for higher wages may enable them to expand their range of desired consumption" (Kymlicka 2002: 192). Abolishing alienated labour could inhibit this pursuit. So for Kymlicka:

> The issue is not whether unalienated labour is a good, but whether it is an overriding good, a good which is necessary to any decent life, and which outweighs in value all competing goods. I see no reason to think unalienated labour is such a good (Kymlicka 2002: 192).

The pursuit of these other values, he concludes, contradicts with creative production. As such, abolishing alienated labour advances, unfairly, one value before others. Likewise, Arneson (1987) observes that conceptions of the good spread out 'in all directions'. "Some seek mystic ecstasy, some suburbia and its comforts, some intellectual and artistic achievement, some varieties of physical culture, and so on, endlessly" (Arneson 1987: 524). His claim is that when a particular notion of the good, intrinsic job satisfaction, arbitrarily subordinates other equally desirable categories of the good, it is unfair to those whose preferences lie elsewhere (Kymlicka 2002: 191–3; Arneson 1987: 524–6). If this is the case, then prioritising creative labour would, quite blatantly, violate the neutrality ideal.

New Economic Democracy and Marxist-Humanism

There is some substance to the critiques covered in the above two sections. Marx does regard the appropriate transformation of the productive sphere as humanity's prime objective, and without revisions to his theory, organising society to satisfy peoples' species being would invoke a comprehensive value. As explained above, his view is that people share an innate need to express their creative capacities freely in their place of work. In the appropriate circumstances, labour becomes a fulfilling and rewarding experience. This clearly involves appealing to a comprehensive value, and can therefore be seen as a perfectionist argument. "Neutrality, of course, rules out the use of such controversial premises" (Klosko 2003: 179). I do not, however, believe that NED's moderate neutrality (civil society) and neutrality (commune system) does rule it out. It is true that Marx's creativity value is highly distinctive. The imperative to create is held above non-productive values. But an endorsement of the former does not need to go this far. A 'softer' usage of this 'controversial premise' is, by way of contrast, fairly non-controversial. The statement that all citizens, given the opportunity, would welcome the prospect of joyful, creative and meaningful work does not strike me as terribly controversial. It may invoke a comprehensive value, but as it is surely something that, generally speaking, is highly desirable, it can appeal to the vast majority of conceptions of the good. As such, it does not violate the neutrality ideal. Rawls recognises that the principles of all reasonable political conceptions require basic institutions that "inevitably encourage some ways of life and discourage others" (2001: 153). But he adds that the state must not justify its actions by appealing to comprehensive conceptions of the good. By focusing on the controversial principle, though, and invoking the reasonable rejection criteria, the overlapping consensus can be supplemented in a way that does not demand the rejection of the neutral state.

Contemporary readers should not then be overly dismissive of Marx's early writings. There is much in them that can, and should, inform constitutional design.[11] *Labour is fundamental, no society can exist without it, and in this respect, labour is unique.* As such, the idea that production should be organised so that it becomes, to the greatest extent possible, a creative and fulfilling experience for all citizens, with the communal appreciation of each others' products, holds, once it is placed on an even par with consumer interests, enormous intrinsic appeal. To overcome the problems of alienation and commodity fetishism, producers must be in a position to democratically control their working environments in a way that they can relate to one another directly. Social relations must be prevented from falling into relations between commodities. For Marx this involves rational planning. NED's planning also aims to fundamentally transform the worker to worker and worker to nature relationships. Although commodity production will continue, the opportunities to engender creative labour are maximised. Citizens will meet each other in capacities other than merely exchangers of products in an impersonalised market. Democracy in the workplace and democracy over investment planning will help compensate for residual commodity fetishism, as there will be direct relations both *within* organised groups of workers and *between* workers and consumers. Here relations are not just through commodities, and producers will not be transformed into 'things' due to the dependence on capital. Recall that the arguments in Chapter Three, in NED capital, understood as a self-expanding dynamic, do not exist. That said, I do not hold that creative labour is an 'overriding good', nor do I insist it 'outweighs in value all competing goods'. NED does not prioritise the productive sphere. Part of the role of the consumer councils is to maintain an adequate standard of material consumption. Production is not the primary domain of fulfilment. Although no other set of values is ranked higher, consumption is, in terms of importance, situated alongside it. This is how NED softens its commitment to Marxist-humanism. Marx's argument that creative co-operative production is the key *single* characteristic to human excellence is not fully endorsed. Production is not elevated at the expense of non-productive values. In Rawlsian terms, it is no longer 'the privileged locus of our (complete) good'. But as work is clearly a part—and for most of us a central part—of life, I do claim creative labour is an important, even necessary, component to a decent life. And as Rawls unambiguously declares that what people "want is meaningful work in free association with others" (1971: 190), he would, presumably, agree.[12]

NED eliminates alienation not through an equal ownership of private productive property, but by socialising the instruments of production. Note, however, the specific way it does this. Producers are sovereign over the labour process, yet consumers are sovereign over the items produced. This constitutes an alternative interpretation of, and makes an important revision to, Marx's theory. It was explained above that in Marx's thesis there are four main forms in which human beings are alienated from their most distinctive characteristics, their species life: 1) from their species being, what it means to be human, 2) from the product, 3) from each other, i.e. their productive associates and 4) from human life, the essence of humanity. Marxist-humanism pictures a society of co-operative production in which productive assets are socialised and workers freely produce to meet each others' needs. It establishes a system of productive democracies whereby workers will be able to control the dynamics that give rise to the above four forms. Inasmuch, alienated labour will no longer endure. In terms of the power it grants to labour, NED does not go this far. Although workers *will* take control over the work environment, they do *not* determine the items and commodities produced; this task falls to the consumer councils. Workers of course can have their say about the quality and quantity of what gets produced, but it is not through the organisations of the workplace; rather, it is in their capacities as consumers, by virtue of the consumer councils and through the guild regulated markets. The recognition that both productive and consumptive interests are equally valid is central to Cole's political thought. Realising this, he synthesised what is best from syndicalism and Fabian social democracy. In his libertarian socialism, as in NED, neither the productive nor the consumptive sphere takes precedence. This is surely the correct starting point.[13]

Invoking the functional principle as society's demarcating criteria provides the key premise upon which a response to Kymlicka's argument that creative labour poses a threat to non-productive values can be advanced. His position is that citizens should enjoy the freedom to, if they wish, sacrifice quality in their working life in the interests of other values, such as leisure and consumption. I have no call to dispute this claim, but as people will still need to work in order to finance their non-productive pursuits, NED will still ensure that work is, to the greatest possible extent, creative and enjoyable. Kymlicka does not dispute the validity of this proposition. "Phrased as a choice between intrinsically satisfying and intrinsically unsatisfying work, most people will favour creative and cooperative work. The evidence is overwhelming that most workers in capitalism wish that their jobs were more satisfying" (2002: 191). Rather his point is that *if* the people who value their leisure and consumptive interests above their work can fund these interests more economically through wage-labour, then creative labour is detrimental to their value commitments.[14] This, it seems to me, is a hugely suspect if, given the minuscule skill content involved in dull, repetitive and boring labour—all of which are characteristics of alienating labour—it is fair to say that workers performing these tasks are, predominantly, amongst the lowest paid section of society. Furthermore, for the assumption that wage-labourers will systematically be in receipt of higher incomes than cooperative workers—both understood in ideal-typical terms—to be convincing, a number of other circumstances would need to exist. That they are not in any sense exploited, and have the means to resist oppressive measures, would seem essential requirements. Further still, it would have to be shown that wage-labour enterprises are more efficient than co-operative workplaces. And this point is seriously challenged in both the theoretical and the empirical literature. For instance, MaCain states that when viewed through the discipline of economic theory, workplace democratic ideals actually made more economic sense than he had initially anticipated. As he "had expected to pay an economic price for political righteousness", this came as a pleasant surprise (MaCain 2001: A2).[15] Others, too, are keen to stress that "[i]n recent years, evidence has been mounting that small-scale, decentralised, participatory, and labour-intensive organisations may be just as productive and efficient—and by some criteria, more so—as large-scale, hierarchical, and capital-intensive modes of organisation" (Rothschild and Whitt 1986: 111). Great attention should be paid to these arguments. It does not have to hold that co-operative labour is *more* efficient than wage-labour, only that it is *not less* efficient. For then, given that the 'choice between intrinsically satisfying and intrinsically unsatisfying work, most people will favour creative and cooperative work', the *exchange creative labour for an increase in non-productive values* argument loses its plausibility. On the empirically sound provision that, in terms of productive efficiency, co-operative labour compares no less favourably with wage-labour, the scenario that people who freely choose to self-fulfil through their leisure and consumptive endeavours must sacrifice productive creativity is a red herring.

Besides, the idea that citizens seek pleasure in leisure—and *only* leisure—irrespective and independently of their working environment, is just as comprehensive as the equally one-sided view that self-fulfilment must be sought in their capacities as producers. But the softer claim that enjoyable time spent in leisure is essential to the good life can be defended along similar lines as those along which I am defending creative labour, i.e., it is a non-controversial claim that is not dependent upon a particular value for it to make any sense. If, as Kymlicka suggests, many people will prefer to work less and spend more time seeking pleasure and self-fulfilment in their leisure and consumptive activities, then fine. The political structures in NED will enable them to do so. The consumer and civic councils are designed precisely to undertake, democratically, this reasonable task. Moreover, they are indispensable for this purpose; as Kymlicka appreciates, in capitalist society "those with the best jobs typically also have the best consumption and leisure, whilst those with poor jobs often get no compensating increase in leisure or consumption" (2002: 194). It was argued in Chapter Four that POD retains the key institutions of capitalism; as such, it is unclear how political liberalism will resolve this dilemma. The imperative must be to structure society so that all citizens are presented with the genuine opportunity to seek fulfilment in both democratised spheres of life. That person A may at a given time choose the latter over the former, and person B vice-versa, does not undermine the relatively non-controversial substance of this claim. One does not need to be a Marxist-humanist to recognise the benefits of creative labour, nor a liberal to recognise that the freedom of consumers is essential to a well-ordered society.

Care needs to be taken though in drawing this conclusion because, as the insights of others indicate, there are further complexities to consider. The following two are good examples. Arneson (2003) is a fierce critic of neutrality. He argues that the state should self-consciously promote conceptions of the good, even if they are controversial. Conversely, Gaus (2003) is an advocate of a strict neutrality ideal. He stresses that, properly understood, neutrality severely restricts the use of the coercive power of the state. Yet irrespective of their polarised positions, they both express a similar concern with regard to the comparativeness and the ranking of values. As their critiques have a direct bearing upon my present discussion, I will briefly summarise, and then respond to, the issue raised. Arneson contends that sound yet controversial aspects of the good can suitably inform state policies. On the list of candidates he provides is 'meaningful work', 'pleasurable experience and especially enjoyment of the excellent', 'satisfaction of reasonable life aims', 'intellectual and cultural achievement', 'relationships of friendship and love' and such like. These are, he insists, objective human goods, and should be promoted by the state. He is aware that a likely objection will be that these goods are, at the abstract level, uncontroversial. But when described in greater detail, he insists, they become controversial. The guiding of policy requires principles that may serve to compare and contrast these goods, and reasonable citizens will not agree on each comparative value. It is such disagreements that make the list of goods controversial. "Regarding comparison and measurement, one should expect to find partial commensurability. For many possible mixtures of goods, there may be no fact of the matter as to which package is best" (Arneson 2003: 216). But partial commensurability, Arneson concludes, does not amount to neutrality (Arneson 2003: 215–6).

Gaus argues that most public policies cannot survive the strict neutrality test he adheres to. His claim is developed partly through a response to the view that substantive values can inform public reason if they are shared by competing conceptions of the good. For this to stand, one of three conditions needs to hold: a) if a value is equally held by all understandings of the good, b) if a value is essential to the realisation of all understandings of the good and c) when empirical evidence suggests that certain actions are needed to advance common uncontroversial values, i.e. non-coercive strategies to promote good health. Gaus notes that, in one sense, these claims are correct. "If the claims are not rationally controversial, they do not run afoul of liberal neutrality" (2003: 157). But, he immediately adds, although it can be argued that a given value is endorsed by all rational citizens, it does not follow that this value provides a neutral reason to justify a policy. The problem is the 'ranking of values'; a reason is an impartial justification for a policy only if it is accepted by all rational citizens. But some citizens may reject a reason because it asserts a ranking of values they do not agree with, that is, there is a difference in the way citizens piece together value hierarchies:

> . . . our main disagreements about the good are not about what is of value, but the relative importance of values. After all, what is a ranking of values but a 'conception of the good'? Liberal neutrality requires justification by impartial reasons, and reasons that presuppose a controversial value ranking do not qualify (Gaus 2003: 157).

For Gaus, state policies cannot be justified on the grounds that citizens accept the same values or goods; there must also be a ranking of values that is equally acceptable to all rational citizens. So his radical neutrality principle precludes the state policies that invoke such trade-offs, and as this includes most of them, it rules out the majority of state actions (Gaus 2003: 157–8, 162).

Whether it is in regard to the comparison or the ranking of competing values, these critiques present us with a challenge. As NED is not a utopian paradise, attempts to finalise a non-controversial hierarchy of values that meets with universal approval are unlikely to succeed. Even if one did, its probable inflexibility would not be particularly desirable. Nevertheless, the above critiques are, I think, somewhat exaggerated, and a valid response may at least be approximated. In regards to the former, Arneson's objective goods only become controversial, he acknowledges, when they are described in detail; citizens will disagree about the comparative values of each good, and about which package of mixed goods is preferable. This seems reasonable, but the confusion intensifies when the promotion of the good in question is to guide the policy of an undifferentiated state. When it informs the policies of demarcated institutions like the economic / civic guilds and the consumer / civic councils, the 'partial commensurability' can be more easily clarified. From Arneson's list, meaningful work obviously relates to citizens' capacities as producers, whereas the others require time spent in consumption and leisure. When they are accounted for in accordance with the functional principle, disagreements about many of the comparative values—those that can be clearly represented by one demarcated body, such as creative labour or the enjoyment experienced through the consumption of a product—will, as they can be pursued *simultaneously* through both structured channels, no longer exist. Of course some of the objective goods Arneson lists apply to citizens' productive *and* consumptive interests, but then allowing them expression in both respects is, given that the whole point is to determine policy through meaningful dialogue, and in a way equally accessible to *all* citizens, relatively non-controversial. Indeed, it was this point that largely constituted my counter to Kymlicka's critique. Nevertheless, when these goods are being evaluated through one demarcated institution, i.e., when a consumer council is determining which products or services its members would like the two sets of guilds to provide, there may still be reasonable disagreement as to which particular amalgamation of goods is best, and in this respect the problem is not fully erased, even though it is made more visible.

The same reasoning informs my response to Gaus. He stresses that if a claim is non-controversial, it does not violate the principle of neutrality. But, he adds, although there may be no disagreement that a certain good has value, the problem is the 'relative importance of values'; a 'controversial value ranking' is not impartial, and so cannot be held up in justification of liberal neutrality. But again, by demarcating citizens' interests between the two general headings of producer and consumer, and institutionalising the articulation and expression of both, the number of possible value rankings is reduced. Producer and consumer values are not ranked in the same index; both represent only one set of differentiated interests. The ranking of values *within* each functional body will, as conceded above, remain. But as they are not *complete* organisations, their value hierarchies will not constitute a conception of the good, at least not in the same sense as they are liable to do when formulated through the structures of the state. The problem is not fully resolved, but if the democratic process of evaluating values—and, crucially, the ranking of values—within and between the functional bodies can proceed with transparency and clarity, may this not at least reduce some of the controversies in the way values are ranked? And minimising the controversies at the same time minimises, as all parties seem to agree, the threat to the neutrality ideal.

Conclusion

As the arguments in this chapter have been fairly detailed, I will not attempt to provide an extensive summary. Rather, I will highlight the key findings that entitle the conclusion to be drawn that between NED and POD, in analytical terms, the former is in a superior position to sustain the overlapping consensus. In NED, politics is returned to revitalise local communities. The economic and civic guilds and the consumer and civil councils are the decentralised associations, smaller than the state yet still formidable enough to stimulate a community spirit. During the second decade of the twentieth century, it was reflections upon their most desirable organisational design that preoccupied the libertarian socialists. One of the key questions central to their discourse was how to construct a concept of citizenship in the absence of sovereignty. This chapter has shown how this may be done in relation to the non-economic civic sphere. POD consists of more than atomised individuals pursuing their own advantage. It can also, to some extent, sustain a sense of community. It is though NED which has the democratic structures capable of bringing politics closer to the daily lives of citizens. Far from ignoring the values of liberal individualism, the intermediate functional organisations are a prerequisite for their realisation. It is the totality of these interacting demarcated bodies that provides a base in which the political values of freedom, autonomy, equality, justice, etc. can be stabilised in a way that enhances an ethic of community.

In regards to forging a stable practical agreement, the aim of Rawlsian philosophy is to assimilate comprehensive standpoints into part of a wider allegiance by advancing a standard they can all endorse. Different political viewpoints are not regarded as rival factions on disputatious issues. The hope is that co-existence will then become possible. Rawls is alert to the objection that there are insufficient political and social forces to stabilise the overlapping consensus. He agrees that this is an 'intricate question'. His solution is to establish how, once the principles of justice as fairness has been accepted as a modus vivendi, it may develop into a stable overlapping consensus. As we have seen, of particular significance is that, according to Rawls, most views are articulated only partially, and not fully, comprehensively; they admit to 'certain looseness'. As there is 'lots of slippage'; a political conception can 'cohere loosely' with partially comprehensive views. For Rawls "this allows scope for the development of an independent allegiance to a liberal conception" (2001: 197). He suggests that as people come to appreciate that this is in the common good, if an incompatibility later arises, it is the comprehensive view that may be adjusted. These revisions occur slowly and become stronger over time. In sum, the political conception of justice as fairness has a limited scope, and most comprehensive doctrines are not general but loose; together, they allow for "the eventual development of a modus vivendi into an overlapping consensus" (2001: 192–4, 197–8). In my opinion, Rawls is too optimistic here. It was argued in the first section that, in political liberalism, the relation between the two moral powers will not always be harmonious. Certain comprehensive doctrines will find it intolerable to prioritise their public identity before their private values, i.e., the denial of the revisability principle in associational life may well come before a commitment to the political conception. If so, the reasonable will not subordinate the rational; the just will not dictate the good. It is true, however, that no plural liberal society can fully extirpate this problem. But if one excepts the value of Rawls' overlapping consensus, in particular the two moral powers he ascribes to free and equal citizens, as NED does, then the task is to re-think the political arrangements of the basic structure of society so that these ideals can be more successfully realised.

In accepting this challenge, I have stressed that the emphasis should be directed towards a 'non-statism'. Indeed, NED seeks to socialise and democratise civil society, in both the economic and civic spheres, at the expense of a private property market forces–state redistributive economy. In other words, NED deliberately prioritises one set of economic and civic relations over another. The sound neutral justification is the realisation of the two principles of justice, a realisation that materialises in civil society. Some critics of perfectionism insist that no state is suitable for promoting the good, that those who come to hold seats of political power are ill-suited for this task. Ackerman (1980), for instance, stresses that bureaucratic structure is a permanent fixture of modern government, and notions of the good are difficult to impose by 'bureaucratic decree'. The danger is the sense of the grandiose engendered through the subjective experience of holding office. Bureaucratic minions will, he fears, manipulate notions of the good so that they come to serve their own inflated purposes[16] (Ackerman 1980: 362–3). However, it is as well to take note "that the considerations often invoked to call into question the state's competence to promote the good would also call into question its competence to pursue other political goals, such as social justice" (Wall and Klosko 2003: 16).[17] These remarks capture the logic behind the argument developed not just in this chapter, but throughout the entire book. It will now be clear why I view the state as an inappropriate arena in which to articulate a conception of the good and to secure social justice. These tasks are more suited to the functionally demarcated organisations in civil society.

This assertion is central to my entire argument. To reiterate, the Rawlsian state is not neutral in regards to *all* controversial conceptions of the good, only those that do not violate the basic liberties of the first principle. A policy that would subordinate a racial minority in an attempt to enhance material production—perhaps by denying it, and only it, the minimal wage—is clearly in breach of political equality, and therefore a non-starter in justice as fairness. But there are other, more controversial examples that are also ruled out. Recall the conclusion drawn in the first section of the previous chapter: in class divided societies like POD, the state cannot possibly be conceived in neutral terms. In order for it to be, Rawls would have to proscribe controversial conceptions of the good that invoke huge concentrations of private capital. Large economic inequalities render, and he is adamant about this, the basic liberties of the first principle merely formal, and void of any real substance. Presumably then the Rawlsian state would, in these cases, be distinctly non-neutral. The difference is that in the former example, policies that are overly detrimental to already marginalised groups are generally more easily identified than policies which fail to prevent unacceptable levels of economic inequalities. The first section of the previous chapter exposed why such inequalities cannot be fully erased from POD. By way of contrast, the basic institutions in the social and economic system of NED contain the egalitarian and democratic property relations which enable the commune system to be what the state in POD's mixed economy is not: a genuinely neutral body politic.

Finally, Rawls takes established yet opposing comprehensive doctrines, uncovers a consensus, and with it derives a collective adherence to a liberal constitution. This is a sound strategy, but the overlapping consensus is, as it stands in political liberalism, insufficiently thin to realise its objective—to provide the stability justice as fairness needs in light of the reasonable pluralism of modern liberal societies. Conversely, the overlapping consensus is more substantive in NED. The objective list of primary goods is more extensive; it includes the adoption of creative co-operative labour at the political convention so that it is treated as a basic political right. The political conception is thicker than it is in POD. As democratic procedures have been introduced into the economic and civic spheres, the common ground is more extensive. An adequate range of conceptions of the good can also be sustained within these political arrangements, thus providing for a richer and more extensive treatment of Rawls' second moral power. That is, the worthy conceptions of the good that are not self-supporting yet survive public scrutiny, through the evaluation of what Rawls calls public reason, can be advanced non-coercively. Although this will invoke a soft perfectionism, it was shown in section two that it is not in diametrical opposition to the neutrality ideal. In addition, representing consumer interests as rights of citizenship also goes some way towards strengthening the overlapping consensus; the same can be said of meeting the basic needs of all citizens collectively and inclusively—both instances appeal to common interests. Section three responded to the predictable objection that in the endeavour to strengthen the overlapping consensus so that it may fulfil its rightful purpose, I have only succeeded in elevating a controversial conception of the good. It has been argued that democratising economic and civic relations the way NED has need not betray the neutrality ideal. In NED the Marxist-humanist position has been appropriately softened so that the common ground is suitably thickened and given greater substance, yet with a procedure that does not subordinate other conceptions of the good, such as those related to self-fulfilment in private life. Only this course of action, I contend, can secure in the basic structure the political arrangements by which the two principles of justice can be adequately sustained.

Notes

1 A distinction not explicitly drawn in *Theory*.

2 The notion of 'public reason' is given content by the formulation of a political conception of justice, which has three aspects: a) it secures basic rights, liberties and opportunities, b) it grants them a special priority and c) it assures to all citizens all-purpose means so that these basic rights and liberties are not simply formal. It is clear that, along with other liberalisms, Rawls' two

principles of justice 'fall under this general description', any of which citizens can appeal to in their exercise of public reason (1993: 223; Larmore 2003: 388).

3 As such, they are open to the communitarian critique that they embody a non-neutral conception of the good (Mulhall and Swift 2003: 473).

4 Or, as Rawls says, the justice as fairness of *PL* 'recasts' the social contract (1993: 23).

5 Also see Caney 1991: 467.

6 Kymlicka, who is an advocate of the liberal neutral state, acknowledges the relevance of this point (1989: 894).

7 See part three of this chapter for further elaboration and analysis on this point.

8 Here NED's civic services may also follow Gutman's suggestion and endorse "perfectionist arguments that do not threaten anyone's basic liberties or opportunities" (2003: 195).

9 Kymlicka stresses this point clearly in his riposte to Ronald Beiner's (1989) critique of state neutrality. He stresses that "the argument for state neutrality presupposes, rather than denies, social nonneutrality" (1989: 895–6).

10 By adopting the term 'non-alienating co-operative labour', I do not mean to imply that all co-operative work is by definition stimulating and meaningful, nor do I wish to infer that all non-alienating labour is co-operative, as the work of self-employed individual artisans is often creative. But it is, I think, the case that where associative effort is required, and democratic worker input into the internal relations of the firm is essential to sharing control over the working environment, the two terms are complementary. For an interesting account of how to balance stimulating and tedious tasks within the productive process, see Albert and Hahnel's idea of 'diverse job complexes' (1991: 19–21).

11 Marx does not address this question. For a summary of his position that 'writing recipes for cookshops of the future' is pointless, and the argument that Cole inadvertently makes explicit what is only implicit in the young Marx, see Wyatt (2006).

12 Incidentally, Rawls acknowledges that the question of whether workplace democracies in competitive market economies should initially be allocated subsidies 'so that they can get going' needs 'careful examination' (2001: 178–9). This may be an excellent idea, but would it not be bordering upon promoting a particular conception of the good?

13 For an intriguing discussion on why self-realisation at work is preferable to consumption activities, see Elster (1986: 103–10); this article also contains a sophisticated exposition of the concept of self-realisation (99–101).

14 Arneson makes a similar point (1987: 526–7). My response to him would be the same as that given to Kymlicka.

15 For the bibliographic references which support this, see MaCain (1993).

16 In this latter respect Ackerman follows Michels. The exercise of power, Michels warned, creates a metamorphosis in those commanding it (1999: 205–11).

17 Caney also contends "that the state might make mistakes about the right and justice: but this does not lead neutralists to conclude that the state should not promote justice and rights" (1991: 461).

Conclusion

As the analyses throughout this book have been quite substantial, it will, I think, be helpful to take stock of the key points established. I will bring these arguments together in order to verify the central claim of this book: as the demands of the difference principle are far more easily realised in NED than they are in POD, it is the institutions in the former that are just.

New Economic Democracy: A Summary

The principles of justice dictate institutions which Rawls believes are compatible with both private and social ownership schemes (1971: 280). He insists that markets decentralise power and are favourable to liberty and equality of opportunity (1971: 272). But in the case of public goods and externalities, state action must amend markets. The economy sketched is therefore mixed. I have argued however that it is NED which represents a genuine and more realistic third way. As market and command planning systems either distort or limit information about production and consumption, both create instrumental decision making. Markets have a poor record in meeting the basic needs of people, they generally cannot deal with externalities, and by elevating competition they tend to advance antisocial behaviour. Central planning is implemented through rigid hierarchical command structures. In these systems both producers and consumers are typically denied the opportunity to input democratically into economic matters; they are also prone to the epistemological critique explained in Chapter Three. The denial of the basic political liberties of Rawls' first principle of justice in state socialist regimes, together with the excessive regulation of all aspects of individuals' lives, did much to tarnish the image and reputation of socialism, and in doing so presented apologists for liberal capitalism with an open goal. Cole makes it clear that his concern is not with all experience, only social experience. By this he means actions taken through organised groups. He makes a clear distinction between a 'community' and a 'society'. The former is the broadest and most comprehensive. It is a complex of social life in which people live together sharing customs, conventions and traditions. A complex community clearly has a diversified social organisation. It will contain a section that is legally regulated and is directed by formally organised associations. This labyrinth of organised associations he calls society. It is "neither the whole complex of community, nor any particular association or institution, but the sum total of organised social structure which is the resultant of the various associations and institutions within a community" (1920a: 30). Society (the essential associations being the guilds, consumer and civic councils, and communes, as well as their interaction and co-operation) is not a complete circle of common life, only its organised section. It follows that society cannot express the whole life of any one person. The community is fundamentally a centre of feeling, whereas society centres on deliberation and planning. What cannot be organised therefore escapes society. For Cole, the finest sentiments, like love and devotion found in personal relationships, are best left unorganised (1920a: 25–32). As a libertarian society, NED fully respects this principle. Not only will it grant all the civil liberties liberal democracy does, it will not attempt to regulate the total sum of citizens' affairs, only those which correspond to organisation.

In contrast to command, market and Rawlsian mixed economies, NED retains Cole's commune system, his advocacy of workplace democracy, his non-capitalist system of consumer representation and his institutionalisation of dialogue between the key interests inherent in all citizens—most notably in their capacities as producers and consumers.[1] Cole's proposals for democratic planning, though, will now only apply to the goods deemed necessary to meet basic human needs; here the functional bodies will democratically decide the just price. The production and distribution of other products, those connected to the satisfaction of wants and preferences, will be determined by the guild-regulated markets. This idea represents the most original innovation put forward in this book. The other main addition is the assimilation of a strategy to subject new investment to democratic adjudication, which in NED has been functionally demarcated. In a line, NED articulates a democratically planned economy which has a role for a subordinated market. Price setting of 'need' goods through democratic deliberations is, in NED, an inclusive system which grants all citizens, even the poorest, the right and opportunity to have their say about what is produced. That is, the opening for people without wealth to actively participate in what is produced *in advance of purchase* is provided. One of the most attractive features of Cole's libertarian socialism is that it seeks to give consumers the opportunity to express their wishes in a manner that is not wholly dependent upon market considerations. The idea is that the power of consumers to initially help determine productive output will not be thoroughly dependent upon the ability to pay. Quantity and quality will be determined through discourse. The dialogue between producers and consumers ensures that the latter cease to be simply buyers of goods. In NED, as citizens' basic needs will be determined by extra-market criteria, the needs of the poor will not be neglected as they often are in market economies. The capacity of what remains of the market to foster the inequalities capable of inhibiting legal and political equality is undermined. POD does not prioritise the provision of an opportunity for economic self-governance. In contrast, NED makes it a prerogative. Rather than control over production being under the command of private individuals, NED redistributes economic power along egalitarian lines. Workplaces are prevented from ploughing profits back into their firms in the quest to maximise profit margins. NED's functionally demarcated democratic investment planning is arranged so that financial power is accountable. Private interest cannot determine the flow of capital, and, therefore, the direction of the economy. As wealth cannot concentrate in the hands of a few powerful individuals, the distribution of economic power is equalised. Insofar, the substance of sovereignty has been reconstituted so that it comes to rest largely with the interacting functional bodies in civil society. The commune's authority remains as a final court of appeal, but in the manner in which it can assert itself, it is confined. Neither is there a small dominant class possessing the financial muscle capable of wielding a disproportionate influence upon the commune's action. These are the key institutional contours of NED.

Property Owning Democracy and New Economic Democracy

Rawls' principles of equal political liberty and equality of opportunity, when regulated within POD, will, I have claimed, allow a minority class to seize positions from which they will hold the power to subordinate the majority. Political rights may be equal, but in class-divided societies they are not experienced equally. Liberal equality and freedom are undermined when set within a private-property regime in which huge concentrations of wealth are inevitable. Marx made this point long ago, most notably in *On the Jewish Question* (1843). For Marx, the political state–civil society dualism ensures that inequalities and exploitation are confined to the latter, where they are seen as non-political. Rawls is no Marxist, and although his redistributive government is extensive, he would retain a substantial divide between state and civil society. Nevertheless, he too is troubled by vast economic inequalities. He introduces the notion of the fair value of political liberties to answer the familiar socialist critique that these liberties are actually only formal. While it seems the basic rights and liberties are equal, this critique goes, inequalities in the background economic institutions are so huge that the wealthy are able to dominate political life and effectively control the legislating procedure. Rawls proposes that the gain permitted to the most favoured must be limited, even if it is sanctioned by the difference principle, otherwise "there would be unjust effects on the political system" (1971: 81). Further on he repeats that political liberty is de-valued when the powerful are able to settle social questions through their control of the 'course of public debate' (1971: 225). POD aims to distribute property ownership as broadly as possible. Indeed, "[f]ree market arrangements must be set within a framework of political and legal institutions which regulate the overall trends of economic events", and that "it may be worthwhile to recall the importance of preventing excessive accumulations of property and wealth" (1971: 73). Although he adheres to a competitive economy, he insists that within "an open class system excessive inequalities will not be the rule" (1971: 158). The reader's clarity is not helped when he immediately adds that 'nothing guarantees' that inequalities will not be substantial (1971: 158). Despite these ambiguities, his chief concern is to justify the inevitable inequality in life prospects of those in different social classes (1971: 78). The solution offered is of course the difference principle, that those better situated must work as part of a scheme in which the conditions of the worst-off are improved as much as can be expected (1971: 75). Rawls' re-introduction of the social contract is intriguing, but the real issue is how to reduce the huge gulf in class so that it may be accepted by everyone. Within POD, in the likely event that the worst-off receive gains at a disproportionate ratio to the best-off, the difference principle would authorise large economic disparities. The first section of Chapter Four explained the problematic significance of this.

As a corollary, although POD can be understood as a moderate from of socialism, on the grounds that social democracy may still pass for this, the premises to Rawls' theory dictate a far more radical vision of economic and political arrangements. Barry claims that *A Theory of Justice* "introduces a principle of distribution which could, suitably interpreted and with certain factual assumptions, have egalitarian implications. If socialism is identified with public ownership or with equality, then this form of liberalism is compatible with socialism" (1973: 166). He is, I believe, right. But then, to attract interest, this socialism will need to explain how its public ownership functions, and what will be the structural means by which its equality is sustained. These are the tasks undertaken in this book. To reiterate, the argument that democracy cannot be realised in the state whilst private interest and unaccountable power reign supreme in civil society has been augmented. The goal must be, as it was for Marx and Cole, to abolish the political domain as a detached, unaccountable and alienated sphere of power. In the words of the latter:

> . . . such democracy as is recognised is conceived in a narrowly 'political' sense, as applying to a quite peculiar sphere known as politics, and not in a broader and more comprehensive sense, as applying to all the acts which men [sic] do in association or conjunction. The result is that theoretical 'democrats' . . . ignore the fact that vast inequalities of wealth and status, resulting in vast inequalities of education, power and control of environment, are necessarily fatal to any real democracy, whether in politics or in any other sphere . . . [and] if, in the sphere of industry, one man is a master and the other a wage-slave, one enjoys riches and gives commands and the other has only an insecure subsistence and obeys orders, no amount of purely electoral machinery on a basis of 'one man one vote' will make the two really equal socially or politically (1920b: 14–5).

This insight is as true today as it was when Cole theorised his libertarian socialism. Appeals to democratic control will be in vain as long as the possessing minority can, through their economic power, stifle the political pursuits of the majority—a point fully recognised by Rawls. *Production must be brought under the control of a politically organised community.* Those who control productive resources (in any system) are able to assert an inordinate influence upon the political domain. Economic decisions constrain the latitude of state activity. In capitalist society this implies that the state must stabilise the conditions which are favourable to a market based accumulation of private wealth—it was shown that this logic applies, perhaps to a lesser extent, to POD. Democratically controlling production, however, helps realise the principles of representative government more adequately. In NED's functionally demarcated economic democracy, in which key interests of individuals, and not the individuals themselves, are represented politically, control is as widespread and as egalitarian as is realistically possible. Commentating on a closely related issue, Macpherson recognises that even in non-capitalist societies, economic classes may exist:

> But these need not create unequal liberties and rights since they are not necessarily either the result or the means of domination, of gaining at the expense of others. Rawls's principles of justice, applied to such a society, would probably make very good sense (Macpherson 1973: 90).

I have contended that this society is NED.

Finally, with regards to Rawls' mature writings, it has been shown in Chapter Five that the same conclusion can be drawn: NED, not POD, is the just society. In political liberalism, the difference principle is still an important aspect of a political conception of justice. It forms part of the overlapping consensus of reasonable people. For Rawls, reasonable means that citizens are, firstly, prepared to engage in the fair terms of social co-operation—to respect the political principles of justice—and, secondly, given the burdens of judgements, they will acknowledge that there will be disagreement over conceptions of the good. Perhaps the most immediate problem here though is that the 'constitutional consensus'—which the overlapping consensus develops from—is, in political liberalism, not solid enough to realise the role Rawls ascribes to it: the satisfaction of the principles of political justice. It is, as Rawls says, neither 'deep' nor 'wide' (1993: 159). Although the overlapping consensus is supplemented with liberty of conscience, freedom of thought and fair equal opportunity (1993: 164), I have argued why it too requires a more substantial treatment. For Rawls, a modus vivendi is stable in a suspect way. In contrast, he thinks the principles of justice will be stable in the proper way. That is, they will be welcomed firstly in terms of the same reasons accepted by all reasonable free and equal citizens—the political values of public reason—and secondly for reasons internal to the various comprehensive doctrines, the non-public reasons. His conclusion is that the two principles will be accepted for their own sake—or, as he puts it, a political conception is supported 'on its own merits' (1993: 148; Freeman 2003: 36–41). In my opinion, Rawls is right that even though a stable social order needs more than a mere modus vivendi, it requires less than a strong form, or 'statist', communitarianism. I have claimed, however, that only a re-politicised civil society, using the functional principle as a method of organisational demarcation, provides the appropriate solution—and in a way that strengths the overlapping consensus without bringing forth a leviathan. Indeed, in NED the overlapping consensus will be embraced more enthusiastically, i.e., citizens will, I believe, feel NED is a society worth belonging to.

New Economic Democracy: The Good Society

Rawls' endeavour is to establish the principles of justice which can regulate the social interactions that all rational people will regard as fair, and from this to formulate a set of social and political institutions that individuals will conform to irrespective of their unequal status. The difference principle, I have repeatedly stressed, is an impressive device by which society ought to plan its economy; it can serve as an ongoing yardstick with which to inform guild legislation. When applied to a classless society—and if class is understood in terms of inequality, domination, exploitation, ownership, etc., then NED is a classless society par excellence—the difference principle makes good sense. To press the point, in the attempt to work through the Rawlsian method of the four-stage sequence, following the process of quasi-pure procedural justice, and accommodate Rawls' two principles of justice into the political structures of NED, the latter has not had to be altered in the slightest, such is their compatibility. More than this, it has enabled a tighter degree of coherency in the theorisation of NED. On the revision that the rights and liberties of Rawls' first principle include, firstly, creative co-operative labour, and secondly, consumer interests as rights of citizenship, his two principles are basically sound. As this book has shown, though, the society that can more easily accommodate them is NED. An appraisal of NED's basic structure—the reformed guilds, the consumer and civil councils and the commune system—has revealed them to be the logical conclusion to Rawlsian premises. Although I do believe Rawls should have been committed to NED as the *only* viable means of implementing justice, I have not made that argument here. What I have claimed is that NED is at least as good as—and in many respects better—than POD. To conclude, the society whose political structures are best suited to implement the difference principle is NED, not POD.

Notes

1 Rawls believes that everyone should have "at least one community of shared interests to which he belongs and where he finds his endeavours confirmed by his associates" (1971: 442). Although worker-controlled market socialism, with its avocation of producer co-operatives, can also harbour communities of shared interests, NED goes much further. Workplace democracy is still indispensable, but this is supplemented with consumer and cultural councils. Each individual has an equal chance, and would be encouraged, to become active within these institutions. The endeavours of what in my scheme will be citizens—citizenship rights, it will be recalled, are to include the entire remit of consumer interests—will be 'confirmed' by their 'associates' not just in the productive sphere, but in their capacities as consumers, users and neighbours.

Bibliography

Ackerman, B.A. (1980) *Social Justice in the Liberal State*, New Haven: Yale University Press.

Albert, M. and Hahnel, R. (1991) *Looking Forward: Participatory Economics for the Twenty First Century*, Boston: South End Press.

Amdur, R. (1980) 'Rawls and his Radical Critics', *Dissent*, Summer.

Arneson, R.J. (1987) 'Meaningful Work and Market Socialism', *Ethics* Vol. 97, No. 3. April.

——— (2003) 'Liberal Neutrality on the Good: An Autopsy', in Wall, S. and Klosko, G. (Eds.) *Perfectionism and Neutrality: Essays in Liberal Theory*, New York: Roman and Littlefield.

Arthur, C.J. (1970) *The German Ideology*, London: Lawrence and Wishart.

Bardhan, P.K. (1993) 'On Tackling the Soft Budget Constraint in Market Socialism', in Bardhan, P.K. and Roemer, J.E. (Eds.) *Market Socialism: The Current Debate*, Oxford: OUP.

Bardhan, P.K. and Roemer, J.E. (1992) 'Market Socialism: A Case for Rejuvenation', in *Journal of Economic Perspectives* Vol. 6, Summer.

——— (1993) *Market Socialism: The Current Debate*, Oxford: OUP.

Barker, R. (1975) 'Guild Socialism Revisited', *The Political Quarterly* Vol. 46.

Barry, B. (1973) *The Liberal Theory of Justice*, Oxford: Clarendon Press.

Black, A. (1984) *Guilds and Civil Society in European Political Thought from the Twelfth Century to the Present*, London: Methuen and Co.

Blaazer, D. (1998) 'Guild Socialism and the Historians', *Australian Journal of Politics and History* Vol. 4, Part 1.

Bottomore, T.B. (1963) *Karl Marx: Early Writings*, London: C.A. Watts and Co. Ltd.

Briggs, A. and Saville, J. (1971) 'Guild Socialism: The Storrington Document', *Labour History 1886–1923*, London: Macmillan.

Butler, E. (1983) *Hayek*, Hounslow: Maurice Temple Smith.

Caney, S. (1991) 'Consequentialist Defences of Liberal Neutrality', *Philosophical Quarterly* 41, No. 165, January.

Carpenter, L.P. (1973) *G.D.H. Cole: An Intellectual Biography*, Cambridge: CUP.

Carpenter, N. (1922) *Guild Socialism: An Historical and Critical Analysis*, New York: D. Appleton & Company.

Clark, B. and Gintis, H. (1978) 'Rawlsian Justice and Economic Systems', *Philosophy and Public Affairs* 7, No. 4, Summer.

Cole, G.D.H. (1913) *The World of Labour*, London: G. Bell.

——— (1914) October. London Fabian Lecture, Guild Socialism, Cole Collection. Nuffield College. Box A1/46/1–8.

——— (1914a) '*Conflicting Social Obligations*', Proceedings of the Aristotelian Society, Vol. XV.

——— (1915) 'State Sovereignty and the Guilds', *New Age*, 15 April.

——— (1972) [1917] *Self-Government in Industry*, London: Hutchinson Educational.

——— (1919) Unnamed pamphlet on the possible creation of a national railway guild. Cole Collection. Nuffield College. Box A1/48/1–5.

——— (1920) March 4th. Kingsway Hall, Lecture. Cole Collection. Nuffield College. Box A1/49/1–8.

——— (1920a) *The Social Theory*, London: Methuen & Co.

——— (1920b) *Guild Socialism Restated*, London: Leonard Parsons.

——— (1920c) May 6th. Kingsway Hall, Lecture. Cole Collection. Nuffield College. Box A1/49/1–8.

——— (1920d) October 27th. South Place Institute, Lecture. 'The Prospects of the Guilds', Cole Collection. Nuffield College. Box A1/49/1–8.

——— (1920e) *Co-Operation and the Guilds*, Cole Collection. Nuffield College. Box A1/49/1–8.
——— (1921) January 12th. Mortimer Hall, Lecture. Cole Collection. Nuffield College. Box A1/50/1–6.
——— (1921a) Unnamed paper, Cole Collection. Nuffield College. Box A1/50/1–6.
——— (1921b) October. *The Aims of Guild Socialism*, Cole Collection. Nuffield College. Box A1/51/1–7.
——— (1956) *A History of Socialist Thought: Volume III, Part I. The Second International 1889–1914*, London: Macmillan.
——— (1957) *A History of Socialist Thought: Volume II. Marxism and Anarchism 1850– 1890*, London: Macmillan.
——— (1958) Foreword in Pribicevic, B. (Ed.) *The Shop Stewards' Movement and Workers' Control 1910–1922*, (1959) Oxford: Blackwell.
——— (1958a) *A History of Socialist Thought: Volume IV, Part I*, London: Macmillan.
——— n.d. 'Outline of a pamphlet on the control of industry—during and after the war', Cole Collection. Nuffield College. Box A1/46/1–8.
Cole, M. (1971) 'Guild Socialism and the Labour Research Department', in Briggs, A. and Saville, J. (Eds.) *Labour History 1886–1923*, London: Macmillan.
Colletti, L. (1975) *Karl Marx: Early Writings*, London: Penguin.
Corina, J. (1972) Introduction to Cole, G.D.H. *Self-Government in Industry*, London: Hutchinson Educational.
Corlett, J.A. (1991) *Equality and Liberty: Analysing Rawls and Nozick*, Hampshire: Macmillan.
Crocker, L. (1977) 'Equality, Solidarity, and Rawls' Maximin', *Philosophy and Public Affairs* 6/3, Spring.
Daniels, N. (1989) *Reading Rawls*, California: Stanford University Press.
Devine, P. (1988) *Democracy and Economic Planning: The Political Economy of a Self-Governing Society*, Cambridge: Polity Press.
DiQuattro, A. (1983) 'Rawls and Left Criticism', *Political Theory* Vol. 11, No. 1, February.
Dreben, B. (2003) 'On Rawls and Political Liberalism', in Freeman, S. (Ed.) *The Cambridge Companion to Rawls*, Cambridge: CUP.
Dunleavy, P. and O'Leary, B. (1987) *Theories of the State*, Hampshire: Macmillan.
Elliott, W.Y. (1925) 'Sovereign State or Sovereign Group', *The American Political Science Review*, Vol. xix. No. 3.
----- (1968) *The Pragmatic Revolt in Politics*, New York: Howard Fertig.
Ellis, E.D. (1923) 'Guild Socialism and Pluralism', *The American Political Science Review* Vol. xvii.
Elster, J. (1986) 'Self-Realization in Work and Politics: The Marxist Conception of the Good Life', *Social Philosophy and Policy* 3:2, Spring.
Estrin, S. (1989) 'Workers' Co-Operatives: Their Merits and their Limitations', in Le Grand, J. and Estrin, S. (Eds.) *Market Socialism*, Oxford: Clarendon.
Estrin, S. and Winter, D. (1989) 'Planning in a Market Socialist Economy', in Le Grand, J. and Estrin, S. (Eds.) *Market Socialism*, Oxford: Clarendon.
Freeman, S. (2003) 'Introduction: John Rawls—An Overview', in his *The Cambridge Companion to Rawls*, Cambridge: CUP.
Gaus, G.F. (2003) 'Liberal Neutrality: A Compelling and Radical Principle', in Wall, S. and Klosko, G. (Eds.) *Perfectionism and Neutrality: Essays in Liberal Theory*, New York: Roman & Littlefield.
Glass, S.T. (1966) *The Responsible Society: The Ideas of the English Guild Socialists*, London: Longmans.
Gray, A. (1946) *The Socialist Tradition*, London: Longmans.
Greenberg, E.S. (1984) 'Producer Cooperatives and Democratic Theory: The Case of the Plywood Firms', in Jackall, R. and Levin, H.M. (Eds.) *Worker Cooperatives in America*, London: University of California Press.
Gunn, C. (1984) 'Hoedads Co-Op: Democracy and Cooperation at Work', in Jackall, R. and Levin, H.M. (Eds.) *Worker Cooperatives in America*, London: University of California Press.

Gutmann, A. (2003) 'Rawls on the Relationship between Liberalism and Democracy', in Freeman, S. (Ed.) *The Cambridge Companion to Rawls*, Cambridge: CUP.
Held, D. (1989) *Political Theory and the Modern State*, Cambridge: Polity Press.
Hewes, A. (1922) 'Guild Socialism: A Two Years' Test', *The American Economic Review* Vol. xii, No. 2.
Hirst, P.Q. (1989) *The Pluralist Theory of the State*, London: Routledge.
——— (1990) *Representative Democracy and its Limits*, Cambridge: Polity Press.
——— (1990a) 'Democracy: Socialism's Best Reply to the Right', in Hindess, B. (Ed.) *Reactions to the Right*, London: Routledge.
——— (1994) *Associational Democracy*, Cambridge: Polity Press.
Hobson, S.G. (1920) *National Guilds: An Enquiry into the Wage-System and the Way Out*, London: G. Bell.
Hoover, K. et al (1989) *Conservative Capitalism*, London: Routledge.
Houseman, G.L. (1979) *G.D.H. Cole*, Boston: Twayne.
Howard, M.H. (2000) *Self-Management and the Crisis of Socialism: The Rose in the Fist of the Present*, Oxford: Rowman and Littlefield.
Hsiao, K.C. (1927) *Political Pluralism*, Torquay: Devonshire Press.
Jackall, R. and Levin, H.M. (1984) *Worker Cooperatives in America*, London: University of California Press.
Keane, J. (1988) *Civil Society and the State*, London: Verso.
Klosko, G. (2003) 'Reasonable Rejection and Neutrality of Justification', in Wall, S. and Klosko, G. (Eds.) *Perfectionism and Neutrality: Essays in Liberal Theory*, New York: Roman and Littlefield.
Kornai, J. (1993) 'Market Socialism Revisited', in Bardhan, P.K. and Roemer, J.E. (Eds.) *Market Socialism: The Current Debate*, Oxford: OUP.
Kukathas, C. and Pettit, P. (1990) *Rawls: A Theory of Justice and its Critics*, Cambridge: Polity Press.
Kymlicka, W. (1989) 'Liberal Individualism and Liberal Neutrality', *Ethics* Vol. 99, No. 4, July.
——— (2002) *Contemporary Political Philosophy: An Introduction*, Oxford: OUP.
Laborde, C. (2000) *Pluralist Thought and the State in Britain and France, 1900–25*, Hampshire: Macmillan.
Larmore, C. (2003) 'Public Reason', in Freeman, S. (Ed.) *The Cambridge Companion to Rawls*, Cambridge: CUP.
Lawler, J. (1998) 'Criticism of Ollman', in Ollman, B. (Ed.) *Market Socialism: The Debate Among Socialists*, London: Routledge.
Levine, A. (2002) *Engaging Political Philosophy*, Oxford: Blackwell.
McCain, R. (1993) 'Cooperation: The Proper Study of Economics', *International Journal of Social Economics* Vol. 20, No. 10.
——— (2001) http://william-king.www.drexel.edu.
Macpherson, C.B. (1973) *Democratic Theory*, Oxford: Clarendon.
——— (1973a) 'Rawls' Model of Man and Society', *Philosophy of the Social Sciences* Vol. 3, December.
Magid, H.M. (1966) *English Political Pluralism*, New York: AMS Press.
Martell, L. (1992) 'New Ideas of Socialism', *Economy and Society* Vol. 21, No. 2, May.
Marx, K. (1970) in O'Malley, J. (Ed.) *Karl Marx: Critique of Hegel's Philosophy of Right*, Cambridge: CUP.
——— (1975) in Colletti, L. (Ed.) *Karl Marx: Early Writings*, London: Penguin.
——— (1977) in McLellan, D. (Ed.) *Karl Marx: Selected Writings*, Oxford: OUP.
Mathews, F. (1979) 'The Ladder of Becoming: A.R. Orage, A.J. Penty and the Origins of Guild Socialism in England', in Martin, D.E. and Rubinstein, D. (Eds.) *Ideology and the Labour Movement*, London: Croom Helm.
McLellan, D. (1971) *Karl Marx: Early Texts*, Oxford: Blackwell.
——— (1986) *Marx*, Second Edition. London: Fontana.
Michels, R. (1999) *Political Parties: A Sociological Study of the Oligarchical Tendencies of Modern Democracy*, London: Transaction.

Miller, D. (1989) 'In What Sense Must Socialism Be Communitarian?' *Social Philosophy and Policy* 6/2.

Miller, R.W. (1989) 'Rawls and Marxism', in Daniels, N. (Ed.) *Reading Rawls*, California: Stanford University Press.

Mills, C. (2000) 'Not a Mere Modus Vivendi: The Bases for Allegiance to the Just State', in Davion, V. and Wolf, C. (Eds.) *The Idea of a Political Liberalism: Essays on Rawls*, New York: Rowman & Littlefield.

Mulhall, S. and Swift, A. (2003) 'Rawls and Communitarianism', in Freeman, S. (Ed.) *The Cambridge Companion to Rawls*, Cambridge: CUP.

National Guild League (1917) April 7/8th. *Annual General Meeting: Agenda / Minutes*, Cole Collection. Nuffield College. Box D3/3/1, 2.

Nicholls, D. (1994) *The Pluralist State*, Second Edition. Hampshire: Macmillan Press.

Nielsen, K. (1978) 'Class and Justice', in Arthur, J. and Shaw, W. (Eds.) *Justice and Economic Distribution*, Englewood Cliffs: Prentice Hall.

Ollman, B. (1998) 'Market Mystification in Capitalist and Market Socialist Societies', in his *Market Socialism: The Debate Among Socialists*, London: Routledge.

——— (1998a) 'Criticism of Lawler', in his *Market Socialism: The Debate Among Socialists*, London: Routledge.

——— (1998b) 'Response to Lawler', in his *Market Socialism: The Debate Among Socialists*, London: Routledge.

O'Malley, J. (1970) Introduction to *Karl Marx: Critique of Hegel's Philosophy of Right*, Cambridge: CUP.

Putterman, L. (1993) 'Incentive Problems Favouring Noncentralised Investment Fund Ownership', in Bardhan, P.K. and Roemer, J.E. (Eds.) *Market Socialism: The Current Debate*, Oxford: OUP.

Rawls, J. (1971) *A Theory of Justice*, Harvard: HUP.

——— (1975) 'Fairness to Goodness' *Philosophical Review* 84, No. 4, October.

——— (1980) 'The Dewey Lectures on Kantian Constructivism in Moral Theory', *The Journal of Philosophy* 88.

——— (1982) 'The Basic Liberties and Their Priority', in MacMurrin, S. (Ed.) *The Tanner Lectures on Human Values*, Cambridge: CUP.

——— (1985) 'Justice as Fairness: Political Not Metaphysical', *Philosophy and Public Affairs* 14, Summer.

——— (1987) 'The Idea of an Overlapping Consensus', *Oxford Journal of Legal Studies* 7.

——— (1988) 'The Priority of Right and Ideas of the Good', *Philosophy and Public Affairs* 17.

——— (1989) 'The Domain of the Political and Overlapping Consensus', *New York University Law Review* 64.

——— (1993) *Political Liberalism*, New York: Columbia University Press.

——— (2001) *Justice as Fairness: A Restatement*, Delhi: Universal Law.

Raz, J. (1986) *The Morality of Freedom*, Oxford: Clarendon.

----- (1996) 'Liberty and Trust' in George, R.P. (Ed.) *Natural Law, Liberalism, and Morality*, Oxford: Clarendon.

Reynard, H. (1920) 'The Guild Socialists', *The Economic Journal*, Vol. xxx.

Roemer, J.E. (1993) 'Can there be Socialism after Communism?', in Bardhan, P.K. and Roemer, J.E. (Eds.) *Market Socialism: The Current Debate*, Oxford: OUP.

----- (1994) *A Future for Socialism*, London: Verso.

Rothschild-Whitt, J. (1976) 'Conditions Facilitating Participatory-Democratic Organisations', *Sociological Inquiry* Vol. 46 (2).

Rothschild, J. and Whitt, J.A. (1986) *The Co-Operative Workplace: Potentials and Dilemmas of Organisational Democracy and Participation*, Cambridge: CUP.

Schecter, D. (2007) *The History of the Left from Marx to the Present*, New York: Continuum.

Schweickart, D. (1978) 'Should Rawls be a Socialist? A Comparison of His Ideal Capitalism with Worker-Controlled Socialism', *Social Theory and Practice* Vol. 5, No. 1.

——— (1993) *Against Capitalism*, Cambridge: CUP.

——— (1998) 'Market Socialism: A Defence', in Ollman, B. (Ed.) *Market Socialism: The Debate Among Socialists*, London: Routledge.

——— (1998a) 'Criticism of Ticktin', in Ollman, B. (Ed.) *Market Socialism: The Debate Among Socialists*, London: Routledge.

——— (1998b) 'Response to Ticktin', in Ollman, B. (Ed.) *Market Socialist: The Debate Among Socialists*, London: Routledge.

Swift, A. (2001) *Political Philosophy: A Beginners Guide for Students and Politicians*, Cambridge: Polity.

Taylor, C. (1985) *Philosophy and the Human Sciences: Philosophical Papers* Vol. ii. Cambridge: CUP.

——— (1985b) 'Alternative Futures: Legitimacy, Identity and Alienation in Late Twentieth Century Canada', in Cairns, A. and Williams, C. (Eds.) *Constitutionalism, Citizenship and Society in Canada*, Toronto: TUP.

Ticktin, H. (1998) 'The Problem is Market Socialism', in Ollman, B. (Ed.) *Market Socialism: The Debate Among Socialists*, London: Routledge.

Ulam, A.B. (1951) *Philosophical Foundations of English Socialism*, New York: Octagon.

Vernon, R. (1980) Introduction to Cole, G.D.H. *Guild Socialism Restated*, London: Transaction.

Von Mises, L. (1951) *Socialism*, London: Bradford and Dickens.

Wall, S. and Klosko, G. (2003) *Perfectionism and Neutrality: Essays in Liberal Theory*, New York: Roman and Littlefield.

Weber, M. (1990) [1924] 'Legitimate Authority and Bureaucracy', in Pugh, D.S. (Ed.) *Organization Theory: Selected Readings*, Third Edition. London: Penguin.

Weisskopf, T.E. (1993) 'A Democratic Enterprise-Based Market Socialism', in Bardhan, P.K. and Roemer, J.E. (Eds.) *Market Socialism: The Current Debate*, Oxford: Oxford University Press.

Wright, A.W. (1974) 'Guild Socialism Revisited', *Journal of Contemporary History* Vol. 9, No. 1.

——— (1979) *G.D.H. Cole and Socialist Democracy*, Oxford: Clarendon.

Wyatt, C. (2004) '*G.D.H. Cole: Emancipatory Politics and Organisational Democracy*', D. Phil., in the Department of Social and Political Thought, University of Sussex, England.

——— (2006) 'A Recipe for a Cookshop of the Future: G.D.H. Cole and the Conundrum of Sovereignty', *Capital and Class* 90, October.

Index